all about food

PRACTICAL HOME ECONOMICS

Helen McGrath

Oxford University Press 1982

Oxford University Press, Walton Street, Oxford OX2 6DP

London   Glasgow   New York   Toronto
Delhi   Bombay   Calcutta   Madras   Karachi
Kuala Lumpur   Singapore   Hong Kong   Tokyo
Nairobi   Dar es Salaam   Cape Town   Salisbury
Melbourne   Auckland

and associate companies in
Beirut   Berlin   Ibadan   Mexico City

© **Oxford University Press 1982**

ISBN: 0 19 832713 7

Acknowledgements

Illustrations are by David Ashby, Patricia Capon, Bill le Fever, Kate Simunek and Lynne Willey. Cartoon by Marie-Hélène Jeeves. The cover illustration is by Alan Austin.

Photographs are by Roger Charlesson (p.19 and p.68), Alison Souster (p.115 and p.68 inset) and by kind permission of Bedfordshire Area Health Authority (p.12).

The publishers would like to thank the following examination boards for permission to include questions from previous examination papers:

East Anglian Examinations Board (EAEB)
East Midland Regional Examinations Board (EMREB)
Middlesex Regional Examining Board (MREB)
Oxford Delegacy of Local Examinations (O)
South-East Regional Examinations Board (SEREB)
Southern Regional Examinations Board (SREB)
Welsh Joint Education Committee (WJEC)
West Midlands Examinations Board (WMEB)

The author would like to thank Mrs Patty Fisher and Dr R Passmore for their kindness in reading the nutrition section of the book and for their helpful criticisms and suggestions for improvement. She would also like to thank Mr Tom Matson for his invaluable help in typing the manuscript of the book, and all her family and friends for their constant encouragement and interest.

Photoset by Rowland Phototypesetting Limited, Bury St Edmunds, Suffolk and printed in Great Britain by William Clowes (Beccles) Limited

Preface

This book is designed to cover the work on nutrition, food, practical cookery, and housecraft required for the various C.S.E. and O-level syllabuses in home economics.

The aim of any scheme for teaching nutrition should be to effect an improvement in the eating patterns of those who are taught. It is recognized now that nutrition teaching is much more effective if the emphasis is placed on 'food', which interests everyone, rather than on 'nutrients'. When children and adults choose what they are going to eat, they think in terms of food. The idea of nutrients is often considered just as theory for the classroom, unrelated to everyday life.

The emphasis in the nutrition section therefore is on the dietary goals and recommendations which are recognized as being of major importance in relating patterns of nutrition and good health in our society. Briefly, these include:

1 We should eat less sugar.
2 We should eat less fat, particularly animal fat.
3 We should eat more unrefined carbohydrate foods and increase our intake of dietary fibre.
4 Babies should be breast-fed whenever possible.

In a home economics course, this nutrition teaching can conflict with the teaching of traditional cookery skills. To achieve good results in practical cookery examinations, pupils have to acquire a high level of manipulative and craft skills. This can lead to over-concentration on making such dishes as rich cakes and pastries, just those foods high in fat and sugar which we are advised to cut down on in our diets. I have therefore included many recipes which may encourage the use of brown or wholemeal flour, bran, pulses, brown or white pasta and rice, and textured vegetable protein, foods which may replace the highly-processed foods and those foods rich in fat and sugar which as a nation we tend to eat to excess.

The cake-making section includes several recipes which use comparatively small amounts of fat and sugar, or which can be made with ingredients like wholemeal flour, black treacle, and soft margarine. As we shall doubtless continue to enjoy making cakes and other baked goods, it is more realistic to provide plenty of recipes for these less rich cakes than to exhort pupils to avoid them altogether.

For examination work, advice is given on choosing suitable menus, working out the cost of recipes, and preparing time plans. Assignments of various lengths and difficulty are included, suitable for shorter or longer practical lessons. Every dish suggested in the menus is included in the recipe section, which makes it possible to plan and cook complete meals working only from this book.

All of the recipes have been used and tested in the classroom, with the usual range of pupils of varying abilities. I hope that this book will encourage interest in good nutrition through the enjoyment of preparing and eating good food.

Contents

Choosing good food

The food we eat affects the way we feel and the way we look throughout our lives. If we want to feel lively and fit, to be healthy and slim, and to have good teeth and a clear skin, then we should consider carefully the food we eat. We don't always realize how much our diet affects our feeling of well-being, because we don't see the results straight away. We could exist on biscuits, sweets, sticky cakes, and 'pop' for a day or two and not feel much the worse for it. But if we lived on this kind of diet for several months we would soon feel weak and unhealthy, and our skin, hair, teeth, and general appearance would suffer.

What effects can the wrong kinds of food have?

In our country, and in countries where people eat the same kinds of food as we do, many people suffer from disorders which are closely connected to their diet. These include obesity (being very overweight), anaemia, decayed teeth, and constipation and related diseases. Some of these disorders are more serious than others, but all are unpleasant. There is also evidence that high blood pressure and heart disease are related to diet.

In some countries people can't get enough to eat, or they have a very poor diet. This results in a high rate of child mortality (death in childhood), poor physical growth, a low standard of health, and a shorter life.

Our problem in this country is not usually shortage of food, but the opposite. We are much more likely to eat too much. Often it is too much of the kinds of food that are not very good for us and which cause us to become overweight and unhealthy.

The people who make and sell food and drink spend vast amounts of money on advertising in order to persuade us to buy their products. Look at all the advertisements for food and drink which are shown on television and in magazines. There is also such a huge variety of foods of all kinds in the shops that it is difficult to know what to choose. We need some simple guidelines to follow to help us choose wisely which foods we are going to buy and eat.

Sometimes a few small changes in our diet could make a great deal of difference to the way we feel and look. If we ate rather more of some foods and rather less of others, then we could be a much fitter and healthier nation.

Eat less of these.   Eat more of these.

There is general agreement amongst medical experts that as a country we should follow these recommendations concerning the food we eat:

1 We should eat less sugar.
2 We should eat less fat, especially less animal fat.
3 We should eat more unrefined carbohydrate and plant foods.
4 Babies should be breast-fed.

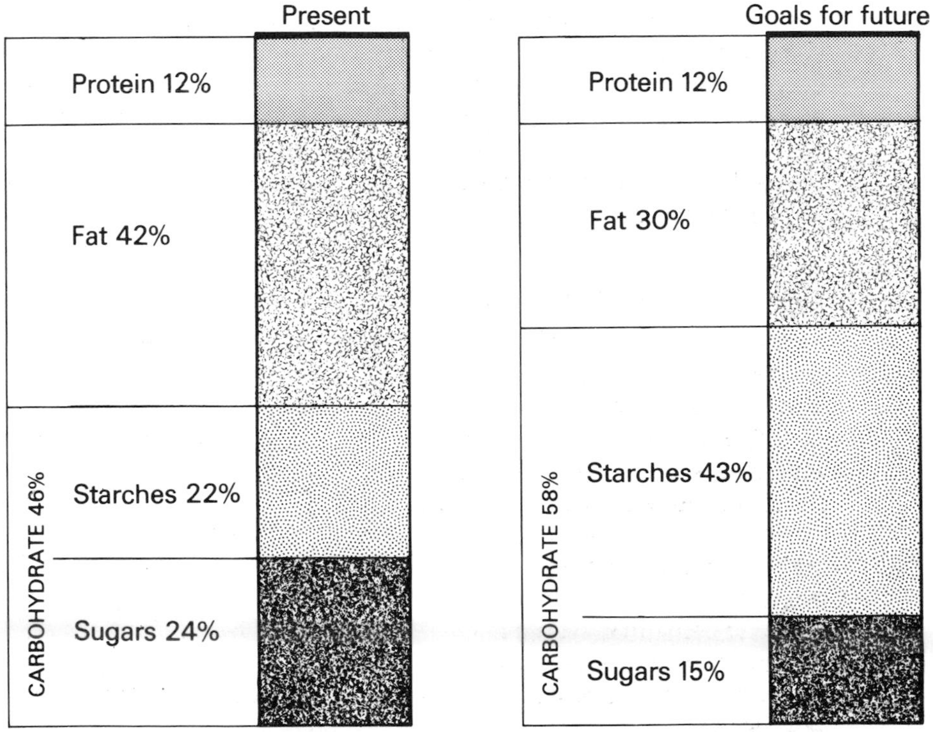

Present

Protein 12%

Fat 42%

CARBOHYDRATE 46%

Starches 22%

Sugars 24%

Goals for future

Protein 12%

Fat 30%

CARBOHYDRATE 58%

Starches 43%

Sugars 15%

This graph shows the changes in diet recommended for people in the U.S.A. by their government. As our pattern of diet is similar, we could also benefit from following these recommendations.

Questions

1 **If you choose the foods you eat carefully, what good effects can this have on you?**
2 **If you lived on a poor diet for several weeks or months, how might you feel and look?**
3 **Make a list of the diseases and disorders which people who live in this country can suffer from, if they eat the wrong kinds of food.**
4 **In some countries people do not have enough to eat. What are the results of this?**
5 **What kinds of food should we try to cut down on?**
6 **What kinds of food should we include more of in our meals?**

We should eat less fat

It is recommended that most people in this country should cut down on the amount of fatty foods they eat. If you eat too much fat you will not only become overweight, but you will also be much more likely to suffer from coronary heart disease. This is becoming a very common cause of illness and death in our society. To cut down on fat, you need to know which foods contain a lot of it. You cannot always tell just by looking. Some fat is 'visible' and can be seen, but many foods have the fat spread through them so that you cannot see it.

Foods which are obviously fatty include butter, margarine, suet, lard, dripping, cooking fats, cooking oils, fat on meat, and fried foods.

Foods which are less obviously fatty, where the fat is 'invisible', include pastry, cakes, biscuits, chocolates, sauces, salad creams, nuts, milk, cream, cheese, pork, bacon, ham, and sausages.

These are the foods you should cut down on, especially if you are overweight or don't take much exercise. We do need a certain amount of fat to make our diet appetizing and balanced. Those people who lead very active lives can eat more fat, but people who lead sedentary lives cannot use up all the energy which fat provides. Most of us should therefore aim to eat less fat.

How can we reduce the amount of fat we eat?

1 Instead of fatty foods, eat more cereal foods, preferably wholegrain, and including bread. Eat more fruit and vegetables of all kinds.
2 Avoid fatty meat. Choose lean meat, chicken, and white fish.
3 Avoid frying as a method of cooking, because it adds a lot of fat. Grill instead, on a wire rack, so that excess fat is drained away.
4 Do not spread margarine or butter thickly on bread. You could use a slimmers' low-fat spread instead if you wanted to.
5 Use skimmed milk for drinks and in cooking. This has had the creamy 'top of the milk' skimmed off. It can be bought powdered or in liquid form.
6 Cottage cheese has a very low fat content compared to other cheeses. Of the harder cheeses, Edam has a lower fat content.
7 Have cream only as an occasional treat. Yoghurt, which is low in fat, can be used instead of cream in some recipes.
8 Cut out puddings and cakes except for the odd occasion; eat fresh fruit instead.
9 If you want to make cakes, look for recipes with a fairly low fat content: for example, tea-breads, scones, yeast recipes, and whisked sponges. But do not spread them with lots of butter, cream, or icing when they are cooked.

Coronary heart disease and fats

The number of people with coronary heart disease has increased and it is now the most common single cause of death in Great Britain. There are several factors which seem to make people more likely to develop it. These are:

1 Cigarette smoking
2 High blood pressure
3 A high level of cholesterol in the blood
4 Being overweight

5 Tension or stress
6 Lack of regular exercise
7 Heredity, that is, a family history of heart disease

   If people have a high risk of developing coronary heart disease they may be advised to reduce the risk by following a special diet designed to lower the level of cholesterol in the blood.

   Cholesterol is a substance normally found in the blood. It is only when the amount in the blood becomes too great that someone is said to have 'a high blood-cholesterol level'. This high level is often found in people who eat large amounts of certain fats or oils. These fats and oils are called 'saturated fats' because of their chemical composition. They are mainly hard, solid fats which come from animals.

   If people are advised to follow a diet low in 'animal fats' or 'hard fats' or 'saturated fats', then they must avoid butter, dripping, lard, suet, hard margarine or vegetable cooking fats, cream, fat on meat, and many cooking oils (see below).

Polyunsaturated fats

Instead of the fats listed above, they should use special soft margarines or cooking oils which are labelled 'high in polyunsaturated fats'. Only these fats and oils should be used for spreading, baking, or cooking. The oil in oily fish is also polyunsaturated, so this can be included in the diet.

   Although all oils look 'soft' rather than 'hard', the only polyunsaturated oils are corn oil, soya bean oil, sunflower oil, safflower oil, and cotton oil. All other oils should be avoided.

   Our first priority should be to cut down on the overall <u>amount</u> of fat we consume. Then we can try to replace some of the animal fats we eat with vegetable fats or oils.

High blood pressure and salt

Some experts have suggested that there is a link between high blood pressure and eating large amounts of salt with our food. Although there is no definite medical agreement about this, it is advisable for those people who have high blood pressure to reduce their salt intake.

Questions

1 **Give two reasons why most people should not eat too many fatty foods.**
2 **Name three fats which people might spread on bread.**
3 **Name two fats which might be used for (a) making pastry, (b) making cakes, (c) frying, and (d) roasting a joint.**
4 **Many people do not realize that certain foods contain a lot of fat, because they cannot see it. Name six foods of this type.**
5 **You have decided to try to reduce the amount of fat you eat. From the nine suggestions listed above, list the five which would be most helpful for you.**
6 **List the factors which may make people more likely to suffer from coronary heart disease.**
7 **Explain the meaning of these terms: (a) blood-cholesterol level, (b) saturated fats, (c) polyunsaturated margarine.**

We should eat less sugar

Most experts agree that in this country we eat far too much sugar and it is not good for us. In fact, the average person in the United Kingdom eats over 100lb (45kg) per year. Not only do we use it in tea and coffee and on breakfast cereals, but we also use it in cakes, biscuits, puddings, tinned fruit, sweets, and drinks. Honey, syrup, treacle, jam, and marmalade contain such large amounts of sugar that they also count as sugar.

Why can sugar by harmful?

1   Sugar is very bad for your teeth. If you are always eating sweet things, your teeth are coated in a sweet, sticky layer most of the time. This is a major cause of decayed, painful, unattractive teeth. Find out how to take care of your teeth and do so. Cutting down on sugary foods is an important part of dental care. Try to eat crisp foods such as apples and raw carrots as snacks, instead of sweets.

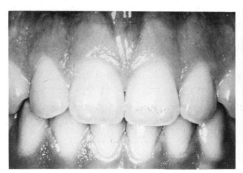 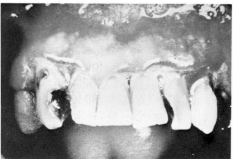

Cutting down on sugary foods helps to keep your teeth looking like the teeth on the left . . . and not those on the right.

2   Too much sugar can make you overweight. We seem to have a natural liking for sweet foods, but we should try to control it as we don't need them. Eating too much sugar is likely to make you fat. Obesity (being very overweight) is not only unattractive and uncomfortable, but very unhealthy too. Fat people are much more likely than slim people to suffer from all kinds of complaints and illnesses (see p. 70).

3   Sugar is an 'empty' food. This means that it provides us only with energy and nothing else. Other foods, like bread and potatoes, provide us with energy but they also provide other valuable nutrients, protein, vitamins, and minerals, so it is much better to get your energy from them. Brown and white sugar are very similar in this respect; there is no nutritional advantage in using the more expensive brown sugar.

How can we cut down on sugar?

1   Try gradually to cut sugar out of tea and coffee. It is quite possible to do this if you reduce the amount a little at a time. You will become accustomed to the taste if you make the change slowly. You could use artificial sweeteners, but it is better to try to lose the need for sweet drinks altogether if you can.

2   Try to control your taste for sweet foods. Replace them with savoury foods as far as possible. For example, for a packed lunch for school you could have sandwiches and fruit rather than chocolate biscuits and sweets.

3   If you want to bake at home, look for recipes with relatively low amounts of sugar, such as tea-breads, scones, fruit loaves, and yeast recipes, rather than rich iced cakes. With many recipes you can safely reduce the amount of sugar in them a little and still get good results.

4   Cut down on puddings with your meals. You don't need them and they are nearly all made with lots of fat and sugar. Try to make reasonable rules for yourself about this, so that you will find it possible to keep to them. For example, you could have fresh fruit instead during the week, and have puddings just at the weekend. This may be more realistic for you than trying to give up all sweet foods completely. If you are <u>too</u> strict, you may find that you suddenly cannot stand it any longer, go on a 'binge', and eat several bars of chocolate all at once!

Questions

1   **Name ten foods which contain large amounts of sugar.**

2   **Name four foods which are savoury rather than sweet, which you could spread on bread or toast.**

3   **Describe three harmful effects of eating large amounts of sweet food.**

4   **Why is it much better to get the energy you need from bread or potatoes rather than sugar?**

5   **Some people think that brown sugar is 'better' for you than white sugar. Do you agree with this?**

6   **If someone wanted to cut out sugar from tea and coffee, how would you advise them to do it?**

7   **Name five items you could bake which contain a fairly small amount of sugar compared to the amount of flour.**

We should eat more fibre-rich foods

We should all be eating more foods containing plenty of 'dietary fibre' or 'roughage'. This means more unrefined, untreated plant foods, such as wholemeal flour and whole grain cereals.

What is dietary fibre?

Fibre makes up the cell walls of plant foods, such as cereals, vegetables, beans, and fruit. We eat food for the nutrients it contains, and the nutrients are contained within this fibrous wrapping.

nutrients —————— fibre or bran wrapping

Grain of wheat.

The fibre is the part of the food which is not digested and absorbed by the body, but is passed out as waste. Because of this it has not always been recognized as being a very important part of our diet. In fact when foods are processed and refined, most of the outer, fibrous layers are removed and discarded. For example, when grains of wheat are milled to make white flour, the whole grain of wheat is broken open and all the outer layer of bran is discarded so that the flour is smooth and white.

'Wholemeal' flour has the whole grain of the wheat ground, including most of the bran layer, so it contains a good amount of fibre.

Why do we need dietary fibre?

We have said that fibre isn't absorbed and used by the body but is just passed out as waste in the stools, so why is it important?

Fibre is bulky and very absorbent. It holds a lot of water. This means that the contents of the bowel (the faeces) remain soft and are easily passed out of the body. This prevents constipation and other disorders related to it. Fibre may also 'mop up' poisonous substances from the bowel, which might be harmful if left.

Fibre acts like a sponge, mopping up water and other substances.

Foods rich in fibre

This list gives fibre-rich foods roughly 'in order' according to how much fibre they provide, with the best sources first:

1 Bran — in breakfast cereals, or it can be bought cheaply as miller's bran from chemists and supermarkets.
2 Wholemeal flour and bread. Ordinary brown flour contains less fibre than wholemeal, but it is still much better than white flour in this respect.
3 Wholegrain cereals, including whole wheat breakfast cereals, brown rice, brown pasta, and barley.
4 Peas and beans of all kinds, and lentils.
5 Root vegetables such as potatoes (if eaten with their skins), carrots, and turnips.
6 Dried fruit such as figs, raisins, dates, and nuts.
7 Other fruit and vegetables.

How can you include more high-fibre foods in your diet?

1 Eat wholemeal bread, or at least brown bread, whenever possible.
2 Use wholemeal flour when cooking. It is very suitable for bread, scones, chocolate, ginger, and fruit cakes, pizzas and some pastries (see recipe section), and biscuits.
3 When buying breakfast cereal, look for 'bran' or 'wholewheat' on the packet and choose that kind.
4 Use brown rice, spaghetti, and other pasta.
5 Use plenty of beans, peas, and lentils in soups and casseroles.
6 Eat plenty of root vegetables, including potatoes baked in their skins.
7 Sprinkle miller's bran onto stewed fruit or any breakfast cereal, or add a little to cakes, bread, or biscuits when baking.

Questions

1 **Explain what is meant by 'dietary fibre' or 'roughage'.**
2 **Why does white flour contain less fibre than wholemeal flour?**
3 **Fibre is not a nutrient, so why is it important in the diet?**
4 **Name five foods which provide a lot of fibre.**
5 **You want to include more fibre in your diet, but you do not like wholemeal bread. How can you achieve this?**
6 **Name five recipes in this book which could be made using wholemeal flour.**
7 **Name five recipes which include (a) some pulses (peas, beans, or lentils), (b) brown rice or pasta.**

The value of food

Nearly everyone enjoys eating. We eat because we feel hungry, because we like eating, and because we feel that food is 'good for us'. Good food enables children to grow properly and to be healthy, with strong bones and teeth. It enables us to be fit and energetic, and to resist infections and disease. When people don't have enough food they cannot grow and develop properly, and they are likely to suffer from ill health.

Food has this effect on our bodies because of the substances it contains. It contains many different chemical substances which are called nutrients. It is these nutrients which enable the body to grow and to function properly. If there are not enough nutrients in the food we eat then the body cannot grow and work as it should. We suffer from poor growth, lack of energy, and ill health.

There are many different nutrients. Each one has a particular function (or job) to perform if the body is to work efficiently. The body is like a car, with many different parts. Each individual part must work properly if the whole car is to run smoothly.

The names of the nutrients are:

protein,
carbohydrate,
fat,
minerals,
vitamins.

We also need dietary fibre. This is not exactly a nutrient as it is not absorbed by the body, but it is still necessary for our digestive systems to work properly.

Water is also very important in our diet. We could not live for long without it. About three-quarters of the body is made up of water. It transports materials within the body, and removes waste substances. We need to drink about 1½ litres (3 pints) of water every day.

What do the different nutrients do?

Protein is necessary for the proper growth of the body. Even when people are fully-grown adults they need protein to repair and replace cells which have become worn out.

Carbohydrate provides the energy we need to keep fit and active. It is the carbohydrate foods which contain dietary fibre.

Fats are also needed as a source of energy for all our activities.

Minerals and vitamins are only needed in small amounts but they are still essential. There are many different minerals such as iron, calcium, and fluoride, and many different vitamins, often called Vitamins A, B, C, and D. Each has a different function and none of them can be used to do the work of any of the others. They are all involved with the proteins, carbohydrates, and fats in the body's growth, activity, and general health.

Most foods contain a mixture of several different nutrients. For example, here are some of the foods which are good for us, with some of the nutrients they contain:

Bread: Carbohydrate, protein, iron, calcium, fibre, Vitamin B_1

Margarine: Fat, Vitamins A and D

Milk and cheese: Protein, carbohydrate, fat, calcium, Vitamin A, some B-Vitamins

Potatoes: Carbohydrate, protein, Vitamin C

Liver, red meat: Protein, iron, fat, B-Vitamins

Sardines, other oily fish: Fat, Vitamins A and D, protein

Oranges: Vitamin C

Eggs: Protein, fat, Vitamin A, B-Vitamins

A good diet is one which provides all the nutrients we need. If we eat a wide variety of foods then we are likely to get all the nutrients we need. We should not, however, eat more than we need. Eating too much of the wrong kinds of food, especially too much fat and sugar, can lead to as much ill health as eating too little.

Questions

1 **What are nutrients?**
2 **Name the five nutrients and say why they are needed.**
3 **Name some inexpensive foods which contain several different nutrients.**
4 **What do we mean by the term 'a good diet'?**

Protein

Protein is necessary for the growth and repair of all the cells in the body. They all contain protein which has to be replaced at regular intervals. We get the protein we need from proteins in the plant and animal foods we eat.

In this country, because we all have enough to eat, a shortage of protein in the diet is very unusual. We do not need large quantities of meat, eggs, milk, and so on, to supply us with enough protein. This is because nearly every food we eat, except refined sugar, processed fat, and alcoholic drinks, contains some protein and so contributes a useful amount to the total we need. Generally, even in poorer countries, where people have enough to eat they have enough protein.

Both animal and plant foods are valuable sources of protein in our diet. As well as meat, fish and dairy produce, it is not always realized what a useful source of protein plant foods are, particularly bread, flour, beans, peas, and rice. Proteins from different plant foods, when eaten together (e.g. beans with toast) can provide as good a source of protein as, for example, grilled steak or chops which are far more expensive.

It is much more economical to have our proteins provided by plant foods rather than animal foods. When so many people in the world are short of food it is wasteful to use plant food to fatten animals for meat. An acre of land can feed many more people if it is used to produce a food crop than if it is used to rear animals.

Textured vegetable protein (T.V.P.)

Soya beans are a good source of protein. Because of this they are used to make T.V.P. This is used as a substitute for meat because it is much cheaper to produce.

T.V.P. may be shaped, flavoured, and coloured to resemble meat, and may be sold in packets or tins. It is more often used, though, in large scale catering institutions like hospitals or canteens, as a meat extender. That means that it is mixed with fresh meat to make the meat go further and so cut down costs. When it is mixed with fresh meat, the taste and appearance blend quite well and it is widely used in this way. You can buy packets of soya mince in the shops to mix with fresh mince. This gives quite good results in dishes like shepherds' pie, meat pies, and spaghetti bolognese. It reduces the cost and makes the meat go further.

From a nutritional point of view, T.V.P. is as good a source of protein as meat, but it does not provide all the other nutrients which meat supplies, such as iron, in a form which is as easily used by the body.

Although it is less expensive than meat it is still not a particularly cheap source of protein, because of course it has to be processed in a factory, packed, and advertised, and this adds to the cost.

It would be much simpler and cheaper if we could just become used to the idea that we do not need meat every day. We could add soya and other beans to casseroles and stews and eat them as they are, rather than spend money trying to make them look and taste like meat.

Questions

1 **Why is protein needed in the diet?**
2 **Name the foods which do not contain any protein.**
3 **Why is it not necessary to eat a large portion of meat every day in order to get the protein we need?**
4 **Name three animal foods and three plant foods which are good sources of protein.**
5 **Why do you think that protein-rich animal foods are more expensive than protein-rich plant foods?**
6 **What is textured vegetable protein? Name five recipes where you could use this instead of meat, or mixed with meat. (See page 135.)**

Fats and carbohydrates

Fats

Fats may come from either animal foods or plant foods. If they are animal fats they are usually hard, like butter, suet, or lard. If they are from vegetables or plants they are usually soft and sold in the form of oil, though sometimes these are hardened to make margarine.

In this country we are recommended to cut down the amount of fat we eat to about 30% of our calorie intake, from the present level which is often about 40% (see page 9). This is mainly because in our country many people are very overweight and coronary heart disease is a major killer. In less developed countries where they eat much less fat (and usually much less sugar and more cereal foods too), obesity and coronary heart disease are much less common.

Fat in reasonable quantities is nevertheless a good food and adds a lot of flavour to our meals. If we had no butter or margarine for our bread and could never roast or fry any food, then our daily meals would be much less appetizing.

Fat is also a useful food because:

1 It is a very good source of energy.
2 Some fats contain Vitamins A, D, E, and K.
3 We have a layer of fat under our skin which insulates us from too much heat or cold.
4 There is a layer of fat round some of our organs, such as the kidneys, to protect them from damage.
5 Fat in a meal helps us to feel full for longer afterwards, because it stays in the stomach for quite a long time. We say it has a 'high satiety value'.

It is quite easy to cut down the amount of fat you eat and this will reduce the risk of obesity (being very fat) and coronary heart disease. Do not eat large amounts of fried foods often, do not spread butter or margarine too thickly, do not indulge in lots of cakes, pastry, cream, and chocolate.

Foods which contain a lot of fat
Butter, margarine, lard, dripping, suet, vegetable oils. Cakes, pastry, and biscuits made with these. Crisps and chips. Cheese, cream, fat in meat and bacon, chocolate, salad cream.

Carbohydrates

Carbohydrate foods can be divided into three main types: sugars, starches, and cellulose.

Sugars

These are found in all types of sugar, jam, honey, treacle, syrup, sweets, and foods made with sugar.

We should reduce the amount of sugar we eat because it will cause our teeth to decay and is very likely to make us overweight (see page 12). Sugar provides only 'empty calories'. Most foods provide a variety of different nutrients, but sugar is almost pure carbohydrate and gives us no extra nutrients at all. Although it is a quick source of energy, we do not really need it. It is better to get our supply of energy from foods like bread and potatoes, because they give us protein, minerals, vitamins, and dietary fibre as well.

Even though we seem to have a natural liking for sweet, sugary foods it is in our own interests to avoid them as far as possible and to try not to develop a sweet tooth.

There is not much difference between brown and white sugar from a nutritional point of view. As brown sugar costs about twice as much as white it is not worth the paying the extra unless you particularly prefer the flavour. The same applies to honey.

Starches and cellulose

If we cut down on sugars and fats we can usually eat good amounts of starchy foods without becoming overweight. Starchy foods include bread, flour, potatoes, cereals of all kinds, pasta, pulses, and rice. They are very useful foods as:

1 They provide us with good sources of energy.
2 They contain a variety of other useful nutrients.
3 They contain good amounts of dietary fibre (see page 14).
4 They are relatively cheap to buy, and to produce.
5 They fill us up as they are bulky, so we do not feel hungry and tempted to over-eat.

One of our aims in choosing our meals should be to eat more unrefined carbohydrate foods. 'Unrefined' foods are those which have not undergone too much processing to remove outer skins, bran, and so on. We should make an effort to include foods like wholemeal and brown bread, bran, brown rice and pasta and 'wholewheat' breakfast cereals in our diet. We would probably be much fitter and healthier as a result.

Questions

1 **Why is fat a valuable food in the diet?**
2 **Why is it not advisable to eat very large amounts of fat?**
3 **What is obesity?**
4 **Name some fats which come from animals.**
5 **Name some foods which contain a lot of fat although they do not look 'fatty'.**
6 **What are the three main types of carbohydrates?**
7 **How could you try to discourage a child from having a 'sweet tooth'?**
8 **Why are starchy foods useful in the diet?**
9 **What do we mean by 'unrefined foods'?**

Micro-nutrients (1)

The food we eat is mainly made up of a mixture of proteins, carbohydrates, and fats, with fibre and water. But it also contains several micro-nutrients which we need in tiny amounts to keep the body working properly. These micro-nutrients are <u>minerals,</u> which include iron and fluoride, and <u>vitamins,</u> including Vitamins A, B, C, and D.

Although we only need very small amounts of these micro-nutrients, they are still essential. If any one of them is poorly supplied in the diet over a long period of time, then your health will be affected. For example, people whose diet is short of iron and Vitamin C will become weak and anaemic.

In our country, where we can have a good, varied diet, serious shortages are not very common. Even so, there are still some groups of people whom we call 'at risk'. Because of the foods they eat, or do not eat, some people are likely to suffer from a lack of certain nutrients. This problem could often be overcome quite simply if they included foods which contain the necessary nutrients in their daily meals.

Vitamin D and calcium

Some people in Great Britain do not get enough Vitamin D and calcium. Together with other nutrients, these are essential if bones are to be strong, straight, and properly formed. Vitamin D, or cholecalciferol, enables the calcium to make the bones firm. Both are needed together as neither can work unless the other is there too. Shortage of Vitamin D and calcium causes rickets in children and osteomalacia in old people. With rickets, bones are soft and bend easily, resulting in painful limbs, bow-legs, and knock knees in children. Osteomalacia is a kind of adult rickets found in old people. Bones are brittle and easily broken, even by a slight fall.

How do we get enough Vitamin D?
When you are exposed to sunlight, Vitamin D is formed under the skin. The more time you spend outside in the sunlight, the more Vitamin D will be formed, so both children and adults should be encouraged to spend time out of doors. Sunlight is a more important source of Vitamin D than foods are, and in Great Britain many of us may not be sufficiently exposed to it during our long dark winters.

Vitamin D from foods
Vitamin D is not found in many foods, which is why some people may be 'at risk'. Good sources of Vitamin D in an ordinary diet are fatty fish, eggs, and margarine (by law this has to have Vitamins A and D added to make it at least as good as butter). It can also be taken in the form of drops or in cod-liver oil, if necessary.

Who is likely to suffer from shortage of Vitamin D?
Rickets was once so common that it was known as the English disease. It was particularly common amongst poorer people and those who lived in big, smoky cities. This was because the air in the cities was so smoky and polluted that enough sunlight could not get through to the skin to form Vitamin D. When smoke abatement and clean air acts were introduced, cases of rickets began to decrease.

With the discovery of how to make Vitamin D in a laboratory, it was easier to encourage mothers, through welfare clinics, to give their babies Vitamin D drops. Cod-liver oil was also recognized as a valuable source of Vitamins D and A. National dried milk was produced cheaply for babies who were not breast-fed, and this was enriched with Vitamin D. Margarine, which poorer people ate instead of butter, had by law to be enriched with Vitamins A and D. All these measures contributed towards making rickets disappear from this country, where it had previously been very common.

The reappearance of rickets

Unfortunately, after many years, rickets has begun to reappear in Great Britain. The people most likely to suffer are again poor families, as they have less money to spend on foods providing calcium and Vitamin D, and as free school milk is less widely available.

Rickets is also increasing amongst children in Asian families in Great Britain. Their traditional diet does not include very good sources of Vitamin D and calcium. Their basic foods include ghee rather than margarine, and chupattis rather than white bread. Neither do they receive as much exposure to sunlight in this country. The climate is less sunny, and women and children spend more time indoors. To reduce the risk of their children developing rickets, it would help if Asian families were to make a few adaptations to their traditional diet. Ghee could be made partly or wholly from margarine, or more white bread and margarine could be eaten. Canned fish such as pilchards could be tried in curries. Perhaps chupatti flour could have Vitamin D added to it, and children at risk should be given Vitamin D drops.

Calcium

Calcium is essential, together with Vitamin D and other nutrients (phosphorus, protein, Vitamins A and C), if bones and teeth are to be firm and strong. Calcium is also needed for the nerves and muscles to work properly and for the clotting of blood.

We usually have enough calcium in our food as there is plenty in bread, beans, milk, cheese, and other foods, but it cannot be used properly without Vitamin D from sunlight and from food. We are more likely to be short of Vitamin D as it is found in only a few foods.

Questions

1 **What does it mean when we say that some people are 'at risk' with regard to certain vitamins or minerals?**
2 **Why are Vitamin D and calcium necessary?**
3 **What are the two ways in which the body can make or take in Vitamin D?**
4 **Name two foods which are very good sources of Vitamin D.**
5 **What is rickets, and how is it caused?**
6 **Name two cheap foods which are good sources of calcium.**

Micro-nutrients (2)

Fluoride

For good teeth the same kind of nutrients are needed as for bones. For strong teeth which resist decay we also need fluoride. In areas where it is found naturally in drinking water, people have much less tooth decay than in other areas. Because of this, it is recommended that all water supplies should have fluoride added in the right amounts. This would mean that everyone could receive the benefits of fluoridation. In those areas where fluoride has been added to the water supplies, the amount of decay in children's teeth has been reduced. Where fluoride has been added for some years and then stopped, the amount of tooth decay has increased again. Fluoride toothpaste has also been shown to be helpful in reducing decay. It is very important as well to avoid sweet, sticky foods, especially between meals.

Iron

Iron and vitamin C are both needed if we are to be lively and energetic, both mentally and physically.

If people do not have enough iron in their diet then they may suffer from anaemia. This will make them feel weak and easily tired. They will have little energy and will be unable to concentrate.

Iron is necessary to form the red cells of the blood which carry oxygen around the body to where it is needed. If the body cells do not receive enough oxygen they do not work efficiently. Muscle cells do not work properly so we are not physically energetic. Brain cells do not work properly so we may feel tired, depressed, and unable to concentrate.

Women and girls are the most likely groups of people to suffer from anaemia because of blood losses due to menstruation, pregnancy, and childbirth.

During pregnancy the mother's diet has to supply enough iron for her own and the baby's blood. The baby also has to build up a store of iron in his liver to last him for the first few months of life. There is a little iron in human milk, but only a very small amount in cow's milk.

Teenagers, both boys and girls, need good amounts of iron-rich foods. Because of their rapid rate of growth they have an increased need to build up blood supplies.

The absorption of iron
Only a small amount of iron in the food we eat is actually absorbed and used by the body. The amount you absorb varies from one person to another and depends on:

1   how much you need,
2   the kind of iron in the food,
3   other foods which are eaten with the iron.

The different kinds of iron
Iron is found in foods in different chemical forms. Some of these are much more easily absorbed by the body than others. 'Haem' iron is like the iron in our blood, so it is easy to absorb. It is found in red meat and black pudding.

Non-haem iron is in a chemical form which is more difficult for the body to use. It is found in cereals, pulses, eggs, fish, and vegetables. Other foods eaten with the iron can improve or lessen the amount of iron the body will absorb. Vitamin C (ascorbic acid) from fruit and vegetables will help the absorption of non-haem iron from other foods.

On the other hand, some foods contain substances which make the iron less easy to absorb. Egg yolks were once considered to be a good source of iron, but it is now known that the iron is in a form which the body cannot easily use. It also lessens the amount of iron which can be absorbed from other foods eaten with it. But if Vitamin C is taken with the iron it helps it to be absorbed. So a glass of orange juice with an egg makes a good breakfast. Phytic acid in wholemeal flour, wholegrain cereals, and many vegetables, also binds the iron and makes it less readily absorbed.

Foods which supply good amounts of iron
Beef, corned beef, liver (especially pig's liver), liver pâté or sausage, black pudding, kidney.
Bread of all kinds, bran, curry powder, Oxo cubes, soya and other beans, peas. Chocolate, cocoa, black treacle, dried figs and apricots.

It is better to eat plenty of iron-rich foods regularly than to rely on iron tablets to supply your needs, but it can be a good idea to take some tablets for five days after a menstrual period.

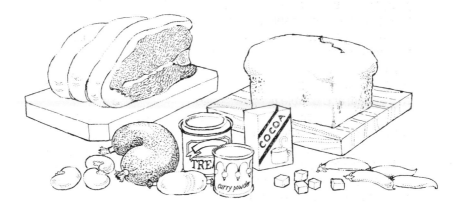

Questions

1. **What is the advantage of having fluoride in drinking water?**
2. **Why is it necessary to eat foods which contain iron?**
3. **What is anaemia?**
4. **Not all of the iron in the food we eat is absorbed by the body. Why is this?**
5. **What kinds of meat are good sources of iron?**
6. **Name some cereal or plant foods which are good sources of iron.**
7. **Why is it useful to eat foods rich in Vitamin C when you are eating foods containing iron?**

Micro-nutrients (3)

Vitamin C – ascorbic acid

This vitamin is involved in many body processes. It helps to keep the body in good repair and helps us to keep active and energetic. Some of its uses are:

1 It makes the protein collagen, the cement which keeps the tissues of the skin, bones, and blood vessels firm.
2 It helps the body to absorb the iron in food.
3 It helps us to resist infection.
4 It helps wounds to heal.
5 Children need it so that they can grow normally.

Sources of Vitamin C

Some fruits and vegetables (but not all) are good sources. These include blackcurrants and blackcurrant syrup, rosehip syrup, tomatoes and tomato juice, citrus fruits (oranges, lemons and grapefruit), and guavas. Potatoes, especially new potatoes, are a good source of Vitamin C in this country, because we eat a lot of them regularly. Green vegetables such as cabbage and sprouts, if carefully cooked, are good sources, and so are red and green peppers. Fruit and vegetables which have been canned or frozen are still good sources of the vitamin.

Lack of Vitamin C

A lack of enough Vitamin C over a long period results in scurvy, a disease where the mouth and gums become swollen and sore, the teeth drop out, and the victim feels weak and may eventually die. Scurvy used to be common among sailors going on long sea voyages where fresh fruit and vegetables were unobtainable. Then it was discovered that the juice of oranges or lemons completely cured the scurvy, and kept the sailors in much better health. We are not likely now to suffer such a severe lack of Vitamin C that we develop scurvy. But if we continually have rather less than we need, then we soon show signs of weakness, tiredness, and lack of resistance to infection.

Although ascorbic acid is found quite widely in plenty of fruits and vegetables, it is easily destroyed. Long storage of vegetables after they have been picked, chopping, soaking them in water, cooking, and keeping them hot for a long time, all tend to destroy Vitamin C. You should prepare and cook vegetables carefully, so that they lose as little Vitamin C as possible.

1 Use fruit and vegetables as soon as possible after they have been picked. Do not store them for a long time (except in a freezer).
2 Do not leave them to soak.
3 Put them into a small amount of boiling water, and cook with the lid on for as short a time as possible. Use the cooking water for gravy.
4 Do not keep vegetables hot for a long time. Serve them as soon as possible.

Suggestions for including plenty of Vitamin C in your diet

Add rosehip or blackcurrant syrup to milk puddings, ice cream, stewed fruit, or cereals. Mix some blackcurrants with apples for a pie or crumble. Have a glass of orange, grapefruit, or tomato juice for breakfast every day, or half a grapefruit or segments. Eat freshly boiled potatoes and green vegetables often. Try Chinese-cooked vegetables. These are cut up small or shredded and cooked in a little hot oil for about five minutes with the lid on. Have plenty of salads with tomatoes, parsley, peppers, and grated raw cabbage or sprouts.

Vitamin A – retinol

Like Vitamin D, this is a fat-soluble vitamin. This means that it is found dissolved in fatty foods rather than watery foods. It is found in good amounts in oily fish and margarine, and in dairy foods. It is also found in cod-liver oil, liver, suet, and eggs. Vitamin A is found in fruit and vegetables as carotene. This is an orangey-yellow substance which can be converted to Vitamin A in the body. It gives the yellow colour to carrots, apricots, peaches, and turnips. It is also present in green vegetables, where the colour is masked by the green of the chlorophyll. In tomatoes and red peppers it is masked by the red colouring.

Vitamin A is needed for the normal growth of children, especially their bones. It keeps the eyes healthy, giving good vision in dim light. It also keeps the mucous membranes, for example in the throat, in good condition so that they can resist infection.

Like Vitamin D, Vitamin A is not easily destroyed. Cooked or canned fruit, vegetables, fish, and milk contain as much carotene or Vitamin A after processing or cooking as before. We are not likely to be short of Vitamin A in this country if we have a good mixed diet.

The Vitamin B group

This includes several different water-soluble vitamins, including thiamin (B_1), riboflavin (B_2), and niacin (B_3). Again, we are not very likely to suffer from a shortage of B vitamins in this country provided that we eat a diet with plenty of variety. This is because these vitamins are found in small amounts in many different foods, particularly unprocessed whole foods. However, more B vitamins are needed after taking a course of antibiotics.

Some foods are good sources of all of the B vitamins – wholemeal flour and cereals, bread, wheatgerm, bran, yeast, yeast extract, pork and bacon, liver and kidney, and nuts. Milk, cheese, and eggs are good sources of riboflavin.

The B vitamins are chiefly needed for muscular energy. They enable us to make use of the energy that is in protein, carbohydrate, and fats. They also keep the nervous system healthy and functioning smoothly.

Questions

1 **Describe some of the functions of ascorbic acid (Vitamin C) in the body.**
2 **Name three fruits which contain a good amount of Vitamin C.**
3 **What are the rules for cooking vegetables, to ensure that they keep as much of their Vitamin C as possible?**
4 **What is carotene?**
5 **Why does the body need Vitamin A?**
6 **Give the names of three of the B group of vitamins. Why are these vitamins needed by the body?**
7 **Name some foods which are good sources of all the B vitamins.**

Summary

Nutrient	Functions in the body	Good sources in the diet
Protein	For growth and repair of tissues. A secondary source of energy.	*Animal* – meat, fish, cheese, eggs, milk *Vegetable* – soya beans, nuts, cereals, pulses
Carbohydrate	Source of energy for all the body's activities. Cellulose provides dietary fibre although it is not a food.	*Sugars* – sugar, treacle, syrup, jam, honey, fruit *Starches* – flour (e.g. in bread, cakes, puddings), other cereals, potatoes *Cellulose* – fruit, vegetables, bran, wholemeal bread, whole cereals
Fat	A very good source of energy. A layer of fat insulates the body, preventing the loss of heat. Some organs of the body, e.g. the kidneys, are protected by fat. Animal fats contain Vitamins A and D. Keeps you feeling 'full' after a meal – it has a 'high satiety value'.	*Animal* – milk, butter, cream, cheese, suet, fatty meat, oily fish *Vegetable* – margarines, salad or cooking oils
Mineral		
Iron	Needed to form the red blood cells which carry the necessary oxygen to all parts of the body. Lack of iron may cause anaemia.	Liver, kidney, red meat, corned beef Green vegetables, bread, cocoa, treacle, dried fruit
Calcium	Development of strong bones and teeth, together with phosphorus, Vitamins D, C, and A. Needed for clotting of blood.	Milk, cheese, eggs Fish bones, e.g. salmon Added to white bread
Phosphorus	Strong bones and teeth.	Present in most proteins

Vitamin	Functions in the body	Good sources in the diet
A (Retinol) *Fat-soluble*	Normal growth of children, especially bones and teeth. Keeps mucous membranes healthy. Healthy eyes, vision in dim light.	*Animal* – fish-liver oil, oily fish, liver, dairy foods, margarine *Plant foods* – as carotene, in orange/yellow fruit and vegetables. Green vegetables
D (Calciferol) *Fat-soluble*	Works with calcium and phosphorus to form strong teeth and bones. Prevents rickets.	Foods — margarine, oily fish, cod-liver oil, eggs Sunlight acting on the fat layer under the skin forms Vitamin D

Vitamin B complex

B_1 Thiamin	For growth of children and good health. Helps liberate the energy from carbohydrate foods. Healthy nervous system.	Found in a variety of 'natural', unprocessed foods. Wholemeal flour, whole cereals Yeast, yeast extract (Marmite) Meat, liver, eggs
B_2 Riboflavin	Similar to B_1.	Similar to B_1, also a useful amount in milk
B_3 Niacin or Nicotinic acid	Similar to B_1 and B_2.	Similar to B_1 and B_2. Milk products do not provide much

Vitamin C

(Ascorbic acid)	Normal growth of children. Clear skin, healthy tissues. Healing of wounds. Healthy teeth and gums. Helps absorption of iron. Prevents scurvy.	Fruit – blackcurrants, rosehip syrup Citrus fruits – oranges, lemons, grapefruit Tomatoes, potatoes, fresh green vegetables

Using the oven

To achieve good results when you are cooking it is important to know how to use the oven properly. Many people spoil the dishes they have prepared by not cooking them correctly. If when you are baking the oven is too hot or too cold, or the shelf is too high or too low, or the baking tray is too big, then the results can be very disappointing. All of the following points are important if you are to use the oven successfully.

Pre-heating the oven

Pre-heating the oven means bringing it up to the right temperature before you put the dish into the oven. To pre-heat a gas oven you light it about ten minutes before you want to use it. To pre-heat an electric oven you switch it on about fifteen minutes before you want to use it. Many electric ovens have a small light on the control panel which comes on when you switch the oven on. When the oven has reached the temperature you have set, the light goes off. You should check to see whether the electric oven you use works like this.

The oven does not need to be pre-heated for dishes like casseroles, stews, or milk puddings. But for good results with most cakes, pastry, and yeast recipes, it is necessary to pre-heat the oven.

The position of the shelf in the oven

You should always put the shelf in the right position for the dish you are making before you switch on the oven. It is much easier and safer to move the shelves when they are cold.

In an electric oven the temperature is fairly even. But in a gas oven the top is hotter and the bottom is cooler than the centre. So if you set the oven to gas mark 5, you will find that the temperature on the top shelf is about equal to gas mark 6 and the temperature on the lower shelf is equal to about gas mark 4.

Sometimes this can be useful as it means you can cook dishes needing different oven temperatures at the same time. On the other hand if you were cooking, for example, three pies, the one on the top shelf would be cooked before the one in the centre, and the one on the lower shelf would take longer.

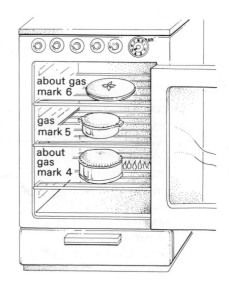

about gas
mark 6

gas
mark 5

about
gas
mark 4

Baking trays

The size of the baking tray you use can also affect your cooking. You should never use a baking tray larger than the one which was provided with the cooker. If you do, you will find that dishes bake unevenly. For example, scones and biscuits on the edges of the tray may burn quickly, before those in the centre are even cooked. You must never let baking trays touch the sides of the oven. There should be a space of about 5cm (2″) all round the edge of the tray, so that the heat can circulate and the food can be evenly browned.

The trays or tins should be placed in the centre of the shelf. Their exact position will depend on the shape of the shelf and the position of the heating elements or gas burners.

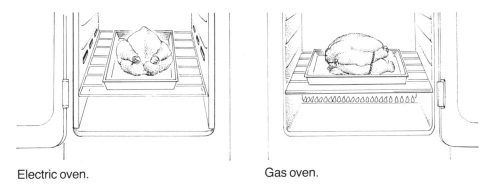

Electric oven.   Gas oven.

Varying temperatures in different ovens

When you are using different cookers for baking in school, you may find that the oven temperatures seem to vary, even though they are set at the same gas mark or temperature. Some ovens can be 'hot' and will brown food too quickly before it is cooked. Other ovens are 'slow' and can take too long to cook, resulting in spoiled food. So it is a good idea to become familiar with the oven you use most of the time at school. Then if you know that your oven tends to be hot (usually gas ovens), you could cook certain items on a lower shelf than the recipe says. If you know that the oven is 'slow', you could set the temperature higher than the recipe says. You may well find that this produces much better results when you are cooking.

Questions

1 **How can careless use of the oven spoil a dish that you are making?**
2 **Name three recipes in this book for which (a) it is necessary to pre-heat the oven, (b) pre-heating the oven is not essential.**
3 **When is the best time to put the oven shelf in the correct position? Why?**
4 **Which part of a gas oven is hottest?**
5 **You want to cook these dishes in the oven at the same time: Swiss roll (Gas 6), ginger biscuits (Gas 4), and apple crumble (Gas 5). What gas mark would you turn the oven to and how would you arrange the dishes on the shelves?**
6 **Describe what might happen if you use a baking tray which is too large for your oven.**

Weighing and measuring

For good results in most recipes, accurate weighing and measuring is essential. It does not make much difference whether you put two onions into a stew instead of one, or whether you put an extra apple into an apple pie. But when you are baking with flour, sugar, and liquids, making cakes, pastry, and so on, you must measure carefully or your cooking will be spoiled. For example, if you do not add enough flour to a cake, or if you add too much sugar or baking powder, the results can be disastrous.

All the recipes in this book have been tested for both metric weights (grams) and imperial weights (pounds and ounces). You must stick to either the metric or the imperial. For example, if a bread recipe says 250g/½lb flour, 125ml/¼pt water, you should not weigh out 250g of flour and then measure a quarter of a pint of water to mix with it, or your dough will be too dry. On the other hand if you measured ½lb flour and added 125ml of water the dough would be too wet. In both cases the bread could be spoiled. So always use either all metric or all imperial measurements and never mix the two.

It is only possible to cook properly with metric quantities if you have metric scales and a metric measuring jug. Unless you have these it is better to stick to imperial measures. There is no point in trying to convert exactly from one to the other. It cannot be done very accurately and it does not work very well.

Kitchen scales

This is a particularly useful kind of kitchen scales, as it will weigh small quantities such as 5g or ½oz accurately. It is much easier to be accurate with these scales than with the more usual kind shown below, as there is much more room on the face to show the markings. These are often called 'diet' scales.

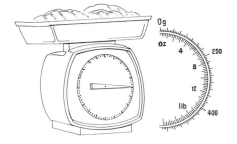

This is the more usual type of scales. It can weigh up to 5kg/10lb. In practice, however, it is more useful to have scales which help you weigh smaller quantities more easily.

These scales are reliable and accurate, once you know how to use them. If you have both a metric and an imperial set of weights then it is easy to use either kind of recipe.

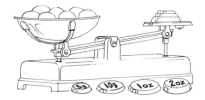

Measuring cups and jugs

These measuring cups are very useful. They are much cheaper than scales and less easily damaged. The quantities corresponding to the weights of most everyday ingredients, such as flour, sugar, currants, and rice, are marked on the inside in both metric and imperial measurements. These cups are very easy to use. They cannot be used to weigh lard or margarine, but it is quite easy to divide blocks or tubs of these into 50g portions.

A measuring jug is needed for liquids. A jug which is marked in mls (millilitres) on one side and pints and fluid ounces on the other, is the most useful kind to have.

You can also buy metric measuring spoons quite cheaply.

A level teaspoon holds 5ml.

A level dessertspoon holds 10ml.

A level tablespoon holds 15ml.

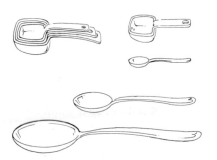

Questions

1 **Why is it important to measure very accurately when you are baking?**
2 **Describe the reasons why imperial and metric quantities should never be mixed.**
3 **What basic equipment is essential before you can cook using metric weights and measurements?**
4 **Describe and draw (a) the kind of weighing scales you would like to have at home, and (b) a measuring cup.**
5 **How much would you expect a level teaspoon, dessertspoon, and tablespoon to hold?**

Basic kitchen equipment

Cook's knife – a large knife for cutting and chopping meat, vegetables, etc.

Vegetable knife – a small knife for preparing fruit and vegetables.

Palette knife – used for lifting biscuits, scones, and so on from a baking tray.

Whisks of different types.

Pastry brush – for brushing pastry with egg and milk before baking, or for greasing tins.

Spatula – for scraping all the mixture from a bowl.

Fish slice – for lifting larger items from a frying pan or baking tray.

Sieve – can be made of nylon, or metal, which is stronger. Clean with a brush.

Colander – for draining vegetables or pasta.

Grater – with different sized cutting surfaces. Metal is best as it is sharpest. Clean with a brush and dry well to avoid rusting.

Flour dredger – for dusting the work surface with a little flour when rolling out pastry, biscuits and so on.

Pastry cutters – they can be plain or fluted. You can also get fancy shapes like gingerbread men, animals, or stars.

Mixing bowl – for all general mixing jobs.

Pudding basins – these are available in different sizes. They are used for steaming puddings, etc.

Wire cooling tray – for cooling cakes, bread, biscuits, scones, and so on.

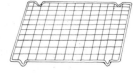

Cake tins and baking tins

Many of these can now be bought with a non-stick finish, but they are more expensive. Non-stick cake tins still have to be greased before they are used. It is usually better to line them with greaseproof paper too, to ensure that the cakes come out of the tin easily. Non-stick tins are easy to wash and dry and they do not go rusty. They must be washed carefully with a soft cloth and must never be scratched with any metal spoon or utensil. Never use a harsh pan cleaner on them, or the non-stick coating will be spoiled.

Cake tins may be round or square. Some have a loose bottom for easy removal of the cake.

Sandwich cake tins are shallower, for cakes which are to be sandwiched together.

Loaf tins are usually made in two sizes, large and small, called 1lb and 2lb tins.

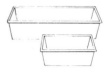

Bun tin, or patty tin, for small cakes and tarts.

Swiss roll tin, for Swiss roll or general use.

Baking tray or sheet for general use.

Roasting tin, for roasting meat.

Yorkshire pudding tins.

Pie plates. Metal plates give the crispest pastry.

Sponge flan tins. They need to be very carefully greased before use.

Flan rings, plain for savoury flans, fluted for sweet flans.

Deep pie dish, for meat or fruit pies with a pastry lid.

Questions

1 **Name and draw three pieces of kitchen equipment which would be useful when you are preparing, cooking, or serving (a) vegetables, (b) scones, (c) cakes, and (d) meat.**
2 **How would you clean (a) a grater that has been used for cheese, (b) a sieve that has been used for flour, and (c) a pastry brush that has been used for greasing a tin?**
3 **What are the advantages and disadvantages of non-stick tins?**
4 **Name the type of tin you would use to cook each of the following: a fruit loaf, some cheese scones, a Christmas cake, a Victoria sandwich cake, an apple pie, some roast potatoes, some sweet mince tarts.**

Basic kitchen equipment

Different types of pans

When you are choosing pans, remember that they get a lot of heavy use. You would expect them to last for many years, so choose carefully. Remember:

1 Heavier pans will last longer and spread heat more evenly, but they should not be too heavy to lift easily.
2 Handles should be heat-resistant and firmly fixed.
3 Lids should fit well.
4 Pans for electric cookers should have a heavy base.

Aluminium pans are very widely used and available in different thicknesses. If they are fairly heavy, they will be strong and hard-wearing. They are easy to clean and reasonably priced.

Vitreous enamel on steel pans often have very attractive patterns and are made in different colours, but they need more care in use than aluminium pans. You cannot use metal utensils in them, nor can you use scouring powder or steel wool to clean them, or they may become scratched.

Stainless steel is very expensive, but it is hard and strong. Stainless steel pans are not really stainless, as if they are not carefully dried after use they will become marked. Pans tend to be thin because of the high cost of stainless steel, so they often have a heavy base added, to spread heat evenly.

A non-stick finish is available on many pans. It makes them easier to clean, but you must be very careful to avoid scratching. Never use metal utensils or pan cleaners in them. They should just be washed in hot, soapy water.

Saucepans, in different sizes. They should have well-fitting lids.	Milk pans have slanted sides or a lip for easy pouring.	Frying pans should be fairly heavy, so that food does not stick easily.

Deep fat pan. This has a basket so that food can be easily removed.	Omelette pan. This has curved edges.	Pancake pan. This is about 15cm/6″ in diameter.

Double pan, for cooking food gently over water, e.g. for lemon curd, porridge, egg custard.	Steamer. This has a lid and will fit over most sizes of pan for steaming puddings or other food.	Jam pan. This is heavy, large and wide, ideal for jam, marmalade and chutney.

Disposable paper and plastic products

Kitchen paper, usually sold on a roll. It can be used for many different purposes, such as mopping up spills, wiping fat from greasy pans before washing them, and draining fried foods.

Greaseproof paper, for lining cake tins. When you are cutting paper to shape to line a tin, it is useful to cut several layers at the same time, so that you have a ready supply for the next time you bake.

Kitchen foil is used for wrapping meat before roasting it, to keep the meat moist and to avoid splashing the oven. Foil is also used for wrapping food to keep it fresh, or before freezing it. It can be used to cover food when you reheat it in the oven, to prevent it from drying out.

Cling film or wrap is very useful for covering food to prevent it from drying out. It will stick to most dishes. It can also be used for wrapping packed meals.

Polythene bags can be bought in different sizes and thicknesses. They are useful for wrapping food to keep it fresh, and for keeping bread dough moist while it rises. Thicker polythene bags can be used for wrapping food before it is frozen; thinner bags are not suitable.

'Roasta' bags. The joint or chicken to be roasted is placed inside one of these special polythene-type bags, with a little flour. The meat cooks and browns inside the bag, keeping in the moisture and flavour, and preventing the oven from being splashed.

Questions

1 **When choosing saucepans what points must you consider?**
2 **Give the advantages and disadvantages of (a) aluminium pans, (b) vitreous enamel on steel pans, (c) stainless steel pans, (d) non-stick pans.**
3 **Arrange the nine types of pan named above in the order in which you think they would be most useful in a kitchen.**
4 **If you could afford to use only three of these paper products, which would you choose and why?**

Hygiene and safety

Food hygiene

It is essential that everything in the kitchen is kept really clean. If people preparing food do not have high standards of cleanliness, there will be a danger of food poisoning. The results of food poisoning can be anything from a mild headache to vomiting, diarrhoea, and even death.

Food poisoning is caused when bacteria are present in large numbers in the food we eat. They increase rapidly in the right conditions. They like a warm temperature, about the same as that of the human body, and moist conditions. They will multiply rapidly in foods such as milk, cream, ice cream, meat, fish, and gravy, so these foods are particularly likely to carry infection if they are not carefully used. Bacteria can be killed by heat and they will not multiply under cold conditions.

Cleanliness in the kitchen

1 Keep all utensils, equipment, and work surfaces clean.
2 Wash up with really hot soapy water, changing it when necessary.
3 Keep kitchen cloths clean. Boil dishcloths often. It is much more hygienic to rinse crockery in hot water after washing up than to wipe it with a tea-towel which is not absolutely clean.
4 Wrap all scraps of food in newspaper, and place them in a covered bin.
5 Sweep up any spilt crumbs or food. Wash the floor at least once a week, using a disinfectant solution.

Hygienic food handling

1 Cook foods such as meat very thoroughly to destroy bacteria.
2 If cooked food must be stored, cool it rapidly. Do not leave it lying around in a warm kitchen.
3 When reheating food, heat it thoroughly. Do not reheat it more than once.
4 Store food in a cool place, preferably a refrigerator. Do not store it for too long.
5 Always keep food covered.
6 Use meat and fish as soon as possible after buying.

Personal hygiene

1 Always wash your hands thoroughly with hot, soapy water before preparing food and after going to the toilet. Otherwise, bacteria from the bowel could be transferred to the food you eat.
2 Never lick your fingers or utensils and then put them into food. There can be harmful bacteria in the mouth, nose, and throat.
3 Wash your hands after using a handkerchief while you are handling food.
4 Do not handle food if you have a heavy cold, sickness, or diarrhoea.
5 Cover all cuts with a clean bandage. Replace it often.
6 Keep your nails clean and your hair out of food.
7 Wear a clean apron or overall.

Safety in the kitchen

The kitchen can be the most dangerous room in the house. Accidents can happen if people are careless, particularly when there are small children in the room. You should always follow these safety rules:

1 Never allow pan handles to stick out over the edge of the cooker. They can easily be knocked over and can cause serious burns and scalds. You can buy a special safety guard for the cooker top if there are small children around.
2 Mop up any spills straight away so that no one will slip and fall.
3 Do not have curtains where they can blow on to a cooker and catch fire.
4 Never leave a deep pan of fat unattended (see page 45).
5 Do not place oven gloves or tea-towels on top of the cooker where they could catch fire.
6 Do not store bleach or household cleaners under the sink if there are small children in the house. Keep them out of reach.
7 Do not leave matches lying around.
8 Use proper, thick oven gloves to lift hot dishes from the oven.
9 Keep sharp knives and utensils out of the reach of children.

Questions

1 **Why is cleanliness in the kichen essential?**
2 **What are the symptoms of food poisoning?**
3 **Describe the foods and the conditions in which bacteria multiply quickly.**
4 **What happens to bacteria under (a) very hot, and (b) very cold conditions?**
5 **You have cooked a joint of beef which you want to eat cold the next day. How would you keep it as fresh as possible?**
6 **Why must you wash your hands after using the toilet?**
7 **Why shouldn't you lick your fingers when preparing food?**
8 **How would you take steps to prevent (a) fires, (b) scalds and burns, and (c) poisoning, from occurring in the kitchen?**
9 **List the hazards shown in the picture above, and explain why each is dangerous.**

Cooking methods (1)

Although many foods, particularly fruit and vegetables, are good to eat raw, most of the food we eat is cooked. We cook it for several reasons:

1 The heat during cooking kills any bacteria which may be harmful to us.
2 Cooking makes food easier to digest. We could not eat raw flour, rice, or potatoes.
3 Food often looks and tastes more pleasant when it is cooked.
4 Cooked meals can be more varied and appetizing than raw foods, especially in cold weather.
5 Sometimes we cook food to preserve it, that is, to make it keep longer. For example, we preserve fruit when we cook it with sugar to make jam or marmalade.

We use several different methods for cooking food. They include stewing, boiling, steaming, roasting, baking, grilling, and frying. The method we choose depends on the kind of food we are cooking and on the kind of results we want.

Stewing

Stewing is a moist method of cooking, which means that the food is cooked in liquid. It is mainly used for meat and vegetables. They can be stewed either in a saucepan with a close-fitting lid, on top of the cooker, or in a covered casserole in the oven.

Because it is a long, slow process, stewing is suitable for tougher, cheaper cuts of meat, which can be made tender and appetizing. During the long, slow cooking the juices and flavour from the meat and vegetables enter the liquid, so producing a very well-flavoured gravy.

Stewing is quite an economical way of cooking, for several reasons. You can use cheaper cuts of meat and can add plenty of vegetables or pulses to make the meat go further. The food is cooked on a very low heat so that it is just simmering. Stews are easy to prepare and the food will 'look after itself' once it is cooking.

A slow cooker is ideal for making well-flavoured stews and casseroles.

Suitable cuts of meat for stewing include:

Beef – shin, blade or chuck steak. These are often just labelled 'stewing steak' or 'braising steak' in supermarkets.
Lamb – neck chops, scrag end of neck, often labelled 'stewing chops', breast or lap. Chicken and liver also make good casseroles.

Recipes in this book which involve stewing or casseroling are beef casserole, liver casserole, chicken casserole, goulash, minced beef, chicken curry, and chili con carne.

Fruit such as apples, plums and rhubarb can also be stewed.

Boiling

Boiling is another moist method of cooking, where food is cooked in just enough boiling water to cover the food.

In fact, however, most foods should <u>not</u> actually be boiled, but should be <u>simmered.</u> This means that bubbles should just rise gently at the side of the pan. When the water is really boiling it bubbles very rapidly, and food tends to break up.

True boiling is mainly used for cooking rice and pasta, as the rapidly moving water prevents the food from sticking to the bottom of the pan. It is also used for jam, to bring it to a stage where it will set.

Recipes in this book where food is cooked by boiling include pasta dishes such as macaroni cheese and spaghetti bolognese, and rice dishes such as pork and apricots and chicken curry with rice. The jams and marmalade are also boiled. Many vegetables are said to be 'boiled', for example potatoes and sprouts, but in fact they should be cooked by simmering so that they do not break up.

Questions

1 **Why do we cook most of our food?**
2 **What kind of meat is suitable for stewing? Give some examples.**
3 **Why is stewing an economical method of cooking?**
4 **Describe what is meant by 'simmering' vegetables.**
5 **Name three foods which should actually be boiled.**

Cooking methods (2)

Steaming

Steaming is another moist method of cooking, but this time the food is cooked by the steam which comes from boiling water. Steamed food does not have the crisp, appetizing flavour of food cooked by dry heat, but it is light and easy to digest. There are three basic ways of steaming:

1   Food is placed in a basin or wrapped in foil or greaseproof paper and placed in the 'universal' steamer. This is specially made to fit over most sizes of saucepan, and has holes in the base to allow steam to pass through.

2   If you do not have a universal steamer, foods such as steamed sponge puddings can be placed in a basin with enough boiling water to come half-way up.

3   Food can be cooked on a plate over a pan of boiling water. It should be covered by another plate or by a piece of greaseproof paper and the pan lid. This method is suitable for thin pieces of fish. Potatoes can be cooked in the water below at the same time.

Whichever method you choose, these points are important:

1   The water should be boiling before you put the food in and should not go off the boil.
2   Keep a kettle simmering to refill the pan with boiling water when necessary so that it does not boil dry.
3   All puddings must be well covered with foil or greaseproof paper so that they do not become damp and soggy.
4   The pans must have close fitting lids so that steam does not escape too rapidly.

Recipes where food is cooked by steaming include fish, for making fish cakes or fish in cheese sauce, and steamed sponge pudding (jam, chocolate, and currant).

Roasting or baking

This is a method of cooking with dry heat. True roasting is done on a rotating spit or rotisserie in front of a fierce heat. But now we talk about 'roast meat' or 'roast potatoes' even though they have really been baked rather than roasted.
        Roasted foods have a good flavour and an attractive, crisp appearance. This method is only suitable for tender cuts of meat (which are more expensive), as cheaper cuts would become tougher in the dry heat. When roasting or baking meat, the meat is first sealed in a hot oven to keep the juices in, then the heat is

lowered and the joint cooked through. It should be basted with hot fat during cooking to keep it moist. Many people now wrap meat in foil before roasting it. This keeps the meat moist and prevents it from shrinking as much. But it does not have quite as crisp a finish, even though the foil is removed for the last twenty minutes of cooking time for the meat to brown.

Suitable cuts of meat for roasting include:

Beef – sirloin, ribs, top side.
Lamb – leg, shoulder, loin, breast. (The latter is not an expensive cut, but it is a little fatty. It can be boned and rolled with stuffing to make a tasty and inexpensive meal.)
Pork – leg, fillet, spare rib, loin.
Chicken and turkey.

Recipes which involve roasting or baking are roast stuffed breast of lamb, baked chicken joints, baked potatoes. Most cakes, bread, biscuits, and puddings are cooked by baking too.

Grilling

Grilling is a quick method of cooking food because the food is close to the source of heat and the heat is quite strong. Grilling is only suitable for foods which can be cooked through in quite a short time. This means that only tender cuts of meat, not too thick, should be used.

Suitable foods include:

Beef – rump, fillet, or sirloin steak. Pork chops, lamb cutlets and chops, liver, kidney, sausages, bacon, chicken joints, and fish.
Grilling can also be used to brown the top of foods such as fish in cheese sauce or macaroni cheese.

Rules for grilling:
1 Brush foods lightly with fat to stop them from drying out.
2 When cooking meat, the grill should be pre-heated until red hot. Seal the meat on both sides under the hot grill to keep the juices in. Then lower the heat while the food cooks.
3 Turn foods occasionally during cooking so that they cook evenly without over-browning.

Questions

1 **How would you expect a steamed sponge pudding to compare with a baked sponge pudding?**
2 **Draw and describe how a Christmas pudding would be cooked in a universal steamer.**
3 **What precautions would you have to take when steaming a pudding?**
4 **Why is roasting only suitable for tender cuts of meat?**
5 **Name two cuts of beef, pork, and lamb which are suitable for roasting.**
6 **Why should a grill be pre-heated when grilling chops or steak?**
7 **Name some kinds of beef steak suitable for grilling, and name some less expensive meats which can also be grilled.**

Cooking methods (3)

Frying

Frying is a quick method of cooking in hot fat or oil. It is a popular method of cooking as the fat gives a good flavour to the food and the cooking time is short. But as we are generally advised to cut down the amount of fat we eat (see Chapter 1), we should avoid eating fried foods too often. Any food which is fried always absorbs a lot of extra fat. Some of the foods we often fry, like bacon or chops, would be better grilled, so that the excess fat drains away.

There are two types of frying, shallow frying and deep-fat frying.

Shallow frying

This is done in a frying pan. Sometimes you do not need to add any fat, for example, when cooking sausages or bacon. There is enough fat in these foods already to prevent them from sticking. For other foods you need just enough fat to cover the bottom of the pan, for example, when frying fish cakes, beefburgers, or eggs.

Deep-fat frying

This is where food is cooked by being completely immersed in hot fat in a deep-fat frier or chip pan. Because the fat is so hot, most foods except potatoes need a coating before they are put into the pan. This stops the food from breaking up and it also helps the food to be cooked through evenly without burning on the outside.

Suitable coatings: Flour, egg and breadcrumbs (e.g. for fish or fish cakes), batter (e.g. for fish or fritters).

Suitable fats to use: beef dripping, lard, or vegetable oil. The fat or oil must be one which can be heated to a high temperature without burning. The temperature will depend on the food being cooked. If the fat is too cool, it will be absorbed by the food, making it greasy. If the fat is too hot, the food will be crisp and brown on the outside before the inside is cooked. The most reliable way of checking that the fat is at the right heat is to use a special thermometer. But as a rough guide, a small piece of bread dropped into the fat should turn a pale golden brown in about 30 seconds. Sometimes a faint haze over the fat shows it is ready. But as some modern fats do not haze, this is not always a reliable guide.

Take care when frying
Be extremely careful when using a deep-fat frier or chip pan. The fat can become very hot and dangerous. If it is overheated to a very high temperature it will burst into flames. Many fires in homes have been started by chip pans. You should never go away and leave the pan unattended. If the door bell or the phone rings, turn the heat off under the pan before you answer it. It is easy to forget about the pan once you start to talk to someone, and this is how fires start.

If the pan does catch fire, cover it with the pan lid, a baking sheet, or a thick towel which is very slightly damp. <u>Never</u> throw water on to it and <u>never</u> try to move a burning pan.

Ideally, you should keep a small fire extinguisher or fire-blanket in the kitchen. They are not very expensive and will put out a fire quickly and efficiently.

Rules for frying successfully

1 Never fill the pan more than two-thirds full. Lower food into it very gently.
2 Keep water away from hot fat or it may spurt and burn you.
3 Do not try to cook large amounts of fried food at once. The fat will become too cool for good results and the pan may become dangerously full.
4 Use clean, suitable fat or oil. Do not let it overheat and burn.
5 Drain fried food on absorbent kitchen paper before serving it, to remove any excess fat.
6 Strain the fat or oil after use, using muslin or a fine metal strainer. This will remove crumbs and particles of food which could otherwise cause the fat to decompose.

Equipment for deep-fat frying.

Suitable foods for frying include:

The more expensive, tender cuts of meat: beef — rump, fillet, or sirloin steak, pork and lamb chops or cutlets. Tougher meat can never be made tender by frying. Sausages, bacon, fish, liver, chicken portions, fish cakes, and beefburgers can all be fried.

Recipes which involve frying include fish cakes, beefburgers, and pancakes. In many stews and casseroles, too, the meat and vegetables are lightly fried before cooking in order to develop the flavour.

Questions

1 **Why is frying a popular method of cooking?**
2 **Give an alternative method of cooking these foods instead of frying them: eggs, bacon, fish fingers, sausages, chops.**
3 **Why do most foods except potatoes have a coating added before being deep-fried?**
4 **How would you know when deep fat or oil was hot enough for frying?**
5 **Chip pans which overheat are a frequent cause of fires in kitchens. What precautions would you always take when using a chip pan?**
6 **If the fat you used for frying chips was rather burnt and full of particles of food, what results do you think you would have?**

Cooking for the family

The way in which people arrange their meals depends on what suits their particular families. Some people like to have a cooked breakfast in the morning, others like a very light breakfast. Some families have their main meal at midday, others prefer it in the evening. This will depend, for example, on whether the mother is at home all day with small children, whether the family have time to come home at midday, whether any of them has a cooked meal at work or at school, or whether they take a packed lunch. The family will decide on the arrangement that suits them best and plan their meals accordingly.

You will see that in the menus in this book meals are described as breakfast, main meal, and lighter meal. This is the pattern most people follow, whatever time of day they choose to eat their main meal. You will notice that all the main meals have three courses. Most of us don't have a three-course meal every day, but as you are now learning to plan and cook well-balanced menus, it is useful for you to have some ideas. There will be times when you want to make a three-course meal, perhaps for a special occasion – or for a practical cookery exam!

Points to think about when you are planning meals

1 Who will be eating the meal? Your family might include an expectant mother, a toddler, an elderly grandmother, a father with a heavy job, a vegetarian, and a daughter on a slimming diet! You don't want to have to make different meals for all of them. As far as possible, choose meals which can be adapted to suit most of your family.
2 How much time do you have for preparing and cooking the meal?
3 How much money do you have to spend?
4 Which fruit and vegetables are good and cheap, because they are in season?
5 Would a hot meal or a cold salad be more suitable for the weather?
6 Is the meal to be an ordinary family meal or is it for a special occasion?
7 With planning, many meals can be made using the top of the cooker only, without having to light the oven. This will save fuel.
8 Make sure the meal is good from a nutritional point of view. Try to include a good variety of fresh foods and not too many sweet, fried, or fatty foods.

Planning main meals – how to make up a menu

1 Choose the main dish first of all. Look at the list of recipes in this book for ideas. Will you use meat, fish, eggs, or cheese, or will you make a vegetarian dish? Think about how much it will cost you, and whether you want a more or less expensive meat or fish. Think about the time it will take, both to prepare and to cook.
2 Choose either potatoes, pastry, rice, or pasta to go with the dish, to make it more filling.

3   Choose vegetables or a salad to go with it. You should include some fresh vegetables or fruit in every meal you make.

4   When you have decided on the main course, choose a first course and a pudding to go with it. If the main course is very substantial, the other courses may be lighter. For example, if you were having chicken and mushroom pie for your main course, then a light pudding like fruit fool would go well with it.

   If you were having a light main course like cottage cheese and pineapple salad, then a more filling pudding like an apple pie or a steamed pudding would balance it.

5   Choose different colours, textures, and hot and cold dishes to give the meal variety. Do not serve onion soup, white fish, boiled potatoes, and cauliflower, followed by rice pudding. (Why not?)

   Do not serve two pastry dishes in one meal, for example, chicken and mushroom pie followed by apple pie.

   Do not serve Florida cocktail followed by meat and salad followed by fresh fruit salad, unless you are on a slimming diet. (Why not?)

Showing your cookery skill

When you are choosing a meal to cook for a practical cookery examination, remember that you not only want to choose a meal which is well balanced and looks colourful, but you also want to show your skill as a cook.

   Dishes which show skills include baked goods like bread, cakes, pastries, biscuits, or scones, a well-made sauce which has a good flavour and is free from lumps, or the attractive icing and decoration of a cake.

Questions

1   **What are the reasons why most families have their main meal in the evening rather than at midday?**

2   **You are in charge of planning the meals of your family for one week. What do you consider are the five most important points you would have to think about when choosing the meals?**

3   **You are deciding on the menu for the family's main meal of the day. Write down the order in which you would choose the food.**

4   **Suggest three sweet and three savoury dishes which an inexperienced cook could probably prepare well.**

5   **Suggest three sweet and three savoury dishes which would show the skill of a more experienced cook.**

Menus

There are plenty of ideas below to help you begin planning menus for yourself. Use these menus as a guide and look at the list of recipes in the back of this book for other ideas.

Main meals

If you want a two-course meal, just leave out the first course. You don't need to have a pudding at every meal, especially if you are cutting down on fat and sugar. You can eat fresh fruit instead. If you do serve a hot pudding, always serve custard or a sauce with it. Notice that plenty of fresh fruit and vegetables are included in these meals. If you want to serve tea or coffee at the end of the meal, page 109 tells you how to make and serve it.

Florida cocktail Beef and vegetable casserole Boiled potatoes Brussels sprouts Jelly whip Shortbread biscuits	Tomato soup Minced beef Dumplings Carrots and sprouts Lemon cheesecake
Vegetable soup Chicken curry Rice Fresh fruit salad Baked egg custard	Ham and cheese roll-ups Beefburgers, tomato sauce Boiled potatoes Cauliflower Apple pie and custard
Onion soup Quiche Lorraine Tomato salad Cucumber salad Steamed jam sponge Jam sauce or custard	Mackerel pâté Pork and apricots Rice Mexican salad Apple charlotte and custard
Lentil soup Fish and cheese sauce Duchess potatoes Buttered carrots Sponge fruit flan	Stuffed tomatoes Liver casserole Baked potatoes Cabbage Pineapple upside-down pudding Pineapple sauce or custard

Lighter meals

Here are some suggestions for menus for the lighter meal of the day, whether it is lunch, tea, high tea or supper. If you take a packed meal to work or school you will find some suitable ideas for food which can be carried on page 78.

Cheese and onion flan
Lettuce and cucumber salad
Fruit fool
Wholemeal fruit cake

Vegetable soup
Macaroni cheese
Baked tomatoes
Apple sponge flan

Cheese pizza
Coleslaw
Bread and butter
Stewed apple
Baked egg custard

Mushroom soup
Sardine and tomato salad
Potato salad
Victoria scones

Beefburgers, bread buns
Fresh fruit salad
Victoria sandwich cake

Tomato soup
Tuna fish salad
Wholemeal bread buns
Sponge sandwich cake

Questions

1 **Write out four menus each for a three-course main meal following the pattern shown here. You can look in the recipe section for ideas.**
2 **Write out menus for four lighter meals, following the pattern shown above.**

Reasons for choice

Sometimes you are asked to give the reasons why you think the dishes you have chosen are suitable. Look at one of the meals on page 48:

Onion soup
Quiche Lorraine
Tomato salad
Cucumber salad
Steamed jam sponge
Jam sauce or custard

Your reasons for including them in your menu might be as follows:

Onion soup – the soup has a good, savoury flavour and provides a hot start to the meal, as the main course is cold.

Quiche Lorraine is an attractive main course dish providing the meal with a good amount of animal protein in the eggs, milk, cheese, and bacon. The dish shows skill in making pastry and in lining the flan ring.

Tomato and cucumber salads – these provide a colourful accompaniment to the main dish. Being crisp, they add a variety of texture to the meal. The tomatoes are a good source of Vitamin C.

Steamed sponge pudding – quite a filling pudding after a fairly light main course. Skill is shown in making the sponge.

Jam sauce or custard – a suitable accompaniment to the pudding.

Here is another example. You have been asked to make a meal for visitors who might be delayed. You could choose the following meal:

Florida cocktail
Beef and vegetable casserole
Baked potatoes
Jelly whip
Shortbread biscuits

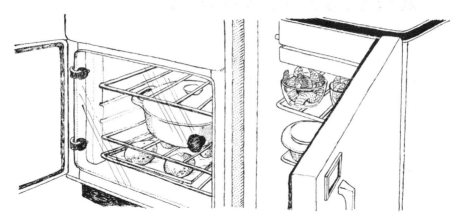

The reasons for your choice this time might be as follows:

Florida cocktail — a cold starter which can be prepared in advance and kept cool until needed. It is colourful, and the oranges and grapefruit are a good source of Vitamin C.

Beef and vegetable casserole — the main dish of the meal, providing a good source of protein and iron in the beef. Plenty of vegetables can be included in the casserole, so they will not need to be kept hot separately. The casserole can be kept hot on a low heat in the oven till the visitors arrive, without spoiling.

Baked potatoes — suitable for serving with a casserole. They too can be kept hot without spoiling.

Jelly whip — a cold sweet contrasts well with the hot main course. It can be kept covered in a refrigerator until needed.

Shortbread biscuits — these are a suitable accompaniment to the jelly whip, providing a crisp texture to go with the soft sweet. The biscuits also show skill in the making and shaping.

You might be asked to make a meal suitable for a small child, an elderly person, a vegetarian, or someone on a slimming diet. You will find suggestions for choosing suitable meals for these and many other occasions in Chapter 4.

Questions

1 **Suggest a three-course menu for a family meal, which includes a fish dish and a hot pudding. Write the menu out correctly as above, then give your reasons for the choice of dishes.**
2 **Write out a menu for a three-course family meal which includes a soup and some freshly cooked vegetables. Give the reasons for your choice.**
3 **Write out a menu for supper or tea, for a family who all have their main meal in the middle of the day. Give the reasons for your choice.**
4 **Write out a menu for a three-course meal which includes a cold starter, a cold pudding and a hot main course. Give the reasons for your choice.**

Working out the cost of recipes

Sometimes it is useful to be able to work out how much it costs to make a certain dish or meal. Then you can plan meals more easily according to whether you have plenty of money to spend, or whether you are trying to economize but still eat well. The price of some foods, like eggs, fruit, and vegetables varies according to the time of year, but you can still work out an approximate price.

Copy this chart into your own exercise book and fill in the spaces. There is a column for the cost of the usual size packet, box or tin, then there is a column for the cost for 25g or 1 ounce of the food. If you fill this in, it is very useful to refer to when you want to know the cost of making any recipe quickly.

	1.5kg (3lb)	25g		500g (1lb)	Each
Flour			*Fresh fruit*		
Plain/S.R.			Oranges		
Strong White			Grapefruit		
Wholemeal			Lemons		
			Eating apples		
Fats	250g (½lb)		Pears		
Butter			Bananas		
Margarine			Grapes		
Lard, Dripping			Plums		
Suet			Cooking apples		
			Rhubarb		
Sugar	1 kilo (2lb)				
Granulated			*Vegetables*		
	500g (1lb)		Potatoes		
Castor			Carrots		
Icing			Onions		
Soft brown			Turnip		
			Swede		
Currants			Cauliflower		
Sultanas			Cabbage		
Raisins			Sprouts		
Coconut			Leeks		
Cherries			Mushrooms		
Dates			Celery		
			Peppers		
Macaroni			Cucumber		
Spaghetti			Lettuce		
Lasagne			Watercress		
			Mustard & cress		
Rice, long grain			Parsley		
Rice, pudding			Radishes		
Semolina			Spring onions		
			Tomatoes		
Lentils					
Split peas					
Dried kidney beans					
Dried butter beans					

Dairy foods		Fish
Milk, 1 pint/500ml		Cod
Cream, small carton, double		Haddock
		Coley
Cottage cheese, small carton		Herrings
Yoghourt, plain, small carton		Tinned foods
Eggs, dozen		Tomatoes
each		Pineapple
Creamy topping, small packet		Pears
		Evaporated milk, small
Cheese, Cheddar, 100g (4oz)		Corned beef
		Mackerel
		Tuna
Meat	500g (1lb)	Concentrated soup
Sausages		Kidney beans
Sausage meat		Butter beans
Bacon		
Cooked ham (¼lb)		Cocoa
Liver, ox		Tea
lamb		Coffee
Chicken livers		
Beef, minced		Bread, large loaf, 25g
Stewing steak, chuck or blade		Cornflour
Lamb, Breast or lap		Custard powder
Shoulder		Digestive biscuits
Leg		Jelly, packet
Pork, Belly		Oil
Spare rib		Potato, pkt instant dried
Fillet		Tomato purée
Chops		Vinegar
Chicken		Yeast, sachet of dried
		Yeast, fresh, 25g

Questions

1 **Work out the cost of each of these recipes: apple crumble, rice pudding, beef and vegetable casserole, cheese and potato bake. Here is an example of how to write out the calculation:**

Apple crumble

500g/1lb cooking apples	**18p**
75g/3oz sugar	**3p**
100g/4oz flour	**3p**
50g/2oz margarine	**4p**
50g/2oz sugar	**2p**
Total cost	**30p approximately**

2 **Work out the cost of some of the meals on page 48. Work out the cost of each dish separately, then add them all to give the total cost of the meal.**

Making a time plan

When you are preparing for a practical cookery exam, you usually have to make a time plan to show how you are going to organize your work within the time available. It may seem complicated at first, but once you understand the idea behind it, it becomes much easier and helps you to avoid making mistakes when you are cooking.

Imagine that you are making these four items:

Sausage rolls (with shortcrust pastry),
Rock buns,
Lemon cake (decorated with butter icing and glacé icing),
Scones.

To help you, make a chart like this which gives you all the details you need to know about each dish you are making:

Dish	Method	Oven temp.	Shelf	Approx. cooking time	Test for whether it is cooked
Sausage rolls	Pastry: rubbing-in	6/200°C	Top	25 mins	Golden brown, crisp
Rock buns	Rubbing-in	7/220°C	Top	15 mins	Golden brown, firm
Lemon cake	All-in-one	5/190°C	Centre	20 mins	Golden brown, firm
Scones	Rubbing-in	7/220°C	Top	15 mins	Well risen, golden

You have to start work at 9.30 and serve the finished dishes at 11.30. You must plan your morning's work so that everything will be cooked and ready in time. Before you decide which items to make first, you will have to think about these points:

1 Two items which need <u>very</u> different oven temperatures cannot be baked successfully at the same time.
2 Sometimes you want to cook two dishes in the oven at the same time and they need only <u>slightly</u> different temperatures. You can manage this if you plan

carefully. For example, you may want to cook an apple crumble at gas mark 5 and gingerbread at gas mark 4. You could do this by putting the oven on at mark 4, then cooking the apple crumble at the top of the oven where it will be hotter, and cooking the gingerbread in the centre of the oven.

3   If you are making a cake which has to be decorated with cream or icing, you will have to make it early, so that it will be cool before you decorate it.

Once you have thought about all the details you will be able to make a plan similar to the following:

Time	Order of work
9.30	Collect the equipment and ingredients you need.
9.35	Light the oven, Gas 5/190°C. Make lemon cake by all-in-one method, divide between two tins.
9.50	Bake near oven centre for about 20 mins until golden brown and firm (out of oven about 10.10). Wash the dishes used.
9.55	Make shortcrust pastry for sausage rolls by rubbing-in method, then shape the sausage rolls.
10.10	Remove lemon cake if cooked, turn up oven to Gas 6/200°C.
10.15	Bake sausage rolls for about 25 mins until golden brown (out of oven about 10.40). Wash dishes.
10.20	Make rock buns by rubbing-in method.
10.40	Remove sausage rolls if cooked. Turn oven up to Gas 7/220°C. Bake rock buns for about 15 mins until golden brown and firm (out about 10.55).
10.45	Make scones by rubbing-in method
11.00	Bake at the top of the oven, Gas 7/220°C, for about 15 mins until well risen and golden brown (out of oven about 11.15).
11.05	Make icings and use to decorate cake.
11.25	Wash up and clear away.
11.30	Serve all the dishes.

Practical work

1   **Choose four simple baked items and make a time plan for them, starting at 9.30 and ending at 11.30.**

 First of all, make a chart like the one on the facing page. Then you will have all the details of the dishes you are making. Carefully check the oven temperatures to make sure you will have time to cook different items at the right temperatures.

 Then try and draw up a time plan like the one above. You will probably find it takes you several attempts to get it to work out, but you will improve with practice!

2   **Make a time plan to fit your own practical cookery lesson. The time you have could vary between about one and three hours. You should be able to make two or more items depending on the time available.**

Time plan for a meal

Sometimes you have to draw up a time plan for a meal, perhaps lunch or dinner. This is rather different from a plan for making several baked items, because not all the dishes are cooked in the oven.

The meal may be like this:

> Stuffed tomatoes
>
> Chicken casserole
> Boiled potatoes
> Sprouts
>
> Apple crumble and custard

When you are making a plan for a meal like this, the most important thing to remember is that all the food has to be cooked and served hot at the same time.

If the meal is to be served at 12 o'clock, it is no good having the potatoes cooked by 10.30, the sprouts ready at 11, and the custard made by 11.30. This may sound obvious but in fact it is quite difficult to organize everything so that all the food is cooked, but not overdone, at the right time.

Any dishes which are to be served cold, like the stuffed tomatoes, can always be made in advance and left to keep cool.

The casserole, which is cooked in the oven, should be made early to make sure it is ready in time. It can then be left to look after itself until it is to be served.

The vegetables need the most careful thought. The potatoes will take about 20 minutes to cook, the sprouts about 15 minutes. If dinner is to be served at 12, you will have to start cooking the vegetables at about 11.30, so that they will just be cooked, but not overdone, by dinner time.

The apple crumble takes about 40 minutes to cook, so it should go in the oven at about 11.15. If you start to make it just before 11, it will be ready at the right time.

The custard has to be made last of all. If it is made too early it will be cold and unappetizing by the time it is to be eaten.

Again it will help you if you make a quick chart before you start the time plan, reminding you of the details you will have to remember.

Dish	Method	Oven temp.	Shelf	Approx. cooking time	Test for whether it is cooked
Stuffed tomatoes					
Chicken casserole		4/180°C	Centre	1½ hrs	Meat should be tender
Potatoes				20 mins	Soft when tested with skewer
Sprouts				15 mins	Soft but still firm
Apple crumble	Crumble: rubbing-in	5/190°C	Top	40 mins	Golden brown, apples soft
Custard				5 mins	

Time	Order of work
10.00	Collect the equipment and ingredients needed.
10.05	Prepare vegetables for the casserole. Make the casserole.
10.30	Put casserole in centre of oven, Gas 4/180°C, for about 1½ hours, until the chicken is tender (out about 12 o'clock).
10.35	Prepare the stuffed tomatoes, leave in a cool place.
10.55	Prepare crumble topping by rubbing-in method. Prepare the apples, add crumble topping.
11.15	Put in oven above the casserole. Bake for about 40 mins until apples are soft and top is golden brown (out about 11.55).
11.16	Put water on to boil for vegetables. Peel the potatoes and prepare the sprouts.
11.30	Simmer the potatoes gently for about 20–25 mins, until soft when tested with a skewer (cooked about 11.55).
11.35	Simmer sprouts for about 15 mins until cooked (about 11.55).
11.45	Make the custard.
11.55	Drain the vegetables.
12.00	Serve the meal.

Practical work

Write out a menu for a simple two- or three-course meal which includes potatoes and vegetables.

Decide on the time you have to start work and the time you will serve the meal. Make a time/order of work plan, similar to the one above.

Before you start, make a quick chart like the one at the top of the page. You will find it makes the time plan much easier to do.

Time plan for a special occasion meal

Mushroom soup, bread rolls

Pork and apricots

Rice

Cucumber salad, tomato salad

Sponge fruit gateau

Coffee

A time plan for this meal, suitable for a special occasion, is a little more complicated. Think about each of the dishes on the menu and think about any special points about the timing and preparation of each.

Mushroom soup – if necessary, this could be made in advance, blended, and returned to the pan, ready to be reheated just before serving.

Bread rolls – these will have to be mixed, kneaded for 10 minutes, shaped, then left to rise for about 30–40 minutes.

The *pork and apricots* and the *rice* should be cooked just before they are needed.

The *cucumber and tomato salads* can both be prepared in advance and left in a cool place. Both of these are served with a French dressing. This can be prepared in advance, but should be shaken and put on the salads about 20 minutes before they are served.

Sponge fruit gateau. The cake must be made early so that it will be cold before you decorate it with whipped cream.

Before you start the time plan, make a rough note of the preparation and cooking details you will need to know.

Dish	Method	Oven temp.	Shelf	Approx. cooking time	Test for whether it is cooked
Soup				25 mins	
Rolls	Mixed, kneaded, left to rise	8/230°C	Top	15–20 mins	Golden brown, hollow sound if tapped underneath
Pork and apricots				30–40 mins	Meat should be tender
Rice				11 mins	Soft, but still firm shape
Gateau	Whisking	6/200°C	Above centre	10 mins	Firm, golden brown

The coffee must be made last, just before the meal is served. Allow 5 to 10 minutes for the coffee to infuse.

As you become better at making out time plans, you may find you do not need to make a chart like this, but can make an order of work plan just by referring to the recipe.

Time	Order of work
9.30	Collect the equipment and ingredients needed.
9.35	Make bread roll mixture, knead for 10 mins, shape.
9.55	Put in a warm place to rise for 30—40 mins (ready to bake about 10.30).
10.00	Make sponge cake by whisking method.
10.10	Put in the oven, above centre, Gas 6/200°C, for about 10 mins, until firm and golden brown (cooked at about 10.20). Prepare the soup.
10.20	Simmer the soup gently for about 25 mins (ready 10.45).
10.30	Put bread buns near top of oven, Gas 8/230°C, for 15—20 mins until golden brown. They should sound hollow when tapped underneath if they are done (out of oven about 10.45). Make the salad, cover and leave in a cool place. Make the French dressing.
10.45	Liquidize the soup. Leave in pan ready to reheat.
10.50	Drain the fruit, whip the cream, decorate the gateau.
11.15	Prepare pork and apricots, simmer until tender (about 11.55).
11.35	Prepare the tray for the coffee, put kettle on low heat. Put water on to boil for rice.
11.45	Boil rice for 11 mins (ready at 11.56). Gently reheat the soup. Spoon dressing over salads.
11.55	Drain the rice, place on serving dish with pork. Make the coffee.
12.00	Serve the meal and tray of coffee.

Practical work

Suggest a menu for a meal of three courses and coffee, which includes an item made with yeast.

Make a time plan for the meal, starting at 9.30 and finishing at 12 o'clock, or starting at 1.30 and finishing at 4 o'clock.

Meals in pregnancy

When a woman is pregnant she should be extra careful to make sure she has a good diet. A healthy, well-nourished mother is much more likely to have a healthy baby than a mother who has not taken much care of herself during her pregnancy.

An expectant mother should:

1 Visit the doctor as soon as suspects that she is pregnant.
2 Make sure she goes to the ante-natal clinic regularly.
3 Try to give up smoking, or at least cut down; and cut down on drinking alcohol, especially spirits.
4 Eat good meals, with plenty of variety and plenty of fresh foods.

Eating for two means that an expectant mother has two people to consider when she chooses what to eat. She is responsible for the baby's healthy growth and development now as well as her own. Eating for two does not mean that she should eat twice as much as she used to. If she did, she would put on unnecessary weight, which might be difficult to lose afterwards. She will need a little more food than usual, though, especially in the later stages of pregnancy and when breast-feeding the baby.

Foods to eat

A pregnant woman doesn't need to eat any particular foods as long as she has a good varied diet. She should not try to 'make do' with sweet, starchy snacks if she is at home by herself during the day. It is quite possible to have a light, well-balanced snack meal such as bread and butter, cheese, an orange, and a milky drink, without spending too much time preparing it.

A pregnant woman should make sure that she eats plenty of fruit and vegetables, potatoes, milk and dairy foods, fish, and iron-rich foods such as liver and red meat. Bread, especially wholemeal bread, whole breakfast cereals, and bran should be eaten daily. They all will provide dietary fibre to prevent constipation, which can be common in pregnancy.

Foods to avoid

Like everyone else, an expectant mother should avoid a lot of sugary, fatty foods. If she suffers from sickness, indigestion, or heartburn, then fried, greasy, or spicy foods could make it worse. Strong tea and coffee can also have this effect. If she is putting on too much weight, she can safely cut out all puddings and cakes and eat fresh fruit instead. She should not take any pills or medicines, including vitamin and iron pills, unless she has talked to her doctor about it. If she has a varied diet with plenty of good foods, then vitamins and iron supplements should not normally be needed and may be better avoided.

Suggested meals for one day

Breakfast	*Main meal*	*Lighter meal*
Wholemeal or bran cereal	Stuffed tomatoes	Vegetable soup
Scrambled egg	Liver casserole	Cheese and onion flan
Brown or white toast	Baked potatoes	Coleslaw
Butter and marmalade	Cauliflower	Banana cake
Tea or coffee	Apple pie and custard	

Ideas for other meals

Mackerel pâté, beef casserole or stew, spaghetti bolognese, chicken casserole, cheese pizza, macaroni cheese, Quiche Lorraine.
Apricot fool, steamed chocolate pudding and chocolate sauce, custard tart, gingerbread, wholemeal scones, fruit cake.

Practical work

1 **Plan a day's meals for an expectant mother who is at home with her two-year-old child during the day.**
2 **State (a) the main nutrients provided by each dish, and (b) the reasons why you have chosen it.**
3 **Cheese is a good food for an expectant mother. Make a main dish for the family tea or supper which includes cheese.**
4 **It is a good idea to include liver in meals once a week, to help form good red blood cells for mother and baby. Prepare a dish for the family's evening meal using liver, and serve it with boiled rice or boiled potatoes.**
5 **Wholemeal flour is a useful source of dietary fibre in pregnancy. Make a cake, bread, or some scones, using wholemeal flour.**
6 **Make a meat dish which could be left to cook in the oven during a visit to the ante-natal clinic. Cook some jacket potatoes and a milk pudding at the same time. Also prepare a cold first course or starter to go with the meal.**

Meals for toddlers and small children

When babies are a few months old they are gradually <u>weaned</u> or introduced to solid foods. Over the months their diet changes from milk to sieved foods and then to the same foods as the rest of the family eat.

A sensible mother will encourage her children to enjoy as wide a variety of foods as possible from an early age. This will help the child not to be 'fussy' about food later on but to fit easily into the family meal pattern. Many of the family's everyday meals will suit the baby. For example, they may be having meat, gravy, potatoes, and vegetables, followed by a fruit pudding and custard. A portion of each course can be sieved or put through a mouli or electric blender to make it suitable for the baby. Cans or jars of baby food can be kept as a useful standby if the family meal is unsuitable.

As the child gets older he will become more used to managing different foods. But while children are still toddlers (about two or three years old), you should remember these points when choosing suitable food for them:

1 Young children often have small appetites and do not like large quantities. They like small portions of food neatly served.
2 Children need food which is easy to manage on a plate. They will not be very skilled with a knife and fork.
3 Young children usually enjoy eating from their own special dishes and using their own cutlery.

4 They may find large pieces of meat difficult to chew and swallow.
5 Do not give them a lot of greasy, fried, rich, or spicy foods, which can be difficult to digest.
6 Encourage them to enjoy a variety of foods. Sometimes they will refuse to eat certain foods, often vegetables. This will not do them any harm if they eat fruit and cereal foods instead.
7 Do not encourage them to want a lot of sugar. There is no need to add sugar to drinks, breakfast cereals, and fruit. Children do not need it and it will spoil their teeth. Do not give them sweets between meals.
8 Train them from an early age to have good table manners, setting them a good example yourself.

Suggested meals for one day

Breakfast

Scrambled egg
Fingers of toast
Milk or fruit juice

Main meal

Fish cakes, tomato sauce
Carrots, peas
Steamed sponge
    pudding, custard

Lighter meal

Sandwiches, brown or
white bread, with a
savoury filling, such as
grated or cottage
cheese, egg and tomato,
sardine, or yeast extract

Jelly whip, Swiss roll
Fruit juice to drink

Ideas for other meals

Beefburgers, chicken or beef casserole, fish and cheese sauce, macaroni
cheese, minced beef, savoury beef and tomato.
Baked egg custard, fruit crumble, apple charlotte, rice pudding, stewed fruit.
Scones, banana cake, cheese loaf, fruit loaf, gingerbread, queen cakes, rock
buns, Victoria sandwich cake.

Practical work

1 **You are helping to look after the children in a day nursery for a week. Plan
a day's meals for the children to include their breakfast, lunch, and tea.**
2 **State (a) the main nutrients provided by each dish, and (b) the reasons
why you have chosen it.**
3 **You are looking after two three-year-old children for a day. Prepare and
cook a dish suitable for their main course for dinner, and some vegetables
to go with it.**
4 **Your two-year-old child refuses to drink milk but you want to include it in
his diet. Cook two dishes he would enjoy, which use milk as a main
ingredient.**
5 **Prepare one sweet and one savoury dish suitable for a packed lunch for a
playgroup outing. Make a drink to take.**
6 **Prepare a selection of dishes suitable for a five-year-old's birthday party.
Include a drink.**

Meals for elderly people

As they get older, many people find that they cannot eat and enjoy the same foods as they once did. They may find that certain foods do not 'agree with them' any more and give them indigestion, or they may not have good teeth and gums and so may find it more difficult to chew and swallow.

Some older people, of course, can continue to enjoy the same foods, but many others will find that a few gradual changes in their diet will make them feel fitter and more healthy.

There are many reasons why the elderly do not always feed themselves very well. These might include:

1   Difficulty in shopping, especially if the shops are a long way off or the weather is bad.
2   Shortage of money, which may lead them to eat mainly starchy, sugary foods because they are cheapest.
3   Difficulty in buying amounts small enough for one, especially if they do not have a fridge in which to keep food fresh.
4   If living alone, an old person may not feel like bothering to shop and cook just for one. Again, this could lead to a diet consisting largely of foods like biscuits, cakes, and bread and jam, because they are easy to prepare and keep. This will mean that their diet lacks the variety of foods they need to feel really well.

Foods to choose

When planning meals for old people include foods which are good sources of the following nutrients, in a form suitable for their needs:

Protein: More easily digested in foods such as chicken, white fish, minced beef, casseroles, lightly cooked eggs, and milk.

Vitamin C: For general good health and good gums, and to help absorb iron. Oranges, grapefruit, blackcurrants, and fruit and tomato juices are good sources, as are tomatoes, potatoes, and green vegetables. Blackcurrant or rose-hip syrup can be added to milk puddings.

Iron: To help prevent tiredness and weakness. Easiest for old people in the form of bread, cereals, liver, corned beef, cocoa, dried fruit, and green vegetables.

Vitamin D and calcium: Help prevent a curved spine and brittle bones. Milk and other dairy foods, and bread, will provide them.

Dietary fibre: Adds bulk and roughage to the diet. Good sources are bran, wholemeal (or brown) bread, cakes, and scones, and fruit and vegetables.

Foods that may be better avoided include fried or fatty foods and strongly flavoured, spicy foods, as these could be hard to digest. Roast or grilled meat may be difficult to chew.

Suggested meals for one day

Breakfast	*Main meal*	*Lighter meal*
Glass of orange juice	Florida cocktail	Macaroni cheese
Lightly boiled egg	Chicken casserole	Baked tomatoes
Brown or white toast	Boiled potatoes	Fruit fool, shortbread
Butter and marmalade	Carrots	biscuits
Tea or coffee	Apple charlotte, custard	Bran tea loaf

Ideas for other meals
Soups, beef and vegetable casserole, minced beef, liver casserole, meat loaf, chicken and mushroom pie, fish and tomato casserole, fish and cheese sauce. Rice pudding, stewed fruit, baked egg custard, fresh fruit salad, sponge puddings and custard, fruit pie or crumble.
Scones, Victoria sandwich cake, fruit loaf, Granny loaf, Swiss roll, queen cakes.

Practical work

1 **Write out a menu for meals for one day for an elderly couple.**
2 **State (a) the main nutrients provided by each dish, and (b) the reasons why you have chosen it.**
3 **Your grandparents are staying with you for a few days. Make a milk pudding for tea and prepare and/or cook some fresh fruit to go with it.**
4 **You are going to visit your grandmother. Bake a loaf or cake and a batch of scones to take with you.**
5 **Some elderly neighbours are coming to dinner with you. Prepare a main dish using chicken or fish, and cook some fresh vegetables to go with it. Also make a suitable first course and a pudding.**

Meals for invalids

Invalids are people who are unwell or recovering from an illness. Special attention has to be paid to the food they are given as it can play an important part in helping them to get well again.

Sometimes the doctor or dietician will prescribe a particular diet for a patient, in which case it must be followed carefully as part of the medical treatment. In other cases it is only necessary to provide the patient with a 'light diet', that is, food which is easy for an invalid to digest and enjoy, and which will help him to get well again.

In the early stages of an illness, when the patient's temperature is high, he may have little appetite and require only a liquid diet – fruit juices, milk, and barley water. As his temperature drops and his appetite returns, a light diet of easily digestible solid food should be introduced.

Planning meals for invalids

1   Choose food that is easy to digest. For main meals choose chicken, white fish, lean lamb, or beef in a casserole.
2   Avoid fried foods, pork, fatty meat, rich pastry, and spicy or vinegary foods.
3   Provide food that is easy to manage, if it is to be served on a tray.
4   For puddings or tea, choose milky puddings, fresh or cooked fruit, and light sponge cakes or puddings.
5   Serve small portions, as the invalid's appetite may be poor; but serve meals regularly, as they break up the invalid's day.
6   Present meals attractively, laid neatly on a tray if necessary.
7   All food should be absolutely fresh and everything used to cook or serve the meal must by spotlessly clean.
8   Remove the tray as soon as the meal has been finished.
9   Provide refreshing drinks such as fruit juices, barley water, lemonade, or milk. Leave a supply of cool drink by the patient's bed, but make sure that it is covered.

Invalids need protein for building up the body tissues. Plan meals around the more easily digested protein-rich foods, and provide a variety of foods. Include plenty of fruit and vegetables, to supply the vitamins and minerals needed for good health. Foods providing Vitamin C and calcium are particularly important. Carbohydrate and fatty foods are not required in large amounts as an invalid does not use much energy.

Suggested meals for one day

Breakfast	Main meal	Lighter meal
Fresh grapefruit or orange juice	Tomato soup	Mushroom soup
Lightly boiled or poached egg	Fish and cheese sauce Boiled potatoes Sprouts	Cottage cheese and pineapple salad Bread and butter
Bread and butter, honey Tea	Rice pudding Stewed fruit	Apple sponge flan

Ideas for other meals

Soups, minced beef, chicken casserole, savoury beef and tomato, beef and vegetable casserole, macaroni cheese.
Eggs — boiled, poached, or scrambled.

Baked egg custard, steamed sponge pudding and custard, jelly whip, fruit fool, whisked sponge cake, Victoria sandwich cake, plain biscuits or scones (without butter icing or cream).

Practical work

1 **Plan the meals for one day for a convalescent.**
2 **State (a) the main nutrients provided by each dish, and (b) the reasons why you think it is a suitable choice.**
3 **Prepare a light breakfast for someone who is ill in bed. Serve it attractively on a tray.**
4 **Prepare an easily-digested savoury dish suitable for an invalid. Use milk or fresh fruit to make a pudding to go with it.**
5 **Make a light cake and a fruit drink suitable for serving to someone on a light diet.**

Meals for vegetarians

Vegetarians are people who do not eat meat. They may have different reasons for deciding not to eat meat. It may be because they feel that eating animal flesh is unpleasant, or they may not like the idea of animals being killed so that we can eat them. Some vegetarians do not eat meat because they feel more fit and healthy if they do not. Others consider that eating meat is a wasteful use of food when so many people in the world are hungry. If farm land is used to produce cereal crops for people to eat, then many more people can be fed than if the same area of land is used for rearing animals to be eaten as meat.

There are two types of vegetarian, lacto-vegetarians and vegans.

Lacto-vegetarians

Most vegetarians are lacto-vegetarians. They do not eat meat or fish, but they do eat milk, cheese, eggs, and butter, as well as fruit, vegetables, and cereals. It is not difficult for them to have a good diet as they have a variety of foods from which to choose their meals.

Vegans

Vegans are very strict vegetarians who will not eat any food at all from animal sources: no meat, fish, milk, eggs, cheese, butter, lard, or dripping. All their food has to come from plants. They may base their meals on beans, peas, lentils, nuts, rice, flour and other cereals, fruit, and vegetables. They use vegetable oil for cooking, or a type of margarine made from vegetable oil.

The complete lack of meat and dairy foods makes it more difficult to provide a good diet for vegans, and particularly for growing children who usually rely on these foods to provide the nutrients which are essential for the normal growth and development of strong bones and teeth.

Health food shops sell a wide variety of vegetarian foods.

Vegetable sources of protein

When you are planning meals for a lacto-vegetarian, you can replace meat and fish with eggs, cheese, and milk, and with good vegetable sources of protein like beans, peas, lentils, nuts, and cereals, including bread.

Not only vegetarians, but also many other people who are interested in having a simple healthy diet, are trying beans and peas of many kinds, including butter beans, red kidney beans, cannellini beans, soya beans, and split peas. They provide a good, inexpensive source of protein, and help to make meat go further. Depending on which you choose, they can be used in soups, in stews and casseroles, and in salads.

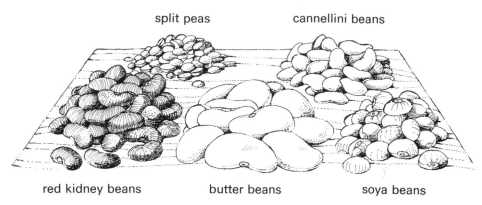

split peas   cannellini beans

red kidney beans   butter beans   soya beans

Meals for one day for a lacto-vegetarian

Breakfast

Muesli, milk
Wholemeal bread buns
Butter and honey
Tea or coffee

Main meal

Stuffed eggs
Cheese and potato bake
Kidney bean salad
Pineapple upside-down pudding, custard

Lighter meal

Lentil soup
Cheese pizza
Coleslaw, lettuce and cucumber salad
Crunchy chocolate flan

Ideas for other meals
Soups, stuffed tomatoes, melon.
Cheese and onion flan, macaroni cheese, cauliflower cheese.
Cheese loaf or scones, cottage cheese and pineapple salad, and other salads and vegetables.
Cakes, scones, yeast foods, and puddings of all kinds.

Practical work

1 **Plan meals for one day for a lacto-vegetarian.**
2 **Write down the main nutrients provided by each dish you have mentioned.**
3 **Prepare a savoury dish suitable for the main meal of the day for a lacto-vegetarian family. Cook suitable vegetables or make a salad to go with it.**
4 **Prepare a complete breakfast for a lacto-vegetarian, and lay the table.**
5 **Prepare a high tea for a family which includes a lacto-vegetarian. Include a home-made soup.**

Slimming diets

In nearly all cases, people become overweight simply because they eat more food than they need. Occasionally there are medical reasons for being overweight, so you should consult a doctor if you seriously want to go on to a slimming diet. But most people just enjoy eating, and it is very easy to eat just a little too much and to start putting on weight. People vary in the way they are able to use up their food. If you are slim you are more likely to be active and energetic, so you will be able to eat normal amounts of food. But once people are fat they usually become less active. So although they may not eat very large quantities, they find it hard to 'burn up' even normal amounts of food. This means they remain overweight or become even more so.

If you are not carrying excess weight around, you will find there are many advantages:

1   You will probably feel that you look more attractive. Clothes will fit you more easily.
2   You will probably feel fitter and more energetic. This will help you to stay slim.
3   You will be more healthy. Fat people are more likely to suffer from all kinds of diseases, including high blood pressure, coronary heart disease, diabetes, varicose veins, and some kidney diseases.

Foods to avoid

These fall into two main groups: sugary foods and fatty foods. All sugary and fatty foods are likely to make you overweight. Look at pages 10–13 to see which foods contain a lot of fat and sugar and for ideas on how to cut down on them.

Bread and potatoes

A lot of people mistakenly think of these foods as fattening, starchy foods, but in fact they are good staple foods which are inexpensive and which provide us with a good amount of the nutrients we need.

If you eat baked or boiled potatoes and wholemeal bread, they will be very good sources of dietary fibre (see p. 14). They are valuable in any diet designed to help you lose weight or keep to your correct weight. As they take quite a long time to chew and digest they will help you to feel full. This is important because many people give up their slimming diets altogether as they cannot stand feeling empty and hungry all the time. If you do not add fat to the bread and potatoes when you cook and eat them, then they will not be very fattening at all, and you may find it easier (and cheaper) to stick to your diet.

'Slimming' foods

To call a product a 'slimming food' is really a contradiction in terms because no foods can be 'slimming'. There are dozens of products for sale in the shops which are meant to help you to lose weight. They may occasionally help you to lose a couple of pounds but they do not solve the main problem. You have to learn to change your food habits so that you not only become slim, but find it possible to stay that way. If you are aiming to eat <u>less</u> overall it does not seem sensible to go out and spend <u>more</u> money on 'slimming foods'.

Planning meals

Remember:

1 Cut down on fatty, sugary foods (see pages 10–13).
2 Plan meals using lean meat, white fish, cottage cheese, eggs, reasonable amounts of bread and potatoes, and plenty of fruit and vegetables.
3 Get into the habit of eating fresh fruit instead of puddings most of the time.

Suggested meals for one day

Breakfast

Half a grapefruit
Boiled egg
Slice of wholemeal toast
(thinly spread with butter
or low-fat spread)
Tea or coffee (skimmed
milk, no sugar)

Main meal

Florida cocktail

Grilled white fish, lemon
and parsley
Grilled tomatoes
Runner beans

Natural yogurt
with fresh fruit

Lighter meal
Tomato soup[1]

Small baked potato
stuffed with cottage
cheese
Green salad

Baked egg custard[2]
Fresh fruit salad[3]

[1] Leave out the potato and use an extra carrot or onion instead.
[2] Made with liquid saccharine instead of sugar.
[3] Use unsweetened orange juice instead of syrup.

Practical work

1 **Suggest meals for one day for someone trying to lose weight.**
2 **Name ten sugary foods and ten fatty foods which a slimmer should avoid.**
3 **Make a meat, fish, or cheese dish, or a salad, for the main meal of the day for a slimmer.**
4 **Prepare a two- or three-course meal for a family which includes one person on a weight-reducing diet. Suggest foods you could add to the meal for those who are not trying to lose weight.**

Cooking for a low-fat diet

Sometimes people are advised to follow a diet which contains only a small amount of fat. Page 10 tells you which foods to avoid and suggests ways of reducing the amount of fat you consume. If the diet is suggested by a doctor he will probably give you a diet sheet to follow, but the following plan gives an idea of meals that would be suitable.

Suggested meals for one day

Breakfast	Main meal	Lighter meal
Fresh fruit juice	Melon	Lentil soup, bread buns
Smoked haddock	Beef and vegetable	Tomatoes stuffed with
Wholemeal toast, thinly	casserole	cottage cheese
spread with low-fat	Boiled potatoes	Salad
spread	Cauliflower	Rice pudding made with
Marmalade	Sponge fruit flan	skimmed milk
Coffee or tea with		Stewed apples
skimmed milk		

If your doctor advises you to eat a diet low in animal fats or saturated fats (see page 11), then you should cut all fats from animal sources out of your diet. These fats are replaced by special margarine and cooking oil made from 'polyunsaturated' fat. This can be used for cooking and baking as well as for spreading on bread. Daily meals similar to those on the plan above would be suitable.

Ideas for other meals

Tomato, onion, or vegetable soup, Florida cocktail. Lean minced beef, grilled beefburgers (made with lean mince), savoury beef and tomato (lean mince), chicken casserole, chicken curries, grilled white fish with lemon, cottage cheese and pineapple salad.

Vegetables of all kinds except roast or fried. Don't add butter after cooking. Salads.

Whisked sponge cake or Swiss roll (filled with jam, not cream), scones, fruit loaves, tea-breads, bread and other yeast recipes. Fruit, fresh or stewed, fresh fruit salad.

Practical work

1 **Suggest meals for one day for someone on a low-fat diet.**
2 **State which nutrients are provided by each food you suggest.**
3 **Prepare and cook a dish for someone on a low-fat diet, using suitable meat or fish. Also cook and serve vegetables to go with it.**
4 **Make a pudding or a whisked sponge suitable for a low-fat diet.**
5 **Your father has been advised to follow a diet low in animal fats. Prepare and cook a meal which would be suitable for the whole family including your father.**

Cooking for a high-fibre diet

Everyone is advised to include in their diet foods which provide a good amount of dietary fibre or roughage (see page 14). The following plan suggests ways of including plenty of dietary fibre in daily meals.

Suggested meals for one day

Breakfast

Bran breakfast cereal and milk
(or wholewheat cereal sprinkled with a little bran)
Wholemeal bread buns
Butter and marmalade
Tea or coffee

Main meal

Lentil soup
Savoury beef and tomato
Baked potatoes in their jackets
Carrots and Brussels sprouts
Apple crumble (mix a tablespoonful of bran into the crumble mixture)
Custard

Lighter meal

Tuna fish salad
Wholemeal bread, butter
Ginger loaf
Bran biscuits

Ideas for other meals

Dishes which include pulses (peas and beans), for example, chili con carne, pork and bacon casserole, lamb and bean casserole, kidney bean salad.
Pasta such as spaghetti or macaroni made from wholemeal flour instead of white, for example, in spaghetti bolognese or macaroni cheese.
Wholemeal bread and scones. Cakes made with wholemeal flour or with added bran, for example, bran tea loaf, ginger loaf, wholemeal fruit loaf, or banana cake. Flans or pies where the pastry is made with wholemeal flour. Vegetables of all kinds. Fruit, including stewed fruit sprinkled with bran.

Practical work

1 **Suggest meals for one day which include plenty of dietary fibre.**
2 **State the nutrients each food contains.**
3 **Prepare and cook a main course for a family meal which includes peas, beans or lentils.**
4 **Make some bread, biscuits, scones, or cakes, using either wholemeal flour or bran as one of the ingredients.**

Cooking for breakfast

Everyone should start the day with breakfast of some kind, not just a cup of tea or coffee. If you have eaten breakfast you will be able to work and concentrate much better. You will not need to have sweet biscuits and drinks during the morning because you feel hungry. Children in particular should not be allowed to go to school without having had breakfast. It is quite possible to have a good breakfast without spending a lot of time preparing it. You could include:

Fruit – half a grapefruit, grapefruit segments, freshly squeezed fruit juice or juice from a carton, bottle, or can. Stewed prunes, apricots, or figs (called a compote).

Cereals – preferably a wholewheat or bran cereal, porridge, or muesli.

Cooked dishes – grilled bacon, sausage, tomato, fried bread, black pudding. *Eggs* – boiled, scrambled, fried or poached. *Fish* – kippers, smoked haddock.

Bread – rolls, toast, or crispbread. Butter, marmalade, jam, and honey.

Breakfast menus

A light breakfast might consist of:

Fresh orange juice Cereal and milk Toast, butter, marmalade Tea

Grapefruit segments Wholemeal bread rolls Butter, honey Coffee

A full cooked or 'English' breakfast would include first fruit or cereals or porridge or muesli, then a cooked dish, then toast or rolls with butter and marmalade, jam, or honey, with tea or coffee to drink. For example:

Muesli Scrambled egg, tomato Toast, butter, marmalade Tea

Half a grapefruit Grilled bacon, sausage, fried egg Toast, butter, honey Coffee

Continental breakfast
A 'continental' breakfast is a light, uncooked meal. It consists of fresh bread, rolls, or croissants, with butter and jam, and coffee. If you have a glass of fruit juice with this continental breakfast, it makes a better meal.

A place setting
for a cooked
breakfast.

Practical work

1 **Suggest a menu for a full English breakfast.**
2 **State the main nutrients provided by each dish you mention.**
3 **Suggest a menu for a light, quickly-prepared breakfast. Include some fruit.**
4 **Prepare and serve a cooked breakfast for two people. Lay the table.**

Cooking for afternoon tea

Not many people have afternoon tea very often these days. It is a light tea, eaten in the afternoon at about three or four o'clock. It would be eaten in homes where lunch is served at about one o'clock and dinner is served in the evening at about seven or eight o'clock. You might serve afternoon tea to visitors, or you might see it on the menu in a hotel, café, or tea room.

An afternoon tea might include thin bread and butter, thinly-cut sandwiches, and scones, cakes, or biscuits, with tea to drink. It would not include anything for which you would need a knife and fork. It is a light, 'dainty' tea, which you could eat on your knee if you were not sitting at a table.

It is traditionally served on an embroidered or lacy tablecloth, with small matching napkins. You would use a china tea set and small tea knives. If you were serving a very sticky cake, you would provide cake forks with which to eat it. These have a wide prong at the side, to cut the cake into mouthfuls. If you were serving afternoon tea at home, you might lay it on a trolley, passing tea and food to guests sitting around the room rather than at the table.

Dishes suitable for afternoon tea
Small, thinly-cut sandwiches with the crusts removed. Thinly-sliced bread and butter, brown or white, small buttered scones, jams. Small fingers of fruit tea bread or fruit load, buttered if necessary. Cakes or biscuits.

Practical work

1 **List some recipes which would be suitable for afternoon tea. Look in the recipe section for suitable sandwiches and fillings, cakes, scones, biscuits, and pastries or yeast recipes.**
2 **Write out a menu suitable for afternoon tea.**
3 **Make and decorate a sandwich cake suitable for afternoon tea.**
4 **Prepare and cook a selection of dishes suitable for afternoon tea.**
5 **Lay the table for tea for four people.**

Cooking for a special occasion

Sometimes you may want to cook a meal for a special occasion, perhaps for a family celebration or when you have invited some friends to a dinner party. Provided that you organize it carefully and plan well in advance, this should not be too difficult.

These are some of the points you should think about when you are planning the meal:

1 Choose dishes which you have made before and know you can do well.
2 Aim to serve three courses, followed by fresh coffee.
3 Have one or two cold courses which can be prepared in advance and left covered in a cold place. This saves a lot of rush at the last minute. You could also make soup in advance and keep it cold, reheating it just when you need it.
4 The simplest main course to choose is one which can be kept hot, in a pan or in the oven, without spoiling. Keep it covered with a lid or foil.
5 Use plenty of colourful garnishes on the food. The simplest dishes can look appetizing if they are attractively served.
6 Make sure that hot food is served on hot plates, and cold food on cold plates.
7 Lay the table very carefully (see page 108).

Menus for special occasions

| Mackerel pâté |
| Toast |
| Chili con carne |
| Baked potatoes |
| Fruit fool and shortbread biscuits |
| Coffee |

| Mushroom soup, bread rolls |
| Pork and apricots |
| Rice |
| Cucumber salad, tomato salad |
| Pineapple gateau |
| Coffee |

| Ham and cheese roll-ups |
| Thin brown bread and butter |
| Chicken casserole |
| Duchess potatoes |
| Hot stuffed tomatoes |
| Sponge fruit flan |
| Coffee |

Other suggestions

Soups: for example onion soup or tomato soup. Serve soup sprinkled with plenty of freshly-chopped parsley and with a little single cream poured over the top, or serve with croutons or fresh bread rolls.

Cold starters: any of the recipes in this book, attractively garnished.

Meat dishes: spaghetti bolognese, chicken curry, sweet and sour pork, lamb and bean casserole.

Cheese dishes: pizza, cheese and vegetable flan, Quiche Lorraine, sausage plait, all served with salads.

Sweet course: fresh fruit salad, perhaps with fresh strawberries or raspberries added, crunchy chocolate flan, sponge fruit gateau, pineapple upside-down pudding with pineapple sauce. Many of these could be decorated or served with fresh whipped cream.

To drink: lemonade, ginger punch, coffee.

Practical work

1 **Suggest a menu for a celebration meal for your family, which you could cook.**
2 **Work out the approximate cost of the meal (see page 52).**
3 **Prepare and cook a main course suitable for a dinner party. Serve suitable vegetables or a salad with it.**
4 **Make a cold sweet for a special occasion which will show your skill at decorating.**
5 **Prepare and cook a three-course meal for a special occasion.**

Cooking for packed meals and picnics

Like any other meal, packed meals should be varied and nutritionally well balanced. They should not contain only starchy carbohydrate foods like bread and cake, just because they are easy to carry. They should include a good source of protein like meat, fish, eggs, or cheese, and some fresh fruit or salad vegetables.

Many people, including school children, have a packed lunch every day rather than a cooked meal. When a packed meal is one of your main daily meals, it is particularly important to see that it is a good meal. A well-planned packed lunch can be just as nutritious and appetizing as a cooked meal.

The amount and kind of food you provide will depend, of course, on the person for whom it is intended. It may be for a school child with a small or large appetite. It may be for a man with a heavy job or for an office worker who needs only a light meal. A picnic might be for a hiker who is going to carry it all day, or it might be a more elaborate meal if you are travelling by car for a day's outing.

Whatever kind of packed meal you are preparing, check all the following points to make sure that the meal will be well balanced, and still appetizing when you are ready to eat it:

1 Include a good helping of protein-rich food such as meat, fish, eggs, or cheese.
2 Always include some kind of fruit or vegetables.
3 Choose foods which are easy to pack and carry.
4 Wrap them carefully so that they do not break, spill, or dry out. You could use polythene bags or cling wrap, plastic lunch boxes, or bowls with airtight lids.
5 Provide a suitable drink, perhaps tea, coffee, or cocoa, or lemonade or orange squash. Soup would be suitable in cold weather. You could carry the drink in a flask or plastic bottle, or in a cup with a leak-proof lid.

Suggestions for packed meals

For a school child

Cornish pasty or sausage roll
Tomato
Fruit cake
Apple or orange
Tea or lemonade

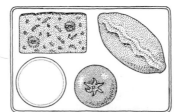
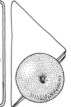

A light lunch for an office worker

Cold cooked meat
Salad
Crispbread and butter
Fresh fruit
Tea or coffee

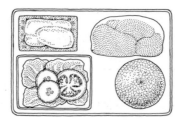

Picnics

If you are travelling by car for a picnic you might like to be more adventurous in your choice of food as you could carry more with you. You could include fruit salad, fruit in jelly, or a larger cake or pie. Remember to take with you napkins, salt, pepper, suitable cutlery, and a flannel for sticky fingers.

On the other hand, if you are hiking and have to carry everything on your back, you will probably stick to plainer food which is easy to carry. Whatever kind of picnic you have, always take your litter home. Don't spoil the countryside for someone else by leaving egg shell, orange peel, and bottles or cans behind you.

Suitable foods to take

Savoury – Cold cooked meat or chicken, hard-boiled eggs, cheese, sausage rolls, meat pies or pasties, sandwiches, and bread buns.

Sweet – Avoid sticky cakes with cream or icing. Fruit loaves and tea breads, gingerbread, scones, rock cakes, and biscuits, are good choices.

Fruit and vegetables – Tomatoes, celery, salad ready-prepared in sealed plastic containers. Fresh fruit salad or jelly whip in individual sealed containers. Fruit pies in foil plates.

To drink – Tea, coffee, cocoa, hot chocolate, soup, lemonade, or squash.

For a day out hiking

Tomato soup
Wholemeal bread buns, cheese filling
Hard-boiled egg
Individual apple pie
Lemonade or coffee

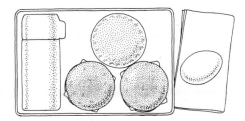

A picnic travelling by car

Cold chicken
Mexican salad
Bread buns
Fresh fruit salad
Apple gingerbread
Tea or coffee

Practical work

1 **Suggest suitable packed meals for:**
a **a journey on a train.**
b **a playgroup outing.**
c **lunch for an outdoor worker with a heavy job.**
2 **Cook and pack a selection of dishes for one of these purposes.**

Cooking for parties

Cooking for a buffet party

A buffet party is an easy and informal way of entertaining. The food and drink are prepared in advance and laid out on a table for people to help themselves.

The table should look attractive and colourful. Choose a brightly-coloured cloth and provide plenty of matching napkins. Have a centrepiece such as a large decorated cake in the middle of the table and arrange the food around it. You will also need serving spoons and forks and plenty of suitable cutlery.

Try to serve a variety of food, both sweet and savoury. Remember that people may be eating standing up or sitting in an armchair, so look for foods that are easy to manage. Choose foods that will look colourful, not just plain sandwiches and pies.

Suitable savoury foods include pizza, sausage rolls or sausage plait, sandwiches or open sandwiches, Quiche Lorraine, cheese scones, and stuffed eggs. Some of these could be served warm. Warm bread buns with butter and a selection of cheeses are popular, as are salads of all kinds, for example rice salad, potato salad, coleslaw, or tomato salad. These always add colour to the table.

For sweet foods, you could serve a decorated cake such as a chocolate cake, a sponge sandwich cake, a fruit gateau, or a lemon cheesecake. A large bowl of fresh fruit salad adds colour and variety, or you could make individual fruit fools, trifles, or jelly whips.

A bowl of lemon and ginger punch, or a jug of lemonade or orangeade, makes a suitable drink.

If the party is for a special occasion such as a bonfire or barbecue, you could serve dishes like beefburgers, baked potatoes, gingerbread, and hot soup.

Cooking for a children's party

When you are preparing food for a party of small children, choose foods which they will be able to manage easily. Provide a selection of sweet and savoury foods and a cold drink. Do not serve too many sweet and sticky cakes with a lot of cream or icing. All the food should be served in small portions as these are more attractive to small children and they are less likely to be wasted.

A birthday cake with candles is usually placed in the centre of the table. A sandwich or sponge cake is more suitable for young children than a fruit cake. If you are adventurous you can make a 'novelty' cake, perhaps in the shape of a train, a fort, a gingerbread house or a football field.

Lay the table with a brightly-coloured cloth and have plenty of napkins and damp flannels ready for sticky fingers. You can buy paper tablecloths, napkins, plates, and cups, in attractive patterns and colours. They are quite expensive but they look very colourful, they save washing up and they avoid any breakages.

Some suitable foods

Savoury: Sandwiches cut into small sizes or into fancy shapes with a cutter. Sausage rolls, cut to a small size before cooking.
Small cheese scones, buttered. Cheese straws, potato crisps.

Sweet: Victoria sandwich cake or sponge cake, decorated with candles. Cakes, not too sticky or creamy. Small fairy cakes with the initials of the children's names in icing are popular.
Biscuits, cut into fancy shapes with a cutter. Small buttered scones.
Jelly whip or fruit fool. These are best served in small individual dishes rather than in a large bowl.

To drink: Lemonade, perhaps with coloured straws.

Older children would probably enjoy hot dogs or hamburgers in bread buns, with tomato sauce and fried onions.

Practical work

1 **Write out menus suitable for each of the following occasions:**
(a) an engagement party; (b) your brother's 12th birthday; (c) an outdoor party on bonfire night.
2 **Prepare a selection of foods suitable for a buffet party. Include a salad of some kind, a decorated cake, and a cold drink.**
3 **Suggest a menu suitable for each of the following occasions:**
(a) a birthday party for five-year-olds; (b) a Brownie's Christmas party; (c) a party for a nine-year-old boy.
4 **Prepare the food and a drink for a birthday party for some seven-year-olds.**

Cooking with convenience foods

Convenience foods are those foods where some of the preparation and cooking has already been done before we buy them. Tinned, frozen, and dried foods, and foods in packets, jars, and bottles are all convenience foods. Many of the foods which once had to be prepared at home from fresh ingredients can now be bought like this. They include soups, stock cubes, meat, fish, vegetables, fruit, puddings, cakes, biscuits, bread, pastry and scones.

Advantages and disadvantages of using convenience foods

1 *Time* Using convenience foods reduces the time spent in preparing meals. This is useful for people who go out to work and have to cook for the family as well.

2 *Flavour* The flavour of convenience foods is not usually as good as that of freshly prepared and cooked food. The home-made version usually tastes much better than the 'bought' or packet one.

3 *Skill* Someone who is not very good at cooking or who has not had much practice might find that he or she could produce better meals with the help of some convenience foods. A more skilled cook could find them useful for adding variety to meals.

4 *Storage* Convenience foods are useful as they will usually keep well in the cupboard or freezer. You can keep a store for times when you can't go shopping, or for when you have unexpected visitors.

5 *Cost* Convenience foods can be more or less expensive than their fresh equivalent; it depends on the food. Frozen vegetables, for instance, are often as cheap as fresh ones, especially as there is no waste at all, and particularly when the fresh vegetables are not in season. Some home-made jams and cakes can cost as much or more than the bought variety.

6 *Food value* The nutritional value of convenience foods is usually about as good as that of the fresh equivalent. The protein, fat, carbohydrate, and mineral content is usually about the same. The vitamin which is most easily lost in foods, Vitamin C, tends to be present in about the same amounts in canned and frozen fruit and vegetables as in fresh foods. This is because manufacturers use only good quality fruit and vegetables, picked when they are at their best. They are usually picked and processed quickly and need only a short cooking and reheating time at home. By the time fresh fruit and vegetables have been bought, stored, prepared, and cooked at home, the Vitamin C content is much the same.

However, the more foods have been pre-prepared, cooked, and processed, the less likely they are to contain dietary fibre or roughage, so from this point of view 'whole', unprocessed foods are better. 'Bought' cakes, biscuits and puddings are also more likely to contain more saturated fat and large amounts of sugar which you would do better to avoid. If you make cakes and puddings at home, you can make them as you choose, using such ingredients as wholemeal flour, soft margarine, eggs, and black treacle. This way you will at least know what you are eating.

Recipes which make sensible use of convenience foods

Try to choose recipes where the convenience food is cooked with some fresh ingredients, rather than just served straight from a tin or packet. This way you will both improve the flavour and show that you have some cookery skill of your own.

Soups: Tomato soup, using tinned tomato and stock cubes.

Cold starters: Florida cocktail using tinned oranges or grapefruit. Mackerel pâté using tinned mackerel.

Meat and fish dishes: Tinned mince for mince pie, savoury beef and tomato, lasagne. Packets of sauce mix for chicken and mushroom pie, fish and cheese sauce, lasagne, fish pie. Instant potato to decorate savoury beef and tomato or fish and cheese sauce, or for fish cakes or corned beef and potato pie. Packets of stuffing for roast stuffed breast of lamb. Tinned tomatoes for chicken casserole, spaghetti bolognese. Pastry mix or frozen pastry for meat pies or pasties. Tinned kidney beans for chili con carne.

Vegetables: Instant potato to use as above, or for duchess potatoes or potato nests. Tinned or frozen vegetables to use in sausage risotto, potato nests, rice salad. Mixed with freshly-prepared vegetables to add colour; for example, mixed buttered carrots and frozen peas.

Puddings and cakes: Tinned fruit or pie filling for fruit pies, crumbles, flans, charlotte, fruit fool, mixed with fresh fruit salad, in pineapple upside-down pudding, and to decorate cakes. Cake or gateau made from a packet mix but decorated to show your own skill.

Food additives

If you look at tins, packets, and jars of food on the shelves in the supermarket, you will see the contents listed on the labels. They usually include chemicals which have been added to improve the appearance, colour, or flavour of the food, and to lengthen its shelf life.

There are many laws governing the use of chemicals in food. A lot of research is done to try to make sure that they are not harmful to us. But of course we cannot be sure what effect they may have on us if we consume them over many years. So it seems sensible to eat fresh and unprocessed foods as far as possible and not to rely too much on packets of pre-prepared or ready-made foods.

Practical work

1 **Suggest a menu for (a) a family dinner, and (b) a special occasion meal, which makes sensible use of some convenience foods.**
2 **Make a cake, some scones, or a fruit or meat pie, first using fresh ingredients and then using convenience foods. Decide which you think tastes better, looks better, is easier to make, and is better value for money.**

Saving fuel when cooking

The cost of fuel for cooking and heating is continually rising, whether it is gas, electricity, or solid fuel. There are a number of ways in which you can save fuel when you are cooking. Careful planning can save you money, and it saves wasting valuable fuel resources.

1 Plan your meals carefully. If you do you will find that you can cook complete meals using the cooker top only, without having to light the oven as well. Or you can make a complete meal in the oven without using the rings as well.

2 Some electric cookers have two ovens, one small and one large. You can save fuel by using only the small one if you are not doing much cooking.

3 Some electric cookers have grills or boiling rings where you only need to switch on half of the grill or ring. This is useful if you are only grilling a small amount of food or using a small saucepan.

4 If your cooker is electric, it is much more economical to use an electric toaster and kettle than to use the cooker for making toast and boiling water.

5 When you put the kettle on, don't overfill it. Only boil as much water as you need, but always make sure that the element in an electric kettle is covered.

6 When you are baking, fill the oven. You could try to bake all you need for the week at once. If you have a freezer you can freeze bread, cakes, casseroles, and other food for use later in the week.

7 A pressure cooker is very economical with fuel. It cooks very quickly and will cook several items together (meat, potatoes, and vegetables, for example), using only one boiling ring on a low heat. It also saves money as you can use it to make cheap, tougher cuts of meat more tender. (See p. 88.)

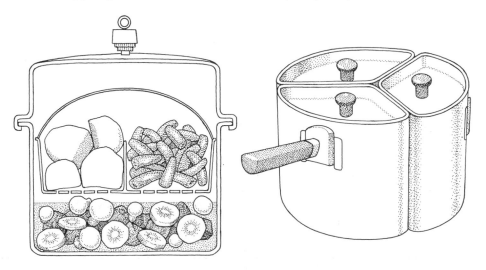

8 You can buy divided pans with three compartments which fit together so that you can cook foods separately, still using only one ring.

9 You can try cooking vegetables together in the same pan, for example, potatoes and carrots, or carrots and peas.

10 When cooking vegetables, cut them fairly small and all to the same size, so that they cook quickly and evenly. Use just a little water and simmer gently. Don't have the heat too high. As well as saving fuel, you will get better-tasting vegetables.

Meals made using the cooker top only

Vegetable soup
Beefburgers, tomato sauce
Boiled potatoes
Brussels sprouts
Stewed apple

Ham and cheese roll-ups
Sweet and sour pork
Rice
Steamed chocolate sponge
Chocolate sauce

Other suitable dishes
Other soups and cold starters.
Minced beef, beef or chicken casserole or curry, cooked on a ring instead of in the oven.
Chili con carne, pork and apricots, spaghetti bolognese, fish cakes, fish and cheese sauce, macaroni cheese, salads.
Fruit fool, jelly whip, fresh fruit salad, crunchy chocolate flan, cheesecake, baked egg custard or rice pudding made in the pressure cooker.

Meals made using the oven only

Florida cocktail
Beef and vegetable casserole
Turnip or swede
Baked potatoes
Rice pudding

Stuffed tomatoes
Meat loaf
Duchess potatoes
Carrots
Plum pie

Other suitable dishes
Most cold starters.
Liver or chicken casserole, toad in the hole, chicken and mushroom pie, mince pie.
Roast stuffed breast of lamb, baked chicken joints, chili con carne, chicken curry, crispy fish bake.
Roast potatoes. For cooking vegetables in the oven, see page 90.
Fruit pies, fruit crumble or charlotte, pineapple upside-down pudding, sponge fruit flan, sponge gateau, baked egg custard.

Practical work

1 **Suggest one three-course meal made using the cooker top only, and one made using the oven only.**
2 **Prepare and cook a hot main course for a family dinner, using the grill and/or the cooker top only. Serve suitable vegetables with it.**
3 **Prepare a hot pudding or cold sweet without using the oven.**
4 **Prepare a two- or three-course meal which can be cooked completely in the oven.**

Cooking with a mixer or blender

Mixers

Mixers can be bought in different sizes, ranging from a small, hand-held mixer to a large, powerful model with its own bowl and stand and a range of attachments.

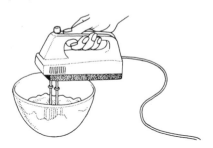 

Hand-held model.   Larger model with bowl and stand.

A small model is sufficient for most cookery jobs. It can be attached to the wall in a convenient place in the kitchen so that it is always ready for use. It can be used directly in a pan to mix a sauce or to cream boiled potatoes.

The largest models are very powerful. They should be kept out on the kitchen work bench so that they do not have to be lifted in and out of a cupboard before they can be used. These large mixers are very useful if you do a lot of cooking for a large family or if you cook in large quantities for a freezer. The wide range of attachments you can buy as extras include:

Dough hook: Extremely useful for taking the heavy work out of yeast cookery. They knead dough efficiently and thoroughly, giving very good results.

Slicer and shredder: This will slice and shred vegetables for soups, salads, coleslaw and potato crisps, or oranges for marmalade. It will shred cheese, nuts or chocolate finely and quickly.

You can also buy mincers for meat or marmalade, juice extractors, bean slicers, coffee-grinders, and tin-openers. Whether or not these will be useful depends on how often you would use them. You have to be prepared to spend time putting them together, taking them to pieces, washing and drying them, and putting them away.

Jobs that can be done with a mixer include:

1 Creaming fat and sugar.
2 Whisking eggs and sugar for sponges.
3 Whipping cream.
4 Whisking egg whites.
5 Mixing a sauce or batter.
6 Rubbing fat into flour. (Some mixers do this more efficiently than others. It is often simpler and better to rub in by hand.)

Recipes made with the help of a mixer
Creaming – cakes, biscuits, puddings. Whisking – Swiss roll, whisked sponge cake and other sponge mixtures, jelly whip. Rubbing-in – (only if your mixer will do this satisfactorily) shortcrust pastry, crumble, rock cakes, fruit cakes, scones.

Blenders or liquidizers

Blenders are very useful. You can buy one as a separate piece of equipment or as an attachment to a mixer.

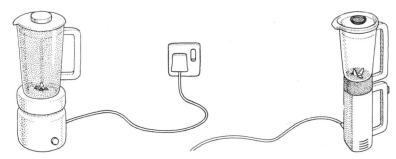

Blender.   Blender attached to a hand mixer.

Blenders can be used for many jobs, including:

1 Making a smooth purée from fruit or vegetables, e.g. stewed apple.
2 Making a purée from soup, instead of sieving it.
3 Making a purée suitable for baby food.
4 Blending cooked fruit and custard for a fruit fool.
5 Making crumbs from fresh or dried bread, cake, or biscuits.
6 Chopping nuts or chocolate.
7 Making granulated sugar finer, like caster sugar.
8 Making pâté.
9 Making batter for Yorkshire pudding or pancakes.
10 Making mayonnaise.

Blenders vary according to their size and the power of the motor. When using a blender follow these guidelines:

1 Always follow the manufacturer's instructions for your particular model.
2 Do not run for longer than recommended, or the motor may burn out.
3 Run at the correct speed.
4 Small blenders may not chop dry food very well.
5 Wash by filling with hot, soapy water, run for a few seconds, rinse and dry.
6 Do not overfill.
7 When blending large amounts or a thick mixture like pâté, you may need to switch off a couple of times while blending, to push the mixture down on to the blades.

Recipes made with the help of a blender
Soups, toad in the hole, mayonnaise, fruit fool. Bread crumbs for stuffed tomatoes, meat loaf, beefburgers, apple charlotte, stuffing. Biscuit crumbs for crunchy chocolate flan, lemon cheesecake.

Practical work

1 **Write out a menu for a three-course meal, where full use is made of the electric mixer and blender.**
2 **Using a blender or mixer to save time and effort, prepare a selection of sweet and savoury dishes.**

Cooking with a pressure cooker

The pressure cooker works on the principle that when the pressure inside the pan is increased by preventing the escape of steam, a higher temperature is produced which cooks food in a shorter time.

Advantages of having a pressure cooker

1 Food can be cooked very quickly, in one-quarter to one-third of the usual cooking time. For example, a stew which would normally take hours can be cooked in about twenty-five minutes, and potatoes can be cooked in six minutes.
2 Fuel can be saved, as food takes less time to cook, and as several foods can be cooked in the pan at the same time – for example, meat, potatoes, and other vegetables.
3 It is particularly useful for foods which would normally take a long time to cook, for example, soups or stews containing dried pulses (peas, beans, lentils), cheaper, tougher, cuts of meat, joints of bacon or ham, steamed puddings.
4 The nutritive value of food is high. Vegetables are cooked in steam rather than water, so there is a smaller loss of vitamins into the water.
5 The cooker can be used for different jobs, like bottling fruit and vegetables to preserve them, sterilizing babies' bottles, making jam and marmalade, and making baby foods.

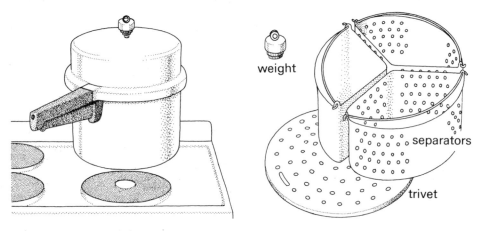

weight

separators

trivet

How to use a pressure cooker

1 Study and follow the instruction book carefully.
2 Do not overfill. The pressure cooker should be no more than half-full for liquids, two-thirds for solids.
3 Put the food in the cooker, put the lid on, and add the weight (the weight you use will vary according to the recipe you are using). Place the cooker over a high heat until it hisses loudly. Start to time the food. Turn the heat down so that the cooker just keeps up a steady hiss.
4 Time the food carefully. Do not overcook it.
5 Cool the cooker either by leaving it for five to ten minutes or by running cold water from the tap over the cooker. The method you choose depends on the food in the cooker (see the recipes).
6 When the hissing stops, remove the weight and the lid.

Suitable recipes

There are many suggestions for recipes in the instruction booklet which comes with the pressure cooker. Here are a few suggestions:

Soups
The cooker is ideal for making soups. If you thicken the soup with blended flour and milk or water, add it after the soup is cooked.

Meat
Suitable for cooking beef or chicken casserole, minced beef, chili con carne, chicken or beef curry, or the meat for mince pie. See each recipe for particular instructions. Always thicken the gravy with blended flour and water after the meat is cooked rather than before.

Vegetables
1 Timing is very important. As they cook so quickly, vegetables can easily become overcooked.
2 Green vegetables should be cooked in the separator. They should not be put in the pan until the water is boiling and the pan is full of steam.
3 Different vegetables can be cooked at the same time. If potatoes and root vegetables are to be cooked with green vegetables, they should be cut fairly small so that they will all cook in the same length of time. Potatoes and carrots can be cooked on the trivet or rack, with the green vegetables in the separator on top of them.
4 Sprinkle salt directly on to the vegetables as the water does not touch them during cooking.
5 Cook at H (15lb) pressure. Reduce the pressure with cold water immediately after cooking.
6 Cooking time for vegetables will vary depending on the size to which they are cut, but a rough guide is: potatoes – 6 minutes; carrots, cut – 4 minutes; cauliflower sprigs, cabbage, sprouts, and diced swede or turnip – 4 minutes.

Puddings
The pressure cooker is very useful for reducing the cooking time of steamed puddings, especially Christmas puddings. See the recipes for steamed sponge puddings for instructions. Rice pudding is delicious when cooked in a pressure cooker, and cooks much more quickly than usual (see recipe). Baked egg custard also cooks successfully in the pressure cooker (see recipe).

Jam and marmalade
The pressure cooker will cook the fruit quickly before the sugar is added (see the recipes). Once the sugar has been added the jam is boiled without the lid on. As the pressure cooker is thick and heavy, it is ideal for making jam if you do not have a jam pan.

Practical work

1 **Make some soup using the pressure cooker.**
2 **Using the pressure cooker, make a main course for the family dinner.**
3 **Cook some potatoes and another vegetable together in the pressure cooker.**
4 **Use the pressure cooker to make either a steamed pudding or a rice pudding.**

Cooking with an automatic timer

Many new gas and electric cookers have automatic oven controls. This means that you can set the oven to switch itself on and off when you are not there. A cooker like this usually has the advantage of a built-in oven timer or buzzer to tell you when food is cooked, and it often has a kitchen clock as well.

With automatic time controls you can leave a meal prepared in the oven, set the oven to switch itself on while you are out at work, and the meal will be cooked for your return. You can cook many kinds of meat and fish dishes, potatoes, vegetables, and puddings like this, with good results. If you buy a cooker with these controls, you will receive a booklet with it which gives you details of exactly what to do, and suggestions for meals which can be cooked automatically.

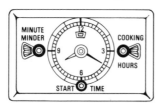 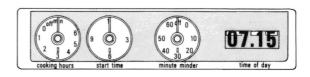

Here are some general points to remember:

1   Choose foods which will cook together at about the same temperature and in about the same time.
2   If any dish requires a slightly higher or lower oven temperature, you can place it on a higher or lower oven shelf.
3   Add an extra ten or fifteen minutes to the normal cooking time, to allow time for the oven to heat up.
4   Choose the cooking dishes carefully so that they will all fit into the oven.
5   Potatoes and root vegetables such as carrots or turnips can be satisfactorily cooked in the oven. They should be cut up evenly to a fairly small size, put in an ovenproof dish with water and salt, and covered with a lid or foil. Potatoes should be brushed with melted fat so that they do not go brown.
6   Green vegetables such as sprouts or cabbage are better cooked on the top of the stove when you come home, otherwise they will be overcooked. Frozen vegetables are a good choice here, as they are ready prepared and can be cooked quickly at the last minute.
7   Many dishes will need to be covered with a lid or foil to prevent drying out or overbrowning.
8   All meat and fish should be absolutely fresh when it is put in the oven. In warm weather, any bacteria would multiply quickly in food which is left in the oven all day. This could cause food poisoning.

Examples of meals which can be cooked automatically

Beef and vegetable casserole
Creamed potatoes
Carrots
Rice pudding

Set the oven temperature to Gas 3, 170°C for about 2 hours.

Special instructions

1   If you wanted a starter to go with the meal, you could prepare a cold starter, cover it with cling-wrap and keep it in the refrigerator.
2   Beef and vegetable casserole – cover with a lid or foil.
3   Creamed potatoes – cut the potatoes into slices about 1 cm/½" thick. Put in an oven-proof dish with a level teaspoon of salt and enough water to come half-way up the potatoes. Brush the top of the potatoes with melted fat to prevent them from going brown and cover with a lid or foil. Before serving, mash the potatoes with a little butter.

4   Carrots – cut into rings or even lengths. Put in an oven-proof dish with a level teaspoon of salt and enough water to come half-way up the sides. Cover with a lid or foil.
5   Rice pudding – cook on the lowest shelf.

| Roast chicken |
| Roast potatoes |
| Turnips, peas |
| Apple crumble |
| Custard |

Set the oven to Gas 5, 190°C for 1½ hours.

Special instructions

1   Roast chicken and potatoes – cut the potatoes into even-sized pieces and place around the chicken. Sprinkle with salt and brush with melted fat. Cover loosely with foil. Fold back the foil while you cook the frozen peas and make the gravy just before serving the meal.
2   Turnips – cut to 1 cm/½" dice. Place in an oven-proof dish with water to come half-way up. Add a level teaspoon of salt. Cover. Drain and mash before serving.
3   Apple crumble – cover loosely with foil or a lid, cook below the chicken.
4   Custard – make just before serving the meal.

Other suitable dishes
Liver or chicken casserole, roast stuffed breast of lamb, meat loaf, chili con carne, chicken curry, crispy fish bake. Apple charlotte, baked egg custard.

Practical work

1   **What is the main advantage of having an automatic cooker?**
2   **Describe the most important points to remember when you are using the automatic time controls for cooking.**
3   **Write out a menu for a two-course family dinner which could be cooked automatically. Describe the special preparations which would be needed for each dish. State the temperature you would set the oven to, the time you would leave it on for, and the position of each item in the oven.**

Cooking for the freezer (1)

A home freezer is very useful for keeping a good supply of foods in store. You can freeze home-grown fruit and vegetables or you can buy them when they are cheap and in season, freezing them for later use. If you are having a party you can make some of the food in advance and store it in the freezer. When you are cooking you can 'batch bake' (see p. 102), freezing some items to use later.

Rules for successful freezing

1 Only freeze food which is in perfect condition. Do not freeze fruit or vegetables which are damaged or overripe, or fish or meat which is not really fresh.
2 Never re-freeze food once it has been thawed. Bacteria increase more rapidly in food which has previously been frozen.
3 All joints of meat and poultry must be completely thawed before they are cooked. If they are not, then they may not reach a high enough temperature in the oven to kill any harmful bacteria.
4 Store food in the freezer only for the recommended time.
5 Food must be completely cold before it is put into the freezer.
6 Open the freezer as little as possible, to keep it cool and so reduce running costs.
7 When you defrost, follow the maker's instructions exactly.
8 Use the fast-freeze switch when necessary (see below).
9 Pack and label all the food carefully. Use stocks in rotation, the oldest food first.

Packaging foods for the freezer

It is important to pack foods carefully or they will be spoiled. They must be wrapped so that they will not dry out, and to prevent odours passing from one food to another. Try to exclude as much air as possible from the package.

Suitable packing materials
1 Polythene bags. These must be fairly thick if they are to protect food properly. They should be sealed with a wire twist or with freezer tape.
2 Polythene sheeting for large awkward shapes. Seal with freezer tape.
3 Polythene or plastic boxes with airtight lids. These are available in many shapes and sizes. Use a type that is recommended for use in a freezer as the lids of other, cheaper types are likely to split if removed when frozen. Larger boxes are useful for decorated cakes etc., to prevent them from being crushed.

If you want to freeze liquid foods, it is a good idea to pour them into a polythene bag standing inside a box (1). Once it is frozen (2) you can take the bag out of the box. The food in the bag is then frozen in a convenient shape for storing (3).

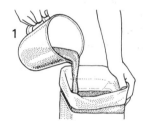

4   Aluminium foil can be used for wrapping most foods and for covering foil dishes.
5   Foil dishes are ideal for stews, casseroles, and pies. Food can be taken from the freezer and put into the oven in the same container.
6   Waxed tubs and cartons with airtight lids are suitable for most soft foods such as sauces, soups, and fruit purées.

Labelling

All food should be clearly labelled with the date and contents. You can buy special freezer labels or use ordinary labels with freezer tape. Marking should be done with a felt-tip or special pen. Ordinary sticky tape will come off in the freezer, so use special freezer tape. It is a good idea to keep a book in which you record all the food you put in and take out of the freezer, so that you know exactly what you have in stock.

Using the 'fast-freeze' switch

When food is frozen the water in the food turns into ice crystals. If the crystals are very large they can break up the cells in the food, spoiling the texture, the flavour, and the appearance of the food. When food is frozen quickly the ice crystals are much smaller, so when the food is thawed it is less 'mushy' and it looks and tastes better. This is particularly true of fruit and vegetables.

        This is why you set the switch to 'fast-freeze' when you add a lot of food to the freezer. The temperature drops, the food is frozen more quickly and so it is better when it is thawed. Once all the food is frozen you set the switch back to normal again. For small amounts (up to about 1kg/2lbs) you will not need to switch to fast-freeze. For large amounts, for example, several joints of meat, you would switch to fast-freeze a couple of hours before adding the food, and leave it on for a few hours. When adding foods which are already frozen you don't need to switch to fast-freeze.

Suitable foods for freezing

The majority of foods can be frozen successfully, including most fresh vegetables and fruit, meat, and fish. Cooked foods which freeze well include bread, cakes, pastry and pies, pizzas, stews and casseroles, sauces and soups. Foods which don't freeze well include salad vegetables, bananas, cooked potatoes, rice, spaghetti, pasteurized milk, milk puddings, and whole eggs.

Questions

1   **What are the advantages of owning a freezer?**
2   **Why should food never be re-frozen once it has been thawed?**
3   **Why must poultry be completely thawed before cooking?**
4   **Why must food be well wrapped before freezing?**
5   **Name some suitable packing materials or containers.**
6   **What information would you put on the label before placing wrapped food in the freezer?**
7   **Explain why the 'fast-freeze' switch is sometimes used.**
8   **Name some foods which do not freeze well.**

Cooking for the freezer (2)

Freezing fruit

There are basically four ways of preserving fruit in the freezer. The method you choose depends on the kind of fruit you are freezing and on the purpose for which you are going to use it. Most fruits can be frozen successfully, except for bananas. Raspberries and strawberries can be frozen, but they tend to lose their shape when they are thawed, so they are best used in recipes where their shape does not matter, for example, in a mousse or a fruit fool.

The methods used are:

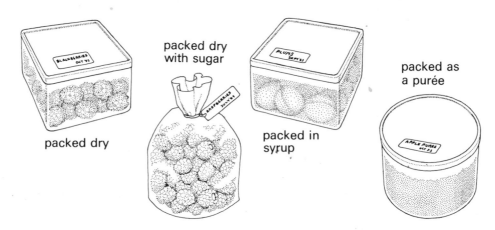

packed dry

packed dry with sugar

packed in syrup

packed as a purée

1   *Dry:* Suitable for fruits that are to be cooked later, in pies, puddings, or jam; for example, raspberries, strawberries, blackberries, gooseberries, currants, rhubarb. The fruit is prepared and cleaned, then packed either into polythene bags or into a firm container if you want to prevent it from being crushed.

2   *Dry with sugar:* Good for raspberries, strawberries, blackberries, and blackcurrants. Prepare the fruit according to its type, but do not wash it unless it is essential. Mix with sugar, about 100g/4oz per 500g/1lb of fruit, then pack into polythene bags or boxes.

3   *In syrup:* This method is used for fruits which are not very juicy, such as plums or rhubarb. You make a syrup, leave it until it is cold, then add the fruit and pack.

   To make the syrup: Put the measured quantity of sugar and water into a pan and warm slowly until the sugar has dissolved. Bring to the boil, then leave it to cool before you use it. If you pour the syrup into a large, cold bowl it will help it to cool more quickly.

4   *As a purée:* Suitable for apples, gooseberries, blackcurrants, raspberries.

   To make a purée: Wash or prepare the fruit. Put it into a pan with the smallest amount of water possible to prevent it from sticking to the pan. This will probably be about 4 tablespoons of water for each 500g/1lb of fruit. Simmer very gently with the lid on until the fruit is very soft. Add sugar, about 75–100g (3–4oz) for each 500g/1lb fruit, and stir to dissolve the sugar, but do not allow the fruit to boil. Either put the fruit into a blender until smooth, or pass through a nylon sieve.

How to prepare fruits for freezing

Apples: (a) Slices for pies and puddings. Prepare a bowl of cold water and add the juice of a lemon. Peel and core the apples and put them into the water. Cut them to slices 0.5cm/¼" thick. Blanch for 1 minute in boiling water. Cool in ice-cold water. Drain and pack in polythene boxes or bags, and label.

(b) Apple purée. Peel, core and slice, and make a purée as explained above. You can sweeten it or leave it unsweetened. Pack in firm containers (not foil) leaving a little room for expansion, and label. Freeze when cold.

Blackberries: Either pack them dry or dry with sugar, using 100g/4oz sugar for each 500g/1lb fruit. Pick over the fruit, mix with sugar if used, pack in polythene containers or bags, label.

Blackcurrants: Wash, dry and remove strings. Either:
(a) pack dry in polythene boxes or bags, label and freeze.
or (b) make a purée and sweeten to taste, using about 75g/3oz sugar for each 500g/1lb fruit. Pack in firm containers (not foil) when cool. Label and freeze.

Gooseberries: Top and tail, wash and dry the fruit. Either:
(a) pack dry in polythene boxes or bags, label and freeze.
or (b) pack in syrup. For each 500g/1lb fruit make a syrup using 250g/8oz sugar and 250ml/½pt water. When the syrup is cold, add the gooseberries, pack in firm containers, label and freeze.
(c) Gooseberry purée, used for fruit fools. Make a purée as above and sweeten to taste, using about 100g/4oz sugar to each 500g/1lb fruit. Pack into firm containers when cold, label.

Lemons: May be scrubbed, then frozen whole. May instead be cut into slices or segments, then frozen in a plastic or polythene container or bag. Can be used as a garnish for cold drinks, fish dishes and so on. The juice can be squeezed and frozen in ice-cube trays, then packed into polythene bags.

Plums: Pack in syrup. Wash and halve the fruit, remove the stones. For every 1kg/2lbs plums, make a syrup using 250g/8oz sugar and 500ml/1pt water. Add 400mg of ascorbic acid tablets to prevent the plums becoming discoloured. When the syrup is cold, add the plums. Pack in firm containers (not foil) and label.

Rhubarb: Wash the rhubarb, trim off the ends. Cut into lengths of about 3cm/1½". Either pack dry or blanch in boiling water for 1 minute, cool in ice-cold water, then pack in syrup in firm containers (not foil) and label. Make the syrup using 100g/4oz sugar, 100ml/4 fluid oz water for each 500g/1lb fruit.

Practical work

1 **Describe the four different methods used for freezing fruit.**
2 **Describe in detail how you would make, pack, and freeze some apple purée.**
3 **Which of the four methods would you use if you wanted to freeze some (a) plums, (b) rhubarb, (c) lemon juice, and (d) slices of lemon to use as a garnish.**
4 **Prepare, pack, and label two types of fruit using two different methods, so that they are ready for freezing.**

Cooking for the freezer (3)

Freezing fresh vegetables

If you have vegetables in the garden or can buy them cheaply, freezing is a good way of preserving them for use later in the year. You should only use vegetables in good condition, and freeze them as soon as possible after they have been picked.

All vegetables must be blanched in boiling water. This stops the activity of enzymes in the vegetables and so keeps them a good colour and flavour. It also helps reduce the loss of Vitamin C.

How to prepare vegetables for freezing		*Blanching time (minutes)*
Beans: runner	Trim the ends, string and slice.	2
broad	Remove from pods.	3
Brussels sprouts	Choose small firm sprouts. Remove coarse outer leaves, wash well.	3
Cabbage	Freeze only if firm and crisp. Shred finely.	1½
Carrots	Peel or scrape if new carrots. Cut into slices, or dice.	4
Cauliflower	Wash and divide into sprigs. To keep them white, add the juice of a lemon to the blanching water.	3
Celery	Scrub well with a brush. Remove any stringy parts. Cut to 3cm/1½" lengths.	3
Courgettes	Cut into 1cm/½" slices. Instead of blanching you could fry lightly in butter before freezing.	1
Peas	Shell. Use when young and sweet for best flavour and results.	1
Potatoes	Better frozen when cooked, as duchess potatoes or croquettes. Chips – freeze when partly cooked. Fry in hot fat for two minutes only, cool and freeze.	
Swedes/turnips	Peel and cut into small dice.	3

Unsuitable vegetables for freezing
Lettuce, cucumber, cress, radishes, whole tomatoes.

How to blanch vegetables

Have ready a large pan, half-full of boiling water. Place about ½kg/1lb of prepared vegetables in a wire basket and put them in the boiling water (1). When the water comes back to the boil, time the vegetables for the recommended blanching time. Then

take them out, cool in ice-cold water (2), drain, and pack them straight away. Use polythene boxes or bags (3) and mark them with the contents and date. If you want separate 'free-flow' vegetables you will have to freeze them open on a baking tray (4), packing them into containers once they are frozen.

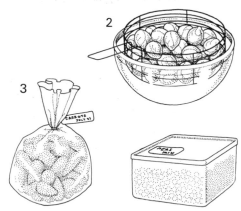

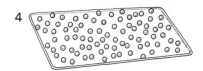

Freezing fresh meat and fish

Chops and steak Separate these from each other with polythene or cling film so that you can remove just the amount you need, without having to thaw the whole pack. Wrap closely in polythene bags, seal and label.

Mince or stewing steak Wrap in useful-sized portions, for example, 500g/1lb packs. Wrap in polythene bags, seal and label.

Joints Wipe with a damp cloth, wrap well and freeze. Do not freeze with stuffing added. Best results are obtained if meat is completely thawed before cooking.

Chicken, turkey and other poultry Freeze without stuffing. Remove giblets, which can be frozen separately if required. Polythene sheeting is useful for wrapping irregular shapes. Wrap carefully, overwrapping if necessary with a large polythene bag or foil. Exclude as much air as possible. Thaw completely before cooking, so that the inside of the bird will reach a temperature high enough to kill any bacteria.

Storage times Follow the guide on your freezer. Approximate times are:

Beef: 8 months	Minced beef: 3 months
Lamb, pork, and veal: 6 months	Bacon – smoked joints or rashers:
Sausages, liver, kidney, etc.: 3 months	2 months; unsmoked: 3 weeks

Fish Only very fresh fish should be frozen. Freeze either fillets or whole fish which have been gutted and washed. For easy removal, separate each fish or fillet with polythene film. Overwrap in polythene bags and label.

Storage times Oily fish: 2 months White fish: 3 months

Practical work

1 **Why are vegetables blanched before freezing?**
2 **Describe exactly how you would prepare, blanch, and pack some Brussels sprouts, a cauliflower, and some courgettes.**
3 **How would you prepare and pack the following before freezing: mince, lamb chops, a chicken, a joint of pork?**
4 **Prepare a selection of vegetables ready for the freezer.**

Cooking for the freezer (4)

Freezing cooked food

1 When you have cooked a dish for the freezer, cool it as quickly as possible, then wrap and freeze it. Do not leave it lying around in a warm room.
2 The flavour of herbs, spices, and seasonings, such as garlic, curry, and salt, can become stronger during freezing, so be careful when you add them. Check the taste when you reheat and season if necessary.
3 Stews and soups are better thickened with cornflour rather than flour, if thickening is necessary. The sauce or gravy will then be less likely to separate.
4 Foil dishes are ideal for freezing foods which are to be reheated later, for example, pies and stews. Or you can use a container such as a pie plate or casserole dish lined with foil and freeze it in that. Once it is frozen, lift the foil and food out, overwrap it and put it back in the freezer.
5 It is best to remove foods you need from the freezer in good time so that they can be thawed in the refrigerator. Some foods can be cooked from frozen. These include vegetables, fish, casseroles, uncooked pies, and steamed puddings.
6 The storage time for keeping foods frozen varies according to the food and the freezer. There is a guide either on the freezer itself or in the instruction booklet which gives you exact details for your model.

Food/approximate storage time	Preparation and freezing
Meat stews and casseroles Soups and sauces 2 months	Cook in the usual way, but do not add much seasoning. When cold, pack in firm containers, foil dishes, or containers lined with foil as above. Wrap well, seal, label, and freeze.
Cooked fish dishes, fish cakes and pies 2 months	Use very fresh fish to make the dishes. Cool quickly, wrap in polythene bags or containers or foil dishes, depending on the recipe. Label and freeze.
Herbs 6 months	Wash and dry. Either chop or leave in sprigs. Wrap in small amounts, enough for a casserole or stew. Bouquets garnis can be prepared. Wrap closely in foil or small polythene bags. Can be added to stews or soups while still frozen.
Bread and rolls 4 weeks	Freshly-made bread, home-made or bought, freezes well, wrapped in foil or polythene. Sliced bread can be left in its wrapper and individual slices removed and toasted when frozen. If you want to keep sliced wrapped bread in the freezer for longer than a week, overwrap it in polythene bags or foil.
Sandwiches 1–2 months	Most kinds freeze well, but avoid salad fillings such as lettuce, cucumber, tomato, cress, or hard-boiled egg. Wrap closely in foil, then overwrap in polythene bags. Sandwiches may be toasted when frozen; they will thaw as they cook.

Food/approximate storage time	Preparation and freezing
Uncooked pastry 3 months	Freeze in packets so that it does not take too long to thaw. It can be rolled out and cut to the shape of your pie plate or tartlet tins and frozen like that. Separate each layer with polythene or greaseproof paper, then overwrap in polythene bags or containers and label.
Uncooked pies 3 months	Make in large or small foil containers or in foil-lined dishes or bun tins, removing from the dish when frozen. Overwrap in polythene bags, label.
Cooked pastry: meat pies 3 months fruit pies 6 months	Make pies as usual with a meat or fruit filling. Cool, wrap in polythene, and freeze. Empty flan cases can be frozen but must be very carefully packed and stored as they are very fragile.
Pizza: uncooked 3 months cooked 2 months	Can be frozen uncooked, with the filling in place, or cooked. Freeze each one separately until firm, then several can be wrapped together in polythene bags or foil.
Scones 6 months	Make as usual, cool, then wrap in polythene bags or containers, label and freeze.
Biscuits 6 months	Make as usual, cool, wrap carefully to avoid damage, in polythene bags or containers. Label and freeze. They may be improved by reheating for 5 minutes in the oven before eating.
Sponge puddings cooked 3 months uncooked 1 month	May be frozen cooked or uncooked. Cooked – make as usual in foil basins or foil-lined basins. If made in a foil basin, cool after cooking, overwrap with polythene or foil to seal well, then freeze. If made in a foil-lined basin, freeze in this, remove basin when frozen and overwrap the pudding in more foil or in polythene. Uncooked – make and put in basin as above, leave room to rise when cooking. Seal well and freeze. The pudding may be cooked from frozen.
Cakes cooked 6 months decorated 2 months uncooked 2 months	All kinds of cakes freeze well: rubbed-in, melted, creamed, fruit and sponge cakes, Swiss rolls and flan cases. Bake in the usual way, freeze whole or cut into slices separated by greaseproof paper. Sponge flan cases should be frozen without a filling. Neither jelly nor arrowroot glaze freezes very well. A decorated cake or gateau should be frozen uncovered until firm, then stored in a large polythene container to protect it. Cream-filled and decorated cakes freeze well but glacé icing does not freeze successfully.

Food/approximate storage time	Preparation and freezing
	Uncooked rich cake mixtures can be frozen in polythene containers or a foil-lined cake tin (1). Remove from the tin when frozen, overwrap in foil or polythene, and return it to the freezer (2). Bake in the same tin.

Butter, margarine, lard, suet *6 months*	Overwrap packets in foil or polythene. Unsalted butter will only keep for 3 months.
Cream *3 months*	Double or whipping cream can be frozen. It is best if half-whipped, with a teaspoon of icing sugar added for each 125ml/¼pt. Small rosettes can be piped on to a tray and frozen open. When they are firm, pack carefully in firm containers to avoid damage. Place in position on the cake or sweet while still frozen.
Milk *1 month*	Pasteurized milk does not freeze well, as it separates. Homogenized milk can be frozen in cartons, but never freeze it in bottles.
Cheese *6 months*	Soft cheeses freeze well, but hard cheeses tend to become crumbly when thawed. Grated cheese freezes well and can be used when frozen. Wrap cheese closely in foil or polythene.
Eggs *9 months*	Do not freeze whole eggs, but whites and yolks may be frozen separately in firm containers. Add a pinch of salt or sugar to each yolk.

Practical work

1 **What are the general rules to follow when freezing pre-cooked foods?**
2 **How would you wrap (a) an uncooked meat pie, (b) a decorated sandwich cake, (c) some biscuits, and (d) some fish cakes, before freezing them?**
3 **You are having a few friends round for the evening next week. Prepare and freeze some suitable dishes for the occasion.**
4 **Prepare and pack a main course and a pudding which it would be useful to have stored in the freezer.**

Reheated food and left-overs

Sometimes food is left over from a meal and to save it from being wasted it can be reheated to make another meal. But if you are going to do this, you must be careful, because of the danger of food poisoning. Remember that bacteria will flourish in food which is left lying around in a warm room. Any food which is to be kept after a meal must be put on to a clean plate, covered, and kept in a cold place. Use it as soon as possible and only use it if it is fresh. When reheating, bring food up to a high temperature from cold as soon as possible. Avoid keeping it at the tepid or warm temperature at which bacteria will multiply rapidly.

How to use up different foods

Reheated meat tends to be dry and lacking in flavour. If you are going to make a reheated dish you should choose a recipe which will add the necessary moisture and flavour. Meat should only be reheated, not recooked, or it will become tough and indigestible. Never reheat meat more than once. If you have any meat left over from a joint or chicken you could use it to make a curry or risotto. If you have a mincer you can mince the meat for mince pie or minced beef and dumplings.

Fish can be used to make fish cakes or fish and cheese sauce.

Potatoes which are left over can be used for fish cakes or meat and potato pie.

Vegetables will have little Vitamin C remaining and should not be counted as a source of this vitamin if they are reheated. But they could be mixed with a cheese sauce to make cheese and vegetable flan.

Fruit Left-over stewed or tinned fruit can be used in various ways, for example in fruit fool, fruit charlotte, or fruit flan.

Bread or crusts If these are stale they can be dried to make raspings (dried bread crumbs). The bread is put into a baking tin and dried in a very low oven until it is golden brown and crisp. Then it is made into crumbs, either in a blender or by placing it between greaseproof paper and crushing it with a rolling pin. When it has been sieved it can be kept for coating fish cakes or other food before frying, or for coating the sides of cakes when you decorate them.

Fresh bread which is not needed can be grated or put in a blender to make fresh crumbs for apple charlotte, stuffing, beefburgers, or a meat loaf.

Cake and biscuits Cake which is not too stale can be used in trifle. Crumbs can be made from plain biscuits for the base of a crunchy chocolate flan or a cheesecake.

Questions

1 **Why is there a risk of food poisoning when using reheated or left-over food?**
2 **How would you avoid this risk?**
3 **What particular care should you take when reheating meat so that it keeps a good flavour and texture?**
4 **Name some recipes for using up (a) left-over roast meat, (b) left-over cooked white fish, (c) cake which has become dry, (d) fresh bread.**

Batch baking

When you are cooking it often takes very little extra time and effort to make double the amount of a basic mixture and use it to make several different items.

For example, if you were making shortcrust pastry you could make a much larger amount than usual and use it to make a pie, some small tarts, and a flan. If you were making a Victoria sandwich cake mixture you could make double the amount at the same time and make both a cake and a pudding.

If you have a freezer you could make a stew or casserole using double the quantities, eat half straight away and freeze half to eat later. This saves time spent in preparation and washing up. It also saves fuel, as you are using the oven to cook several different items at the same time.

Here are some suggestions for making and using larger amounts of basic mixtures:

Shortcrust pastry

Make 400g/1lb pastry using:
400g/1lb plain flour
100g/4oz margarine
100g/4oz lard
Pinch of salt

Suggestions for using

1 Use half of the mix to make a chicken and mushroom pie.   (200g/8oz pastry)
   Use a quarter of the mix to make a cheese and onion flan.   (100g/4oz pastry)
   Use a quarter of the mix to make jam or lemon curd tarts.   (100g/4oz pastry)

2 Use half of the mix to make sausage rolls.   (200g/8oz pastry)
   Use a quarter of the mix to make a Bakewell tart.   (100g/4oz pastry)
   Use a quarter of the mix to make a cheese and vegetable flan.   (100g/4oz pastry)

3 Use half of the mix to make Cornish pasties.   (200g/8oz pastry)
   Use half of the mix to make an apple pie.   (200g/8oz pastry)

Victoria sandwich cake mixture

Make double the quantity of basic mixture using:
200g/8oz self-raising flour
200g/8oz caster sugar
200g/8oz margarine
4 eggs

1 Use half to make a Victoria sandwich cake.
   Use half to make a pineapple upside-down pudding.
2 Use half to make a steamed pudding.
   Use half to make fairy cakes (add an extra rounded tablespoon of self-raising flour to the mixture for these).

Sponge mixture

Make a basic sponge mixture using:
4 eggs
100g/4oz caster sugar
100g/4oz self-raising flour

1 Use half to make a Swiss roll.
   Use half to make a sponge fruit flan.
2 Use half to make some sponge drops.
   Use half to make a sponge fruit gateau.

Rough puff pastry

Make the pastry using:
400g/1lb plain flour
150g/6oz hard margarine
150g/6oz lard
250ml/½pt water

1 Use half to make sausage rolls.
   Use half to make jam and cream slices.
2 Use half to make a sausage plait.
   Use half to make apple turnovers.

Bread

Make a basic bread mix using:

500g/1lb strong flour
2 level teaspoons salt
25g/1oz margarine
15g/½oz fresh yeast
250ml/½pt water
1 × 50mg ascorbic acid tablet

Use half of the dough to make a small loaf.
Use half of the dough to make bread buns.

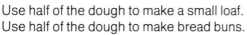

Practical work

1 **You are going to make 400g/1lb of shortcrust pastry (that is, using 400g/1lb flour). Suggest some ways of using this amount of pastry to make several different items.**
2 **Suggest ways of using a basic Victoria sandwich cake mixture made with 200g/8oz flour to make several items from the same mixture.**
3 **Suggest a variety of items suitable for a party that you could make with 400g/1lb rough puff pastry (made with 400g/1lb flour).**

Cooking with herbs

Herbs are green plants which have a distinctive flavour or smell. They are widely used for flavouring foods and for making medicines or perfumes. Different parts of the plant may be used; the leaves, stem, flowers, seeds, or roots. Most herbs can be grown quite easily in this country, either in a garden or in pots on a window sill. They can be used fresh, or they can be dried for use in the winter.

Herbs often used in cookery

Herb	Description	Uses
Basil or sweet basil	Sweet, spicy flavour, rather like cloves.	Tomato dishes, salads, soups, and stews.
Bay leaves	Strong, spicy. The leaf is often used whole, and is removed before serving.	Bouquet garni, savoury dishes of most kinds, milk puddings.
Borage	The leaves and blue flowers are both used.	Salads, fruit salads, cold drinks, flowers used as a garnish.
Chives	Onion family, a delicate onion flavour. Best when freshly chopped.	Salads, cottage or cream cheese. Jacket or mashed potatoes.
Garlic	A bulb divided into cloves. Member of the onion family. Strong flavour and smell.	Many savoury dishes, stews, curries, salad dressings, garlic bread.
Mint	Widely grown and used. Different varieties available.	Mint sauce with lamb. Cooked with new potatoes or peas.
Parsley	Pleasant flavour, more flavour in the stalks than in the leaves.	Widely used as garnish. Stalk used in bouquet garni.
Marjoram	Strong, spicy flavour, used in mixed herbs.	Meat dishes, soups, stuffing, fish, salads.
Oregano	Known as wild marjoram, used as marjoram. Widely used in Italian cooking.	Meats, sausages, cheese and egg dishes, pizzas.
Rosemary	Highly flavoured, so use sparingly. Slightly sweet.	Sprinkled over lamb before roasting. Soups and stews.

basil

mint

bay leaves

borage

chives

marjoram

parsley

garlic

Herb	Description	Uses
Sage	Strong flavour, use with care. Used with rich, oily, meat.	Stuffing for pork, duck or goose, pork sausages.
Tarragon	Distinctive flavour, used for tarragon vinegar, made by infusing the leaves in wine vinegar.	Mixed salads, tomato salad, fish and chicken dishes.
Thyme	A strong, spicy flavour, very aromatic.	Stuffing, mixed herbs, roast meats, soups, and stews.

A bouquet garni is a small bunch of mixed herbs which is used to flavour a sauce or stew. The herbs are enclosed in a piece of muslin and this is cooked with the food. It is removed at the end of cooking.

Mixed herbs are a mixture of such herbs as parsley, sage, marjoram or oregano, and thyme. They are used in stuffings and in many savoury meat and fish dishes.

Fine herbs are a mixture of equal amounts of freshly-chopped parsley, chives, tarragon and chervil. They are often used to flavour omelettes.

Recipes using herbs

Herbs add an interesting flavour to many savoury dishes. They should not be used carelessly but added in small amounts to suitable dishes, such as soups, stews, casseroles, and salads. Mixed herbs may be added to breadcrumbs used for stuffed tomatoes, meat loaf, beefburgers, or stuffing for roast breast of lamb or liver casserole. Garlic may be used in chicken curry, chili con carne, and other casseroles and stews. Chopped parsley is added to many dishes either to add flavour or as a garnish, for example, beef and chicken casseroles, lamb and bean casserole. Oregano can be used to flavour pizzas.

Practical work

1 **Name a herb which is**
a **used to make a sauce eaten with roast lamb.**
b **used to flavour vinegar.**
c **used in many Italian dishes.**
d **chopped and used as a garnish on savoury dishes.**
e **often used in stuffing for roast pork.**
2 **What would you expect to be included in a packet of mixed herbs?**
3 **Prepare and cook one meat and one cheese dish which include herbs in the ingredients.**

rosemary · sage · tarragon · thyme

Cooking with spices

Spices are mainly dried berries and seeds from tropical plants. They have been imported into this country, mostly from the Far East, for hundreds of years, and are valuable for their flavour and aromatic smell. They are sold either whole or ground. Buy them in small quantities as the more recently they have been ground, the better the flavour.

Spices often used in cookery

Spice	Description	Uses
Allspice	Small dried berries, whole or ground. Not to be confused with mixed spice.	Widely used in pickles, sauces, for meats and fish. Also used in cakes.
Cayenne	A hot, sweet, ground red pepper. Use sparingly. Made from small chilies.	Meat, fish, vegetable and cheese dishes, curries.
Chilies (powdered)	This is the whole chili which has been ground. Hot, strong flavour.	Used whole in chutneys, sauces, pickles. Ground for meat dishes.
Cinnamon	Thin inner bark of a laurel tree. Sold as sticks or ground. Sweet smelling, pleasant flavour.	Cakes, gingerbread, puddings, stews, sauces, chutneys.
Cloves	Dried flower buds from the myrtle tree. Strong, fragrant smell and taste.	Apple dishes. Ground for cakes and biscuits.
Cumin seeds	Similar to caraway seeds. Used in chili and curry powder.	Used in Eastern and Mexican dishes to flavour meat and fish. Pickles, sauces, and chutney.
Ginger	The root is used whole or may be ground to a powder. A hot, sweet flavour.	Whole root used in curries and chutneys. Ground ginger used in cakes, biscuits, curries, and in rhubarb and ginger jam.
Mustard	Widely used. Seeds of mustard plant, usually ground.	Used with beef, ham, pork, and cooked cheese dishes.
Nutmeg	May be sold whole, about the size of walnuts, to be grated as required. Also sold ground.	Sweet dishes such as milk puddings, egg custards, potato dishes.
Pepper	Most widely used of all spices. Whole peppercorns – black, freshly ground pepper has very good flavour and aroma; white peppercorns are milder. Also sold ground, black or white.	Pepper blends well with any savoury dish. Whole peppercorns are used for pickling. White pepper is used for light sauces as it does not discolour them.

Spice	Description	Uses
Paprika	A ground red pepper. Like cayenne in appearance but much milder.	Used for goulash and other Hungarian cookery, and for garnishing.
Saffron	Made from stigma of a crocus. Bright yellow in colour, mild flavour.	Used in rice dishes such as paella, to colour.
Sesame seeds	Widely used in Eastern cookery. Sweet, rich flavour.	Fried in butter or toasted, added to salads, chicken, fish. On rolls, etc., before cooking.
Turmeric	Root of a plant similar to ginger, not as strong. Yellow in colour.	Always used in curry powder. Piccalilli, sauces, rice dishes.
Mixed spice	A mixture of several spices such as nutmeg, cinnamon, ginger, and cloves.	Used in cakes, gingerbread, biscuits.
Curry powder	A hot-tasting mixture of many different spices, yellow in colour. Many blends available.	Curries with meat, fish, vegetables.
Chili powder	Mixture of spices including chili, pepper, salt, oregano, cumin seed, and garlic. 'Hot' but less so than powdered chilies.	Chili con carne. Fish, meat, vegetables, sauces.

Salt

Salt is used to bring out the flavour of all other foods. Sea salt or rock salt has a more 'salty' taste, and so goes further than ordinary salt. Salt is usually mined.

Recipes using spices

Use spices in carefully-measured amounts as they have a strong flavour.
Gingerbread, ginger loaf, and ginger biscuits all use ground ginger.
Baked egg custard has nutmeg sprinkled on top.
Chicken and beef curries use curry powder containing turmeric and other spices. Chili con carne contains chili powder.
Fruit loaf contains mixed spice.
Mustard may be added to cheese scones or French dressing.
Salt and pepper are added to almost all savoury foods.

Practical work

1 **What is the difference between herbs and spices?**
2 **Name five spices which are used in sweet dishes.**
3 **Name five spices which are used in savoury dishes.**
4 **What is the difference between (a) cayenne and paprika pepper, (b) allspice and mixed spice, (c) white and black pepper, (d) chilies and chili powder?**
5 **Name the spice you would use in these dishes: (a) baked egg custard, (b) cheese scones, (c) fruit loaf, (d) apple pie, and (e) goulash.**
6 **Prepare and cook a selection of sweet and savoury dishes which include spices in the ingredients.**

Laying the table

1 Choose a clean table-cloth or table-mats, and napkins. Make sure they are well ironed. Try to match the colours of the cloth, napkins, flowers and china if you can. It is easy and fairly cheap to make a table-cloth yourself, from cotton dress or curtain material. You can make matching napkins or buy paper ones in plain, attractive colours.

2 Make a flower arrangement for the centre of the table. Keep it low so that people can see over the top of it. At Christmas, an arrangement of holly, ivy, and red candles looks attractive, especially with a red or white cloth. (See p. 217.)

3 Make sure drinking glasses and cutlery are well polished and free from smears and finger marks. Run them under a hot tap or place them in a jug of hot water and rub each piece with a clean tea-towel as you lay the table.

4 Use thick mats to protect the table from hot serving dishes. Place them where they can be easily reached, with serving knives, forks, and spoons beside them.

5 Place a jug of very cold water on the table, unless you are having wine with the meal.

6 Lay each place setting correctly, according to the food to be eaten. The bottom edge of the cutlery should be in a neat line, 1cm from the edge of the table. Leave enough room for a dinner plate in the centre of the place setting.

7 Use the right cutlery. For a cold first course or starter, place a small knife and fork on the outside of the table knife and fork. For pâté, just a small knife is used. You spread the pâté on to toast. For soup, use special soup spoons. A light sweet course, like a fruit fool, may be eaten with a teaspoon which is laid on the plate. You would not need a dessertspoon and fork on the table.

The table laid for a three-course meal of soup and bread rolls, main course, and pudding.

Serving a tray of coffee or tea

Coffee

Sometimes you have to serve a tray of coffee to a visitor, or at the end of a meal. The simplest way to make coffee is to make it in a coffee pot or jug. If you make it in a percolator you should follow the instructions that come with it. Use freshly-ground coffee if you have it, otherwise use a heaped teaspoon of instant coffee for each person you are serving.

1 Put a kettle of water on to boil.
2 When the water is hot, use some of it to warm the coffee pot and milk jug.
3 Put the coffee grounds into the pot. Use about two rounded dessertspoons for each pint/500mls of water.
4 Pour the boiling water on, stir, and leave in a warm place for five minutes.
5 Warm the milk but do not let it boil. Pour into the warm milk jug.

To serve the coffee, set the tray with a well-ironed tray-cloth, and arrange it exactly as shown here, so that the tray looks neat and the coffee is easy to pour. If you were serving biscuits with morning coffee, you would place them on a doily on a small plate on the tray.

Tea

1 Put the kettle on to boil. Use some of the hot water to warm the pot thoroughly.
2 Put the tea into the pot. A rough guide would be about three rounded teaspoons for a medium-sized teapot.
3 Pour the boiling water on to the tea leaves, stir and leave for about four minutes before pouring. Keep a tea-cosy on the pot to keep it hot.

Serve the tea as shown here, with a bowl of white sugar and a jug of cold milk. If you like, you can put a jug of hot water on the tray to refill the teapot.

Practical work

1 **Lay the table exactly as shown here.**
2 **Lay the table exactly as it should be done for each of the three meals on page 76. Before you start, decide what cutlery you would eat the food with and what cutlery you would need for serving each item.**
3 **Make a pot of coffee and set a tray for morning coffee for two.**
4 **Make a pot of tea for four people.**

Chapter 5: Recipes

Cold starters

Mackerel pâté   *Serves 3–4*

1 tin mackerel
75g/3oz butter
2 tablespoons lemon juice
1 tablespoon vinegar
Salt and pepper
Cress or parsley and lemon slice to garnish

Method
1   Open tin of mackerel, remove skin and bone, drain off the liquid.
2   Cut the lemon in half, cut off one or two neat slices for garnish. Squeeze the juice from the rest of the lemon.
3   Mix the mackerel, butter, lemon juice, vinegar, salt, and pepper in a basin. Beat very thoroughly with a fork and then with a wooden spoon until smooth.
4   Turn into a small dish and smooth the top. Chill.
5   Garnish with a little cress or parsley and a twist of lemon.

You would serve this with fingers of toast or fresh bread buns.

Florida cocktail   *Serves 3–4*

2 oranges
1 grapefruit

Method
1   Cut the top and bottom from the grapefruit, stand it flat on the board, and remove the skin with a sharp knife.

2   Carefully remove all the segments between the dividing skins. Hold over a bowl as you do this to collect any juice.
3   Prepare the oranges in the same way, mix with the grapefruit and chill.
4   Serve in individual glass dishes, standing on a doyley on a small plate, with a teaspoon.

For a decorative effect you can dip the rim of the empty glass dish into egg white and then into caster sugar, to 'frost' the rim.

Ham and cheese roll-ups *Serves 4*

4 slices cooked ham
1 small carton cottage or cream cheese
Lettuce leaves
1 tomato

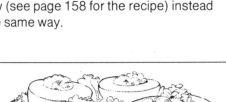

Method
1 Spread the cheese over the slices of ham and roll them up.
2 Wash the lettuce leaves carefully under cold running water, then gently shake them dry. Arrange on a flat serving plate. Slice the tomato thinly.
3 Place the ham rolls neatly on the lettuce and place the tomato slices on top.

You would serve these with thinly cut brown bread and butter.

Ham and coleslaw roll-ups Use coleslaw (see page 158 for the recipe) instead of cottage cheese. Make and serve in the same way.

Stuffed eggs *Serves 2*

2 eggs
25g/1oz cheese
1 level tablespoon salad cream
Lettuce for serving

Method
1 Put the eggs in a small pan, cover with cold water. Bring to the boil and simmer gently for 10 minutes. Leave to cool.
2 Wash the lettuce leaves carefully under the cold tap. Gently shake them to remove the water. Grate the cheese very finely.
3 Shell the eggs, then cut them in half lengthwise.
4 Remove the yolk from the eggs. Mix it with the cheese and salad cream. Either spoon it or pipe it back into the whites.
5 Arrange neatly on the lettuce.

Stuffed tomatoes *Serves 4*

4 firm tomatoes
2 slices of bread
50g/2oz cheese
Salt and pepper
Lettuce for serving

Method
1 Wash and dry the tomatoes. Slice the top off to make a lid (not the stalk end).
2 Use a grater or blender to make breadcrumbs. Grate the cheese.
3 Using a teaspoon, remove the inside of the tomatoes and mix this with the crumbs and cheese. Add a little salt and pepper.
4 Spoon this filling back into the tomatoes, put the lid on.
5 Wash the lettuce and gently shake it dry. Serve the tomatoes on a flat dish, on the lettuce.

To serve the tomatoes hot When the filling has been added, stand the tomatoes on a greased baking tray. Brush with oil or melted butter and bake at Gas 4, 180°C, for about 20 minutes.

Soups

It is easy to make soup at home, and it always has a good flavour when made with fresh ingredients. With many soup recipes you can adapt the vegetables to make best use of those which are cheap and in season.

Always taste the soup before you serve it, to make sure it has enough salt and pepper. If it is too thick, it can be thinned with a little water or milk. If too thin, it can be thickened by blending a level tablespoon of cornflour or plain flour with about 3 tablespoons of cold milk or water in a small basin. Pour this into the soup, bring to the boil and simmer for a few minutes to thicken.

Serve the soup in a soup tureen, garnished with chopped parsley or a few thinly-sliced vegetables. For a special occasion, a little single cream poured over the top of the soup looks attractive.

Tomato soup   *Serves 3–4*

1 medium-sized (14oz) can of tomatoes
500ml/1pt water
1 chicken stock cube

1 potato, 1 onion, 1 carrot
Salt and pepper
Chopped parsley

Method
1 Peel and chop the potato, onion, and carrot. Put them in a pan with the tomatoes, water, stock cube, salt, and pepper.
2 Stir to dissolve the stock cube, then simmer gently with the lid on for about 20 minutes until soft.
3 Liquidize the soup (or sieve). Check the seasoning. Reheat if necessary.
4 Serve in a warm soup tureen, sprinkled with chopped parsley.

Golden vegetable soup   *Serves 3–4*

1 potato
1 carrot
25g/1oz dripping
750ml/1½pts water
Chopped parsley

2 sticks celery or 1 leek
1 onion (2 if not using celery or leek)
1 chicken stock cube
Salt and pepper
1 level tablespoon plain flour or cornflour

Method
1 Peel all the vegetables, grate the carrot and finely chop the other vegetables. Fry in the dripping for 10 minutes.
2 Add the water, stock cube, salt, and pepper. Bring to the boil and simmer for about 25 minutes until all the vegetables are soft.
3 Blend the flour with 4 tablespoons water until smooth. Pour into the soup and simmer for 5 minutes. Check the flavour.
4 Blend in a liquidizer until smooth.
5 Serve in a warm soup tureen, sprinkled with parsley.

Onion soup   *Serves 3–4*

500g/1lb onions
15g/½oz dripping or margarine
1 medium-sized potato
750ml/1½pts water

1 chicken stock cube
Salt and pepper
Chopped parsley

Method
1 Peel and roughly chop the onions and potato.
2 Melt the dripping in a fairly large pan and gently fry the vegetables for 10 minutes, stirring occasionally.
3 Add the water, stock cube, salt, and pepper and bring to the boil. Simmer with the lid on for about 30 minutes until cooked.
4 Put into a blender and run for a few seconds until smooth (or sieve). Check the seasoning. Reheat if necessary.
5 Serve in a warm soup tureen, garnished with chopped parsley.

Mushroom soup   *Serves 3*

100g/¼lb mushrooms
15g/½oz margarine
Half a small onion
500ml/1pt water

1 chicken stock cube
Salt and pepper
1 level tablespoon plain flour or cornflour
125ml/¼pt milk

Method
1 Carefully wash the mushrooms in cold water. Slice one of them very thinly to use as a garnish, and roughly chop the rest. Peel and chop the onion.
2 Melt the margarine in a pan and gently fry the vegetables for 5 minutes. Add the water, stock cube, salt and pepper.
3 Bring to the boil and simmer with the lid on for 25 minutes.
4 Mix the flour with the milk until smooth, pour into the pan and boil for a few minutes. Blend for a few seconds until smooth (or sieve). Check the seasoning.
5 Serve in a warm soup tureen, garnished with mushroom slices.

Lentil soup   *Serves 3–4*

75g/3oz lentils
1 large carrot
1 onion
1 medium potato
½ a small turnip or swede
1 celery stalk (optional)

40g/1½oz margarine
750ml/1½pts water
Chicken stock cube
Salt and pepper
Chopped parsley

Method
1 Wash the lentils in a sieve and drain.
2 Thinly slice the carrot, onion, celery. Cut the potatoes and turnip into small dice.
3 Melt the margarine in a large pan and fry the vegetables for about 5 minutes. Add the lentils, pour in the water, stock cube, salt, and pepper. Bring to the boil, stirring, lower the heat and cover.
4 Simmer very gently for 1 hour (or pressure cook at H/15lb pressure for 20 minutes, then reduce the pressure at room temperature).
5 Liquidize or sieve, and check the flavour.
6 Serve hot, sprinkled with chopped parsley.

Fish

A wide variety of fish is available in Britain. If you don't have a fishmonger near you, you can buy frozen fish from a supermarket or freezer centre. Frozen fish is a good substitute for fresh, though there may be less variety to choose from. The fish is usually frozen quite soon after being caught, so not much flavour should be lost.

There are three main types of fish: white fish, oily fish, and shellfish.

White fish

As the name suggests, these are fish which have white flesh. This group includes cod, haddock, whiting, plaice, sole, and coley or saithe. This last fish is becoming more popular, as cod and haddock become more expensive. The flesh is less white than that of cod or haddock before cooking, but when cooked it has a good flavour and colour and can be used in any recipe which normally uses the more expensive fish.

Food value
White fish is a good source of protein, phosphorus, and iodine. As there is little fat or oil in the flesh of white fish it is easily digested. This makes it a suitable food for invalids and elderly people. The liver of the cod is used to make cod-liver oil, which is a very good source of Vitamins A and D.

Oily fish

This group includes herrings, mackerel, sardines, pilchards, salmon, trout, and tuna. These fish are called oily as they have oil dispersed through the flesh. This makes them darker in colour than white fish.

Food value
They are a good source of protein, phosphorus, iodine, polyunsaturated fats (in the form of oil), and Vitamins A and D. They are particularly useful as a source of Vitamin D as this is not found in many other foods. Canned fish, where the bones have been softened and may be eaten, are also a good source of calcium.

Shellfish

Shellfish are protected by a hard external shell. Lobster, crabs, prawns and shrimps, cockles and mussels, and oysters are all shellfish. They are a good source of protein but not of vitamins and minerals, and they are fairly hard to digest. It is particularly important they are eaten when very fresh, as they may otherwise cause food poisoning. Most of them are cooked before they are sold, except for oysters, mussels, and scallops.

Smoked fish

Some fish may be smoked. This adds flavour and it helps the fish to stay fresh longer. Examples are smoked haddock, kippers (which are smoked herrings), smoked mackerel, smoked salmon and trout.

Choosing fish

It is important that the fish you buy is really fresh, as it does not keep well. Look for these signs:

1 The flesh should be firm and moist.
2 Whole fish should have bright red gills, sparkling scales, and the eyes should be prominent, not sunken.
3 The fish should have a fresh smell.
4 When choosing smoked fish, look for firm flesh, a glossy skin, and a wholesome smoky smell.

Storing fish

As it does not keep well, fresh fish should be eaten the same day it is bought, or the following day at the latest if kept in a refrigerator. A supply of canned fish such as sardines, mackerel, or salmon is useful in the store cupboard. Frozen fish may be stored in the freezer if you have one. There are several kinds available and it is quite cheap if bought in bulk from a freezer centre.

Serving

White fish can sometimes lack flavour and colour. This can be overcome by:

1 Using a method of cooking which adds flavour, e.g. frying in breadcrumbs or butter.
2 Serving with a well-flavoured sauce such as cheese or tomato sauce.
3 Serving with plenty of colourful garnish, such as parsley, cress, lemon slices or wedges, or tomatoes.

Recipes using fish

As well as the recipes below, fish is also included in these dishes: mackerel pâté (p. 110), pizza (p. 198), quick cheese pizza (p. 140), tuna fish salad (p. 159), sardine and tomato sandwiches (p. 181), sardine and tomato salad (p. 159).

Questions

1 **Give some examples of white fish and list the nutrients they contain.**
2 **Make a list of the types of oily fish you have eaten or seen on sale. List the nutrients they contain.**
3 **Name as many recipes as you can in which you would use (a) white fish, and (b) oily fish.**
4 **Why are fish sometimes smoked? Give some examples.**
5 **What are the signs you would look for when choosing fresh fish?**
6 **What foods can be served with fish to add colour and flavour?**

Recipes

Fried fillets of fish   *Serves 3*

3 fillets of any white fish, about 100g/4oz each
1 egg   50g/2oz lard or oil for frying
50g/2oz fresh white bread   1 lemon
Flour for coating   Parsley or cress

Method

1   Wash and dry the fish. Make the bread into crumbs. Beat the egg and put into a shallow dish. Put the flour on to a plate.
2   Dip the fish into the flour, then brush with the beaten egg. Coat with the crumbs, pressing them on to the fish. Shake off any loose crumbs.

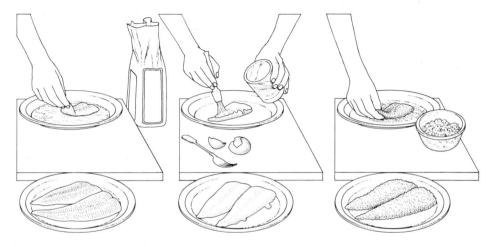

3   Heat the lard or oil in a frying pan. There should be enough fat to cover the bottom of the pan to about 0.5cm/¼″ depth.
4   Carefully lower the fish into the hot fat, placing the skin side of the fish upwards. Cook gently for about 7 minutes, then turn over and cook the other side. When cooked the fish should be white and no longer transparent.
5   While the fish is cooking, cut the lemon into wedges or slices and wash the parsley.
6   Drain the fish fillets on kitchen paper to remove any excess fat. Place them on paper on a warm, flat serving dish and garnish with the lemon and parsley.

To cut the lemon wedges or twists for garnishing fish dishes:

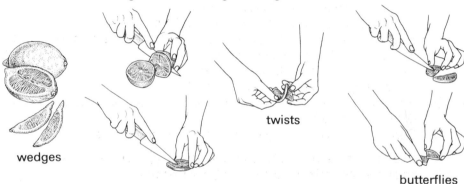

twists

wedges

butterflies

Fish and cheese sauce *Serves 2–3*

250g/½lb white fish
Small packet instant potato (optional)
Parsley to garnish

Sauce
250ml/½pt milk
25g/1oz plain flour
25g/1oz margarine
Salt, pepper, pinch of mustard
100g/4oz cheese

Method
1 Wash the fish, place it between two plates and steam it over a pan of simmering water until cooked (about 15 minutes).
2 Grate the cheese. Make up the instant potato if you are using it.
3 Put the sauce ingredients into a pan. Bring to the boil, whisking all the time. Simmer for 2–3 minutes until thick. Stir in half the cheese.
4 When the fish is cooked, place it in a shallow ovenproof dish. Pour the sauce over, sprinkle the rest of the cheese on top. Pipe the potatoes around the edge.
5 Either grill under a medium heat, or place near the top of a hot oven until golden brown. Garnish with the sprig of parsley.

Serve with creamed or duchess potatoes and another vegetable.

Fish cakes *Makes 6*

100g/4oz white fish (or a can of mackerel, tuna, or salmon)
250g/8oz potatoes (or small packet instant potato)
15g/½oz margarine
Salt and pepper
1 level tablespoon parsley (optional)
1 sprig of parsley for garnishing

For coating
Flour, 1 beaten egg, breadcrumbs
Oil, lard, or dripping for frying

Method
1 Wash and peel the potatoes. Cut them into even-sized pieces, put in a pan and cover with cold water, adding a little salt. Simmer for about 20 minutes until cooked.
2 Wash the fish, place between two plates and place these over the potatoes. Steam for about 15 minutes until cooked.
3 Wash and chop the parsley. Keep a sprig for garnishing.
4 Mash the cooked potatoes, flake the fish and add to the potatoes with the margarine, salt, pepper and parsley.
5 Divide the mixture into 6 pieces, shape into fish cakes. Coat each with flour, beaten egg, and crumbs (see page 116).
6 Heat the oil or fat in a frying pan. Fry the fish cakes carefully, turning over once. Drain well on kitchen paper.
7 Serve on a shallow dish, garnished with the sprig of parsley.

If you are using a can of fish, just open the can, drain the liquid, remove any skin and bone, and mix with the cooked, mashed potato.

Fish and tomato casserole   *Serves 3–4*

About 500g/1lb white fish fillet (e.g. cod, coley, haddock)
Salt and pepper
1 onion
1 medium-sized tin of tomatoes
25g/1oz butter
1 rounded tablespoonful chopped parsley
25g/1oz fresh white or brown breadcrumbs
50g/2oz cheese

Method
1   Wash the fish, place in an ovenproof dish, sprinkle with salt and pepper.
2   Peel and slice the onion, wash and chop the parsley. Drain most of the juice off the tomatoes. Put the tomatoes, onion, parsley, and butter into a small pan, simmer gently for 10 minutes.
3   Grate the cheese. Grate the bread to make breadcrumbs.
4   Pour the tomatoes over the fish. Mix the cheese and crumbs and spread them over the tomato mixture.
5   Bake in the centre of the oven, Gas 4, 180°C for 30 minutes.

Serve with mashed potatoes and fresh vegetables.

Crispy fish bake   *Serves 2–3*

1 tin mackerel or tuna fish
1 tin condensed mushroom or chicken soup
50g/2oz bread
50g/2oz cheese
1 packet of plain crisps
Lemon and parsley to garnish

Method
1   Light the oven, Gas 5, 190°C. Place the shelf in the centre of the oven.
2   Remove any skin or bone from the fish, place it in a greased 500ml/1 pint ovenproof dish.
3   Pour the soup over the fish.
4   Make the bread into crumbs (using blender or grater). Grate the cheese. Crush the crisps in the packet.
5   Mix the bread, cheese, and crisps together, and place over the soup.
6   Bake in the oven for about 30 minutes until hot and lightly browned.
7   Garnish with parsley and lemon twists (see page 116). Serve with freshly cooked vegetables.

Meat

The meat we eat in Britain today comes mainly from the cow (beef), the calf (veal), the sheep (mutton and lamb), and the pig (pork and bacon).

The food value of meat

Meat is a valuable food as it supplies many nutrients. It is a good source of:
> *Protein* − in the lean part of all meats.
> *Fat* − both in the fat you can see on the meat and in the fat spread through the meat.
> *Iron* − particularly in liver and kidney, corned beef, black pudding, and red meat.
> *B-Vitamins* − in most meats.

Storing meat

1 Meat must be kept in a cold place, preferably in a fridge.
2 Cover meat loosely with cling film or foil before placing in the fridge, so that it does not dry out.
3 Uncooked beef, pork, and lamb will keep for 2−3 days in a refrigerator.
  Mince and liver can only be kept for one day uncooked.
  Sausages should only be kept for up to three days.
  Cooked meats should only be kept for 2−3 days.
4 Frozen meat keeps for varying lengths of time, depending on what kind it is. See page 97 for details of how to pack and freeze meat.

Cuts of meat

Meat is cut into different joints or cuts. The more expensive cuts are leaner and more tender. They can be cooked by quicker, dry methods such as roasting, frying, or grilling. Cheaper cuts usually cost less because they are tougher or have more fat. They need to be cooked more slowly, by a moist cooking method such as stewing, boiling, or in a casserole. They have a good flavour and are just as nutritious as expensive cuts.

Beef

Beef should be a bright red colour when freshly cut. It darkens a little when it is exposed to the air but this does no harm. The fat may be creamy coloured or white. There should not be too much gristle in the meat.

Methods of cooking beef
Roasting: sirloin, rib, silverside.
Grilling or frying: sirloin, rump or fillet steak.
Stewing or in a casserole: blade, buttock, or chuck steak. These may be labelled 'braising steak'. Shin − often just labelled as 'stewing steak' in a supermarket.
　　　Mince is made from flank or other cheaper cuts. If it is very fatty it is not very good value for money. You can buy lean stewing steak instead and ask the butcher to mince it for you, so that you can see what you are buying.

Foods served with beef

With roast beef it is traditional to serve Yorkshire pudding and sometimes horseradish sauce. With boiled silverside it is traditional to eat dumplings.

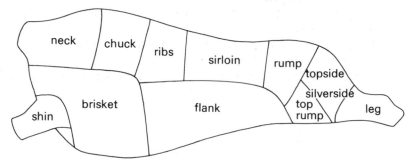

Veal

Veal is meat from the young calf. It is a pale pink colour with a small amount of white fat. The calf is specially fed to produce the delicate flavour and colour. Veal is very lean and tender. It is very expensive and is not eaten much in this country.

Lamb and mutton

Most lamb is from young sheep up to about 6 months old. Mutton is from sheep about 18 months old. The meat of lamb should be pink. In an older animal it is darker. The fat should be a creamy white colour.

Methods of cooking lamb

As lamb is young, most cuts are tender enough to be fried, grilled, or roasted. The only exceptions are the middle or scrag end of neck, sometimes sold as 'stewing chops'.

Roasting: leg, shoulder, breast, loin, best end of neck.

Grilling or frying: loin chops, chump chops, cutlets.

Stewing or in a casserole: middle neck, scrag end of neck.

The traditional sauce to serve with roast lamb is mint.

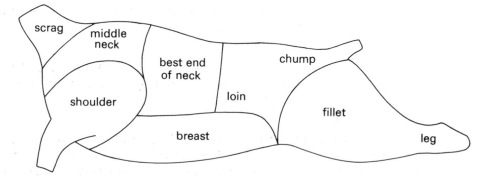

Pork

Pork is the meat from the pig. It should have firm, pink meat and white fat. The skin should be smooth and free from hairs. Pork is a rich meat, containing a lot of fat dispersed through the flesh as well as the fat you can see around the meat. Apple sauce is the traditional sauce served with roast pork. Its sharp, tangy flavour balances the richness of the meat. Sage and onion stuffing, too, is usually served with roast pork. Pork must always be thoroughly cooked.

Methods of cooking pork
Roasting: leg, fillet, loin, spare rib, hand or shoulder, belly (this is a cheaper cut as it is more fatty).
Grilling or frying: loin chops, chump chops, spare rib chops.
In a casserole: belly pork, spare rib.

Sausages may be made from pork or beef. The meat is mixed with a cereal such as breadcrumbs and seasoning.

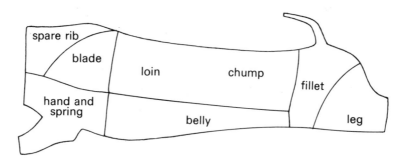

Bacon and ham

Bacon is pork which has been 'cured' so that it can be kept fresh for a longer time. The pork is cut into two sides and cured in brine (a solution of salt and water) for about two weeks. It is either sold as 'green' bacon after curing or it may be further treated by smoking, and sold as 'smoked' bacon. This has a stronger flavour than green bacon.

Gammon is the leg from the side of bacon.

Ham is also the leg of the pig. It is removed from the side of the pig before the pig is cured for bacon. It is then cured separately. The way it is cured decides the type of ham it will be. York ham, for instance, has a mild flavour, or you can buy 'honey cured' ham, or Virginia ham.

Choosing bacon
Look for a deep pink colour and firm white fat. Avoid any which has brownish meat or which has salt crystals on it.

To store bacon
It must be well covered to prevent it from drying out. It may be wrapped in greaseproof paper and then put in a polythene bag or box, or it may be wrapped in cling film. Store in a fridge or cool larder.

Cooking bacon
Most bacon is sold in rashers or thin slices. Cuts include back bacon, middle cut, streaky or collar (shoulder) bacon. Bacon chops may be cut from the back. Rashers or bacon chops are best cooked by grilling to allow any excess fat to drain away. If fried, it should be slowly 'dry' fried without any extra fat added.

Joints of bacon, for example, collar back or gammon, should first be soaked in cold water to remove any excess salt.

The food value of bacon
It is a good source of protein, fat, and B-group vitamins.

Offal

Offal is the term for the internal organs of the animal. It includes liver, kidney, tongue, heart, brains, sweetbreads, and tripe.

Other meat products include pigs' trotters, brawn, oxtail, sausages, and black pudding.

The food value of offal

All offal is very nutritious, and it is good value for money. It is a good source of protein, iron, B-vitamins and Vitamins A and C in liver and kidney.

Poultry

Poultry includes chicken, turkey, duck and goose. Chicken is widely available, both fresh and frozen, and is usually good value for money. It provides a good supply of protein but is fairly low in fat content, so it is a useful food to include often in meals if you are trying to cut down the amount of fat you eat. Chicken is available in joints, for baking, frying, casseroles, or grilling, as well as whole birds for roasting. Roast chicken is usually served with stuffing. Bread sauce, bacon rolls, and chipolata sausages are traditional accompaniments too.

A frozen chicken must be completely thawed before cooking, otherwise the centre may not reach a high enough temperature to kill any bacteria. This could cause food poisoning. Once the chicken is thawed, remove the giblets and wash the chicken inside and out in cold running water. Dry with kitchen paper.

Questions

1 **What nutrients does meat contain?**
2 **Describe how you would wrap each of the following before placing them in the refrigerator. Say how long you would expect each one to keep fresh.**
a **half a pound of lamb's liver**
b **a large joint of beef**
c **a pound of mince**
d **a packet of pork sausages**
3 **Name a cheap cut of (a) beef, (b) pork, (c) lamb which would be suitable for cooking in a casserole, or stewing.**
4 **Name a roasting joint of (a) beef, (b) pork, (c) lamb.**
5 **Suggest meat dishes for the seven main meals in a week. Include a variety of meats from different animals, cooked by different methods. Include some inexpensive meat dishes.**
6 **What are the traditional foods or sauces served with (a) roast beef, (b) roast lamb, (c) roast pork, and (d) roast chicken?**
7 **What is offal? Give four examples. Name the nutrients which are found in one of these examples.**
8 **Why are some cuts of meat less expensive than others? Give three possible reasons.**
9 **What is the difference between**
a **gammon, ham, and a leg of pork?**
b **green bacon and smoked bacon?**
10 **Name five meats or meat products which are good sources of iron.**

Recipes

As well as the meat recipes here, there are others:
In the rice section, page 130: chicken or beef curry, sweet and sour pork or chicken, sausage risotto.
In the pasta section, page 133: spaghetti Bolognese, lasagne.
In the pulses section, page 135: chili con carne, pork and bacon casserole, lamb and bean casserole.
In the pastry section, page 160: mince pie, chicken and mushroom pie, corned beef and potato pie, bacon and egg pie, leek and bacon pie, sausage rolls.

Beef and vegetable casserole   *Serves about 3*

250g/½lb stewing steak
25g/1oz plain flour
25g/1oz dripping
2 carrots, 2 onions
½ a small turnip
1 beef stock cube
375ml/¾pt hot water
Salt and pepper
Parsley

Method
1 Wipe the meat, remove any excess fat. Cut into small cubes and coat in flour.
2 Peel and slice carrots and onions. Peel the turnip and cut into cubes.
3 Melt the dripping and fry the meat and vegetables for about 5 mins. Stir in the rest of the flour.
4 Dissolve the stock cube in the water, add to the pan and bring to the boil, stirring. Add salt and pepper.
5 Pour into a casserole dish, cover and bake in the centre of the oven for 1–1½ hours until the meat is tender. Serve sprinkled with a little chopped parsley.

Beef stew Make as above, but do not pour the meat into a casserole dish. Just leave in the pan to simmer with the lid on for 1–1½ hours until cooked. Stir frequently to prevent sticking (or you could cook in a pressure cooker for about 20 minutes at High (15lb) pressure).

Serve these dishes with potatoes and vegetables.

Beefburgers   *Makes 4*

250g/8oz minced beef
1 small onion
Salt and pepper
For frying: lard, dripping, or oil

Method
1 Peel and grate the onion. Mix with the meat, add salt and pepper.
2 Divide into 4 and shape each into round cakes about 20mm/¾" thick, on a floured board.
3 Either grill for about 10 minutes, turning once, or fry for 5 minutes each side.

Serve with either barbecue sauce or tomato sauce.

Beefburgers with barbecue sauce *Makes 4*

4 beefburgers as above
1 small onion
15g/½oz margarine
2 tablespoons tomato ketchup
1 tablespoon vinegar

1 teaspoon Worcester sauce
Salt and pepper
4 tablespoons water
Tomato and parsley or cress to garnish

Method
1 Grate the onion. Put in a small pan with the other ingredients. Simmer very gently for 10 minutes, stirring occasionally.
2 Make the beefburgers as above. Put them in a grill pan without the grid. Spoon the sauce over and grill gently for about 10 minutes each side, basting occasionally with the sauce.
3 Either serve in bread buns or in a warm, shallow serving dish, garnished with slices of tomato and parsley.

Tomato sauce

1 can tomatoes (14oz size)
1 onion
1 rasher of bacon

15g/½oz margarine
1 level tablespoon cornflour or plain flour
Salt, pepper, level teaspoon of sugar

Method
1 Peel and chop the onion. Chop the bacon.
2 Melt the margarine in a small pan, fry the onion and bacon gently until softened (about 5–10 minutes).
3 Add the can of tomatoes, bring to the boil and simmer gently for about 20 minutes until cooked.
4 Blend the flour to a smooth paste with 3 tablespoons cold water. Pour into the pan, reboil, and simmer for 5 minutes until thickened.
5 Blend in a liquidizer until smooth, or sieve. Check the flavour, adding the salt, pepper, and sugar.

Meat loaf *Serves 4*

500g/1lb minced beef
1 onion
1 tablespoon chopped parsley (optional)

Salt and pepper
1 egg
2 slices bread

Method
1 Light the oven, Gas 6, 200°C. Place the shelf just above the oven centre. Grease a small loaf tin.
2 Peel and chop the onion, wash and chop the parsley. Grate the bread or make it into crumbs with a blender. Beat the egg.
3 Mix the mince, onion, parsley, salt and pepper, and breadcrumbs. Add the egg and bind the mixture together.
4 Put it into the tin, cover with a butter paper or greased greaseproof paper.
5 Bake for about 50 minutes until cooked. To test, insert a skewer into the centre of the loaf and press the loaf gently. The liquid that comes from the centre should not be pink.
6 Turn the cooked loaf on to a flat serving dish. Garnish with cooked vegetables such as carrots and peas, and parsley; or serve it cold instead, with a salad.

Savoury beef and tomato   *Serves about 3*

250g/½lb minced beef
1 level tablespoon plain flour
Small tin of tomato soup
Salt and pepper
Small packet of instant potato

Method
1   Fry the meat in a medium-sized pan until brown. Do not add any fat. Stir in the flour.
2   Add the soup, bring to the boil, then simmer gently with the lid on for 15 to 20 minutes. Stir occasionally and add a little water if necessary.
3   Meanwhile, light the oven, Gas 5, 190°C. Place the shelf near the top of the oven.
4   Make up the potato as directed on the packet and use it to pipe a border around a shallow ovenproof dish. Put this into the oven to brown.
5   When the meat is cooked, pour it carefully into the dish.

You would serve this with freshly cooked vegetables.

Minced beef and dumplings   *Serves about 3*

250g/½lb minced beef
1 large onion
15g/½oz margarine
1 level tablespoon plain flour
250ml/½pt water
Salt, pepper, stock cube

Dumplings
100g/4oz self-raising flour
50g/2oz suet
Pinch of salt

Method
1   Peel and chop the onion. Fry in the margarine in a saucepan for 5 minutes.
2   Put the mince into the saucepan and stir gently over a low heat until it is brown. Stir in the flour.
3   Add the water, stock cube, salt, and pepper. Bring to the boil, stirring. Simmer gently with the lid on for 10 minutes, stirring occasionally. Light the oven, Gas 6, 200°C.
4   Make the dumplings: mix the flour, suet, and salt, and add enough water to make a firm dough. Divide into about 6 dumplings.
5   Pour the meat into an ovenproof dish or tin, adding a little gravy browning if necessary. Place the dumplings on top of the mince and bake near the top of the oven for about 20 minutes until the dumplings are golden brown and crisp.

You would serve this with freshly cooked vegetables.

Toad in the hole   *Serves about 3*

250g/½lb sausages
15g/½oz dripping or lard
100g/4oz plain flour
½ level teaspoon salt
1 egg
250ml/½pt milk

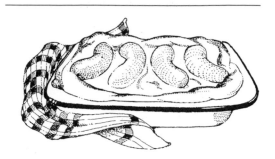

Method
1   Light the oven, Gas 7, 220°C. Put the shelf near the top of the oven.
2   Put the sausages into a large shallow tin or dish. Add the fat and place in the oven.
3   Sieve the flour and salt into a bowl. Drop the egg into the centre of the flour. Add a little milk and beat well until smooth.
4   Add the rest of the milk a little at a time and beat well.
5   When the fat in the tin is really hot and has a faint haze over it, pour the batter into the tin.
6   Bake for about 40 minutes until well risen and golden brown.

Serve with freshly cooked vegetables.

Yorkshire puddings

(To make enough for a 4-hole Yorkshire pudding tin)

50g/2oz plain flour, preferably strong flour
Pinch of salt
1 egg
100ml/¼pt milk
Dripping or lard

Method
1   Light the oven, Gas 8, 240°C. Place the shelf at the top of the oven.
2   Put a small piece of dripping or lard into each part of the tin and heat in the oven until a haze appears.
3   Sieve the flour and salt into a basin, beat in the egg. Add the milk a little at a time, beating well until smooth.
4   When the fat is hot enough, pour the mixture into the tin and put back into the oven.
5   Bake for about 20 minutes until well risen, firm, and golden brown, and serve with roast beef, or as a starter with gravy.

Yorkshire pudding (To make one large pudding)
Make in exactly the same way but use 100g/4oz flour, 1 egg, 250g/½pt milk. Bake in the same way but cook for 40 minutes.

Sausage and onion casserole   *Serves 3–4*

250g/½lb sausages
25g/1oz lard
1 onion
25g/1oz plain flour

Stock
250ml/½pt water
1 beef stock cube

100g/4oz mushrooms (optional)
1 tablespoon tomato purée
Salt and pepper
1 small (8oz) can baked beans
Chopped parsley

Method
1 Fry the sausages gently in the melted lard for 10 minutes until browned.
2 Peel and chop the onion, wash and slice the mushrooms, chop the parsley.
3 Put the sausages on to a plate and keep them warm. Add the onion to the pan and fry till lightly browned.
4 Stir in the flour, add the stock, tomato purée, and mushrooms and stir well.
5 Add the sausages and beans. Cover and simmer very gently for 10 minutes. Taste and season, if necessary.
6 Pour into a serving dish, sprinkle with chopped parsley, and serve with mashed potatoes and vegetables.

Baked chicken joints

1 chicken joint per person
Flour, seasoned with salt and pepper
1 egg
25g/1oz breadcrumbs for each joint
50g/2oz dripping or lard
To garnish, 1 tomato per person, cress

Method
1 Light the oven, Gas 5, 190°C. Place the shelf above the centre. Put the dripping into a small roasting tin and place it in the oven.
2 Make the breadcrumbs. Beat the egg and put it in a shallow dish. Wash and dry the chicken joints.
3 Coat each chicken joint in flour, then in egg, then in breadcrumbs.
4 When the fat is hot add the chicken joints, basting them with hot fat.
5 Bake for 35–45 minutes until tender. Baste during cooking.
6 Cut the tomatoes in half and warm in the oven for the last 10 minutes of cooking time.
7 Place the cooked chicken on kitchen paper to remove any excess fat, then place on a shallow serving dish.
8 Garnish with the tomatoes and plenty of cress.

Chicken casserole   *Serves 2*

2 chicken joints
15g/½oz plain flour
25g/1oz dripping
50g/2oz mushrooms
50g/2oz frozen peas
1 potato
Salt and pepper
250ml/½pt water
1 chicken stock cube

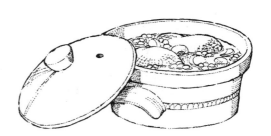

Method
1   Melt half the dripping and fry the washed, sliced mushrooms. Put them into an ovenproof dish.
2   Coat the chicken in the flour and fry in the rest of the dripping until golden brown. Put into the dish.
3   Peel the potato and cut it into slices. Put it in the dish with the chicken.
4   Dissolve the stock cube in the hot water. Put the remaining flour into the pan and stir well. Add the stock a little at a time, stirring until smooth. Add a little salt and pepper. Bring to the boil and pour over the chicken.
5   Cover the dish and cook it in the centre of the oven, Gas 4, 180°C, for about 1½ hours until tender. Add the peas about ¼ hour before the end of cooking time.

Roast stuffed breast of lamb   *Serves 3–4*

1 breast of lamb without the bone
50g/2oz dripping
Salt and pepper

Stuffing
50g/2oz bread
15g/½oz suet
½ a small onion
Pinch of mixed herbs

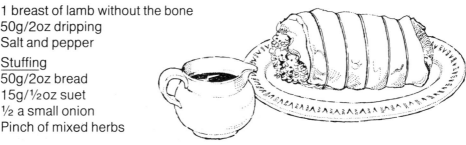

Method
1   Make the stuffing: make the bread into crumbs. Peel the onion and chop it finely. Melt the suet and fry the onion until soft without letting it brown. Stir in the breadcrumbs and herbs, add some salt and pepper.
2   Light the oven, Gas 6, 200°C. Put the dripping in a roasting tin in the oven.
3   Put some salt and pepper on the boned side of the lamb. Spread the stuffing over it. Roll up the meat and secure it with string.
4   Put into the roasting tin and baste it with some of the melted dripping.
5   Roast in the centre of the oven for about 1 hour, basting occasionally. Remove the string when cooked. Serve on a flat, warm plate with gravy.

To make the gravy
When the meat is cooked, put it on to a plate and keep it hot. Pour most of the fat out of the roasting tin, leaving about 1 tablespoonful. Stir in 1 level tablespoon of plain flour, then add 250ml/½pt hot water a little at a time, stirring until smooth. Add a stock cube, seasoning, and browning as required.

Liver casserole *Serves 3–4*

250g/½lb liver
2 rashers bacon
250ml/½pt water
Stock cube
1 teaspoon Worcester sauce
1 level tablespoon plain flour
Parsley

<u>Stuffing</u>
25g/1oz fresh breadcrumbs
1 dessertspoon chopped parsley
1 small onion
About 3 tablespoons milk or beaten egg

Method
1 Light the oven, Gas 5, 190°C. Place the shelf just above the centre of the oven.
2 Wash and dry the liver, cut off any skin. Cut into 3 or 4 portions and lay it in a greased dish or baking tin.
3 Make the breadcrumbs, chop the parsley, finely chop the onion. Mix these ingredients and add enough egg or milk to bind them together.
4 Place some stuffing on each piece of liver and cover it with a piece of bacon.
5 Pour the stock around the liver, cover with a lid or foil and bake for about 30 minutes until the liver is tender. Remove the lid for the last 10 minutes to allow the bacon to brown slightly.
6 Place the meat carefully on a hot serving dish and keep it warm. Add the Worcester sauce to the stock in the tin. Blend the flour with a little cold water and add it to the gravy. Bring to the boil, stirring all the time, and pour round the liver. Garnish with parsley.

Serve hot, with potatoes and vegetables.

Grilled pork or lamb chops

1 loin or chump chop per person
A little oil
Salt and pepper
Watercress and tomato to garnish

Method
1 Light the grill and leave it to heat.
2 Trim any excess fat, skin, or bone from the chops, season with salt and pepper.
3 Brush one side of the chops with a little oil, then grill for 7–10 minutes under a medium heat. Turn the chops over and grill gently for a further 7–10 minutes.
4 Cut the tomatoes in half, add to the grill pan for 5 minutes.
5 Wash the watercress carefully, then place the chops on to a warm, flat serving dish. Garnish neatly with the cress and tomatoes.

For a change you could garnish the pork chops with a slice of pineapple, or half a peach or apricot, which has been warmed under the grill.

Rice

Rice is the staple food in the diet of many millions of people in the East. It is becoming more popular in this country, as it is economical, easy to prepare and cook, and keeps well.

For cooking, there are three main kinds of rice: long, medium, and short grain. Long grain rice such as Patna and Basmati stays fluffy and separate when cooked, so it is best for savoury dishes. Medium and short grain rice becomes softer and stickier when cooked, so it is the best kind for rice puddings, e.g. Carolina rice.

Brown rice is the whole grain of rice, with only the husk removed. White rice has had the bran and germ removed during milling and polishing. Because of this it is less nutritious than brown rice, having fewer B-vitamins, minerals, and proteins, and less fibre. Brown rice takes longer to cook than white rice, about 40 minutes instead of 11. It has a nutty flavour and a more chewy texture.

To cook rice

Allow about 50g/2oz for each person. Wash the rice in a sieve under cold running water. Put it into plenty of boiling salted water, bring back to the boil, then cook for 11 minutes. Drain in the sieve, then serve.

Brown rice is cooked in the same way, but takes 40–45 minutes to cook.

Recipes

As well as the recipes below, see rice pudding (page 191) and rice salad (page 158).

Chicken curry   *Serves about 4*

About 500g/1lb cooked chicken,
   or 1 uncooked chicken portion per person
2 medium onions
1 medium apple
2 cloves garlic
2 tablespoons oil
1 rounded dessertspoon curry powder
   (more or less, as you like)
1 level teaspoon ground ginger
250ml/½pt hot water
1 heaped teaspoon tomato purée
Salt and pepper
250g/½lb long grain rice

Method

1. Cut the cooked chicken into pieces, removing any bones. If using chicken portions, wash and dry them, then brown in a large pan in the oil. Put onto a plate.
2. Peel and slice the onions and apple. Peel and chop the garlic finely.
3. Fry the onions, apple, and garlic for 10 minutes, stirring occasionally.
4. Stir in the curry powder and ginger and fry for another minute.
5. Mix the hot water and tomato purée, stir into the pan. Add the chicken and some salt and pepper.
6. Bring to the boil, stirring. Turn into a casserole dish, cover with a lid or foil.
7. Cook at Gas 3, 160°C, for about 1 hour. Serve on a bed of cooked rice.

Beef curry Make in the same way but use 500g/1lb of stewing steak or mince instead of chicken. Cut into small pieces and brown in the oil before you fry the onions. Cook until the meat is tender, about 1½ hours.

Sausage risotto   *Serves about 3*

250g/8oz sausages
1 tablespoon cooking oil
75g/3oz rice
1 medium onion
100g/4oz mushrooms
50g/2oz green beans or peas
50g/2oz sweet corn
375ml/¾pt hot water
Chicken stock cube
Salt and pepper
1 tablespoon Worcester sauce

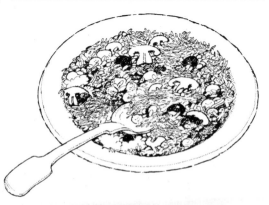

Method

1. Gently fry the sausages in the oil until cooked and brown. Put them on to a plate.
2. Wash the rice in a sieve under a cold tap. Peel and chop the onion. Wash and slice the mushrooms.
3. Add the onion and rice to the frying pan. Fry for about 7 minutes. Keep stirring so that it does not stick.
4. Add the mushrooms, beans or peas, sweetcorn, stock cube, water, sauce, and seasoning. Simmer very gently for about 12 minutes until the rice is tender and all the water is absorbed.
5. Slice the sausages and stir them into the rice.

Serve this hot or cold with a salad.

Chicken risotto Make in the same way but use about 250g/½lb cooked chicken instead of sausages. Cut the cooked chicken into joints and then cut the meat off the bones.

Sweet and sour pork   *Serves about 3*

300g/¾lb belly pork, spare ribs, or pork fillet
1 medium can of pineapple pieces
1 tablespoon oil
½ level teaspoon ground ginger
1 level tablespoon cornflour
1 level tablespoon sugar
1 tablespoon vinegar
1 tablespoon soy sauce
1 level tablespoon tomato purée
150g/6oz long grain rice

Method
1   Grill the meat under a low heat for 20–30 minutes until tender.
2   Drain the syrup from the pineapples into a measuring jug.
3   Put the oil and ginger into a frying pan. Gently fry the pineapple.
4   Add enough water to the syrup in the jug to make 250ml/½pt. Add the cornflour, sugar, vinegar, soy sauce, and tomato purée, and mix until smooth.
5   Carefully pour this into the frying pan. Bring to the boil, stirring all the time. Add the meat, cut into chunks, then simmer for 4 minutes.
6   Serve on a bed of cooked rice (see above).

Sweet and sour chicken Make in the same way, but use 250g/½lb cooked chicken instead of pork.

Pork and apricots   *Serves about 3*

250g/½lb of belly pork, spare ribs, or pork fillet
1 rounded tablespoon plain flour
25g/1oz dripping or lard
Salt and pepper
2 teaspoons Worcester sauce
1 can apricots
150g/6oz long grain rice

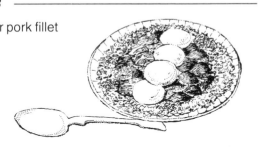

Method
1   Cut the meat into cubes, removing any skin and bone. Coat in the seasoned flour.
2   Melt the dripping in a frying pan and gently fry the meat for about 15 minutes until golden brown.
3   Open the tin of apricots and pour the syrup into a measuring jug. Add enough water to make 250ml/½pt liquid. Save four apricot halves for garnishing and chop the others into small pieces.
4   Put the meat on to a plate. Add the rest of the flour to the pan and stir until smooth. Add the liquid a little at a time, stirring, and boil. Add the Worcester sauce, meat, and apricots to the pan and simmer very gently for about 15 minutes until the meat is tender.
5   Cook the rice in boiling salted water (see above), then drain. Place on a hot serving dish. Pour the meat over the rice and garnish with the apricot halves.

You could serve this with a salad.

Pasta

Pasta can be bought in many different shapes and sizes. Some of the best known kinds of pasta are macaroni, spaghetti, noodles, lasagne, ravioli, cannelloni, and vermicelli.

They are made from a dough of wheat flour and water, sometimes with egg added. The dough is made into different shapes, then dried.

You can buy the traditional white pasta made from white flour, or brown pasta made with wholemeal flour. Like brown flour or brown bread, brown pasta contains more dietary fibre than white pasta. Sometimes green pasta is made, for example, 'lasagne verdi'. This is made by adding cooked spinach to the basic dough.

To cook pasta

Allow about 50–75g (2–3oz) for each person. Drop the pasta into plenty of boiling, salted water and cook for the time directed on the packet, with the lid off the pan. The water should be kept boiling quite vigorously to prevent the pasta sticking. A dessertspoon of oil added to the water will help keep the pieces separate.

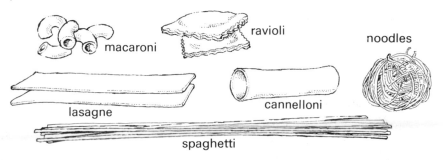

A selection of the different kinds of pasta.

Macaroni cheese   *Serves about 3*

75g/3oz macaroni
100g/4oz cheese
375ml/¾pt milk
25g/1oz plain flour

25g/1oz margarine
Salt, pepper, pinch of mustard
Parsley

Method

1   Put a large pan of water on to boil, add salt. Cook the macaroni in the boiling water for about 12 minutes until tender.
2   Grate the cheese.
3   Make the cheese sauce: put the milk, flour, margarine, salt, pepper, and mustard into a pan. Bring to the boil, whisking all the time. Stir in most of the grated cheese, saving a little for the top.
4   Drain the macaroni when it is cooked, put it into the cheese sauce, then put into an ovenproof dish.
5   Put the remaining cheese on top and grill until golden brown. Garnish with a sprig of parsley.

Spaghetti bolognese *Serves about 3*

250g/8oz spaghetti
1 onion
100g/4oz mushrooms
1 green pepper (optional)
15g/½oz margarine
250g/½lb minced beef
1 rounded tablespoon flour
1 large can tomatoes
100ml/4 fluid oz water
1 stock cube
Salt, pepper

Method
1 Peel and chop the onions and pepper. Wash and slice the mushrooms.
2 Melt the margarine in a large pan. Fry the onions, pepper, and mushrooms for 5 minutes.
3 Add the mince and fry, stirring gently, until it is brown.
4 Stir in the flour, and the tomatoes and stock cube. Add the water if it seems necessary, then add salt and pepper.
5 Bring to the boil, then simmer very gently with the lid on, stirring occasionally, for 30 minutes.
6 Cook the spaghetti: put a large pan of water on to boil. Add salt. Add the spaghetti and when the water comes back to the boil, cook for 10–15 minutes. Drain in a colander and put on a hot dish.
7 Pour the sauce on top of the spaghetti and serve.

Lasagne *Serves 3–4*

175g/3 oz lasagne
1 tablespoon oil

Cheese sauce
375ml/¾pt milk
25g/1oz margarine
25g/1oz plain flour
½ level teaspoon mustard
100g/4 oz cheese

Meat sauce
1 15oz can minced beef
1 small can tomatoes
1 heaped teaspoon tomato purée
1 heaped teaspoon sugar
Pinch of mixed herbs

Method
1 Cook the lasagne in plenty of boiling water, with the oil added, until it is soft (about 15 minutes). Drain.
2 Make the cheese sauce by the all-in-one method: put the milk, flour, margarine, and mustard into a saucepan. Bring to the boil, whisking all the time, until thickened. Add most of the cheese, saving a little for the top. Check the seasoning.
3 Put the meat, tomatoes and juice, tomato purée, herbs, and sugar into a pan, and warm just enough to mix them thoroughly.
4 Put layers of cheese sauce, lasagne, and meat into a shallow ovenproof dish, finishing with a layer of cheese sauce. Sprinkle with the remaining cheese.
5 Bake in the oven Gas 4, 180°C, for about 30 minutes until golden brown.

Serve with a salad.

Pulses

Dried beans, peas, and lentils of many kinds are widely available and are becoming more popular. They are inexpensive, easy to store and cook, and are high in food value. They are a good source of protein, carbohydrate, iron, and B-vitamins. They are also low in fat and high in fibre.

Pulses include orange and green lentils, green and yellow split peas, chick peas, haricot beans, cannellini beans, butter beans, red kidney beans, and soya beans.

To cook pulses

As they are usually dried, all pulses except for lentils must be soaked before cooking. Either soak them overnight in cold water, or for 2–3 hours in boiling water. Drain, then simmer gently in fresh water until soft.

This may take, for example:

Red kidney beans	1 hour
Butter beans	1 hour
Split peas and lentils	30–45 minutes
Soya beans	2–3 hours

A pressure cooker will save you a lot of time if you are cooking pulses.

Red kidney beans *must* be boiled for at least 15 minutes, otherwise they can be dangerous. So never cook them in a slow cooker without boiling them first.

Tinned beans of several kinds are available. They save a lot of time as they are already cooked. They are rather more expensive. You can buy canned red kidney beans, butter beans, and canellini beans, as well as the popular baked beans in tomato sauce. If you are using tinned beans in a casserole, you can add them about 20 minutes before the end of the cooking time to allow them to heat through.

Recipes using pulses include those below, and also sausage and onion casserole, page 127; kidney bean salad, page 158; butter bean salad, page 158; and lentil soup, page 113.

As soya beans are particularly high in protein, they are often used to make meat substitute, or are added to meat to make it go further. Soya products are cheaper than meat and are usually sold dehydrated in packets or in a meat-flavoured sauce ready to use, in cans. These products are made with a texture which is intended to resemble meat, and are known as textured vegetable protein (T.V.P.). They are often used in school and canteen meals. To make sure they are nutritionally good foods, it is recommended that B-vitamins and iron are added to the products when they are manufactured. It is also recommended that they are used only occasionally instead of meat and do not replace it altogether.

Recipes where you could use textured vegetable protein products, e.g. 'soya mince', instead of fresh meat, include these: beef and vegetable casserole, page 123; savoury beef and tomato, page 125; minced beef and dumplings, page 125; chili con carne, page 136; spaghetti bolognese, page 134; beef curry, page 130; and mince pie, page 163.

Always follow the manufacturer's instructions on the packet or tin carefully. If T.V.P. is served with well flavoured, spicy ingredients, and with plenty of freshly cooked vegetables, then this will add flavour to the rather bland taste of the soya product.

Chili con carne   *Serves 4*

2 onions
2 cloves garlic
25g/1oz butter or margarine
1 tablespoon oil
500g/1lb stewing steak (or mince)
100g/4oz bacon pieces
375ml/¾pt water
1 heaped tablespoon tomato purée
Salt, pepper, ½–1 level teaspoon chili powder
A 16oz can kidney beans

Method

1   Peel and chop the onion and garlic. Fry them in the butter and oil for 10 minutes, then put on to a plate.
2   Cut the meat and bacon into small pieces. Add to the pan and fry until browned. Put the onions and garlic back into the pan.
3   Add the water, tomato purée, chili powder, salt, and pepper. Bring to the boil, stirring.
4   Pour into an ovenproof dish, cover with a lid or foil. Bake in the centre of the oven, Gas 3, 160°C, for 1½ hours or until the meal is tender. Drain the beans and stir them in 15 minutes before the end of the cooking.

You could serve this with baked or boiled potatoes, or boiled rice.

Instead of using canned kidney beans you can cook them yourself; this is much cheaper. Wash 100g/4oz dried kidney beans. Soak them overnight. Boil them for 15 minutes, then add them to the casserole when you add the meat.

You could prepare and cook this dish in a pressure cooker. Cook at H(15lb) pressure for 25 minutes. Reduce pressure at room temperature, then stir in the canned beans and simmer for 10 minutes with the lid off.

Pork and bacon casserole   *Serves 3–4*

100g/4oz haricot beans or butter beans which have been soaked and cooked as above <u>or</u>
A 7½oz can of cannellini or butter beans
250g/8oz pork sausages
100g/4oz bacon
1 rounded tablespoon tomato purée
Pinch of thyme or mixed herbs
75g/3oz breadcrumbs
2 onions
2 cloves garlic (if you like it)
1 tablespoon oil
Salt and pepper

Method

1 Put the oil in a frying pan. Chop the bacon and fry it with the sausages for 10 minutes.
2 Peel and chop the onion and garlic. Make the breadcrumbs.
3 Put the sausages and bacon on to a plate. Fry the onions and garlic for 10 minutes until soft.
4 Drain the beans, saving the liquid. Put half the beans into a casserole dish. Add the onions, sausages and bacon. Cover with the rest of the beans.
5 Make the liquid up to 375ml/¾pt of water. Stir in the tomato purée, some pepper, the thyme, and a little salt. Pour into the dish. Cover with a lid and bake at Gas 3, 170°C, for 25 minutes in the centre of the oven.
6 Sprinkle the breadcrumbs on top, return to the oven with the lid off for another 20 minutes until browned. Serve with a salad.

Lamb and bean casserole *Serves 3*

3 lamb chops, any kind
25g/1oz dripping
1 large onion
1 small can butter beans <u>or</u>
75g/3oz dried butter beans,
    soaked and cooked as above
250ml/½pt water
2 rounded tablespoons tomato purée
½ level teaspoon salt
½ level teaspoon sugar
1 teaspoon vinegar
Parsley

Method

1 Trim the chops, brown them on both sides in the melted dripping. Put them on to a plate.
2 Peel and chop the onion, chop the parsley. Boil some water in a kettle, measure it into the jug and stir in the tomato purée and salt.
3 Fry the onions in the pan for 5 minutes, then put them, with the chops, into a casserole dish.
4 Add the drained beans to the casserole, then add the water. Cover, and cook in the centre of the oven at Gas 3, 170°C, for 1 hour. Remove the lid and cook for a further 15 minutes.
5 Just before serving, stir in the sugar and vinegar, and sprinkle with the parsley.

Serve with warm bread rolls, or potatoes and vegetables.

Cheese

Cheese in Great Britain is made from cow's milk. In other countries it may be made from the milk of goats, sheep, or other animals. It takes about one gallon of milk (eight pints) to produce one pound of cheese.

How cheese is made

A 'starter' is added to pasteurized milk to ripen it. Rennet is added and this separates the milk, as it ripens, into curds and whey. The curds are the solid part of the milk which eventually become the cheese. The liquid whey may be used for animal feeding. The curds are drained, and salt is added. The cheese is then pressed. If it is lightly pressed, a soft, crumbly cheese is produced. If the cheese is more firmly pressed, a harder cheese is produced. Then the cheeses are left to mature, to develop a good flavour and texture.

Types of cheese

Hard British cheeses include Cheddar, Cheshire, Double Gloucester, Leicester, and Derby. Softer British cheeses include Wensleydale, Lancashire, and Caerphilly. We import many foreign cheeses into this country. Some of the best known are Edam, Camembert, Brie, Roquefort, Danish blue, Gorgonzola, Parmesan, and Gruyère.

Blue-veined cheeses like Danish blue, Stilton and Roquefort have harmless moulds inserted in them, which spread through the cheese. Originally this kind of cheese was left to ripen in damp caves and the mould grew naturally.

The variations in the different types of cheese are due to the different milks used to make them and to differences in the traditional ways of making the cheeses in the areas from which they come.

Cottage cheese is made from pasteurized skimmed milk. It has a 'starter' added to separate it and to add flavour and texture. As it is made from skimmed milk (with the fat or creamy part removed), it is easy to digest. It is also low in calories and high in protein, so it is useful for a slimming diet.

The food value of cheese

Cheese is really a concentrated form of milk. It contains roughly 1/3 protein, 1/3 fat, 1/3 water. It is a good source of retinol (Vitamin A) and the minerals calcium and phosphorus.

Storing cheese to keep it fresh

1   Wrap the cheese in cling film or foil. Keep it in a cool place.
2   A cheese dish with a lid is also ideal for storing cheese, if it is kept in a cool place.
3   If you keep the cheese in a fridge or cold larder, leave it at room temperature for about half an hour before you eat it. This will bring out the full flavour.
4   Buy the cheese in fairly small amounts, just enough to last for about a week.
5   Cheese can be frozen, though hard cheese may become a little crumbly when it is thawed.

The usefulness of cheese as a food

1 It has high food value, containing many nutrients in good amounts.
2 It can be eaten raw, so is very useful for sandwiches and quick meals.
3 There is no waste.
4 It is relatively inexpensive compared with meat.
5 It has a very good flavour, and there are many kinds to choose from.
6 It can be used in cooking, for example in sauces, scones, cheese pastry, pies, flans, and cheesecake.

Digesting cheese

Some people feel that cheese is hard to digest as it contains a lot of fat (about ⅓). It can be made more easy to digest if:

1 It is grated before being eaten raw.
2 It is cooked lightly, but not for long.
3 It is eaten with a starchy food like bread, potatoes, or macaroni.
4 It is served or cooked with a highly flavoured seasoning, for example with mustard in cheese scones or sauce, or with pickle or chutney for a 'ploughman's lunch'.

Questions

1 **Describe briefly how cheese is made.**
2 **List all the (a) British cheeses and (b) foreign cheeses you have tasted or seen for sale.**
3 **Although all cheeses are made from milk they have different flavours and textures. Give 3 reasons for this.**
4 **Name (a) a French blue-veined cheese; (b) a cheese suitable for someone on a slimming diet; (c) the most popular hard British cheese; and (d) a crumbly Welsh cheese.**
5 **List the nutrients found in cheese.**
6 **How would you store cheese to make sure it did not become dry or mouldy?**
7 **Write out two menus for a family evening meal, both of which contain a hot or cold cheese dish.**
8 **Suggest two cheese dishes suitable for someone trying to lose weight.**
9 **Suggest three cheese dishes suitable for a party.**
10 **Describe fully why cheese is such a useful food.**

Recipes

As well as the recipes below, cheese is used in: fish and cheese sauce (page 117), fish and tomato casserole (page 118), crispy fish bake (page 118), ham and cheese roll-ups (page 111), cottage cheese and pineapple salad (page 159), cheese scones (page 185), cheese and onion flan (page 164), lasagne (page 134), lemon cheesecake (page 193), macaroni cheese (page 133), pizza (page 198), quiche Lorraine (page 163), stuffed eggs (page 111), sandwich fillings (page 181), and stuffed tomatoes (page 111).

Quick cheese pizza *Serves about 3*

150g/6oz self-raising flour
½ level teaspoon salt
50g/2oz margarine
1 egg mixed with 2 tablespoons milk
1 tin tomatoes or 250g/½lb fresh tomatoes
Salt, pepper, pinch of mixed herbs or oregano
100g/4oz cheese
50g/2oz mushrooms (optional)
1 onion
Tin of sardines or pilchards (optional) <u>or</u>
1 rasher of bacon

Method
1 Light the oven, Gas 5, 200°C. Place the shelf near the top of the oven. Grease a baking sheet.
2 Put the flour and salt in a bowl, rub in <u>half</u> of the margarine, add the egg and milk, and mix to a soft dough. Roll out to a large circle, about 22cm/9" in diameter, or make two smaller circles.
3 Drain the tomatoes (or slice if fresh). Grate the cheese. Peel and slice the onion and mushrooms and chop the bacon (if used). Fry in the other half of the magarine until soft.
4 Spread the tomatoes, cheese, salt, pepper, herbs, onions, mushrooms, and bacon over the base. Arrange the fish on top.
5 Bake for about 20–25 minutes until the base is cooked. Cool on a wire tray. Serve warm or cold with a salad.

You can change the topping on a pizza as you like, using for example chopped cooked meat or chicken, olives, or peppers.

Cheese loaf

200g/8oz self-raising flour
Pinch of salt, pinch of mustard
50g/2oz margarine
75g/3oz cheese
1 egg
6 tablespoons of milk

Method
1 Light the oven, Gas 6, 200°C. Place the shelf above the centre. Grease a small loaf tin, and line the bottom with greaseproof paper.
2 Sieve the flour, salt, and mustard together. Rub in the margarine.
3 Grate the cheese and add it to the flour.
4 Beat the egg and milk and save a little to brush the top. Pour the rest into the flour and mix to a fairly soft dough. Shape to a loaf and put into the tin.
5 Bake for about 35 minutes until well risen and golden brown. Cool on a wire tray.

Serve sliced and buttered, the same day it is made. If kept to the next day, serve toasted and buttered.

Cheese and vegetable flan   *Serves about 3*

Shortcrust pastry
100g/4oz plain flour, pinch of salt
25g/1oz lard
25g/1oz margarine

2 eggs
50g/2oz grated cheese
200g/8oz frozen or tinned
    mixed vegetables

Sauce
125ml/¼pt milk
15g/½oz plain flour
15g/½oz margarine
Salt and pepper

Method

1   Light the oven, Gas 6, 200°C. Position the shelf just above the centre. Grease an 18cm 17" flan ring and baking sheet (or use a sandwich cake tin).
2   Make the pastry and line the flan ring. Bake it blind (see page 162).
3   Cook the vegetables as directed on the packet or tin. Grate the cheese. Beat the eggs.
4   Make the sauce: put the milk, flour, and margarine into a pan and bring to the boil, stirring all the time. Add the salt, pepper, and grated cheese. Remove from the heat.
5   Add the eggs and vegetables and mix carefully.
6   Pour into a flan case. Turn the oven down to Gas 4, 180°C, and bake for about 30 minutes until the filling is firm and golden brown.

Cheese and potato bake   *Serves 3–4*

750g/1½lbs potatoes
50g/2oz butter or margarine
2 tablespoons milk
150g/6oz cheese
2 onions

1 egg
Salt and pepper
2 tomatoes
100g/4oz bacon

Method

1   Peel the potatoes, cut to even-sized pieces. Put into a pan, cover with cold water, add salt. Bring to the boil and simmer for about 20 minutes until cooked. Drain and mash with the milk, butter, about half of the cheese and the beaten egg.
2   Peel the onion and chop it finely. Add to the mashed potato. Add a little salt and pepper.
3   Put the potato into a shallow heatproof dish. Place the sliced tomato on top, then the chopped bacon. Sprinkle the rest of the cheese on top.
4   Bake near the top of the oven, Gas 6, 200°C, for about 20–30 minutes until the top is golden brown. For a vegetarian dish, leave out the bacon.
Serve warm.

Eggs

Eggs are an extremely useful food as they are used in making so many different kinds of dishes. They can be used for many different purposes, including:

Whisking They will hold a lot of air when whisked, for example when making a Swiss roll, a whisked sponge cake, or meringues. All the air held in the mixture by the eggs makes the cake light and well risen.

Eating on their own Eggs can be eaten boiled, fried, poached, or scrambled, to make a quick nutritious meal.

Setting Eggs enable a liquid mixture to set, for example in a quiche Lorraine, a baked egg custard, or in lemon curd.

Binding You can add an egg yolk to beefburgers or fish cakes. It will help them to stick together.

Coating Beaten egg can be used to coat fish, fish cakes, or chicken portions before they are dipped into breadcrumbs and fried. This provides a crisp and attractive finish.

Emulsion When you add an egg or egg yolk to mayonnaise it helps the oil and vinegar to stay smoothly blended together.

Enriching other foods You can add a beaten egg to mashed potato or a milk pudding to improve the food value and make the dish more nutritious.

Glazing If pastry or scones are brushed with beaten egg and milk they will have a shiny golden brown appearance when cooked.

The food value of eggs

Eggs are a valuable food as they contain many nutrients. They contain all the nutrients that would have been necessary for a chick to develop from the egg. These nutrients include protein, fat, Vitamins A, B, and D, calcium, and iron.

Tests for freshness

1   A fresh egg is heavy because none of its moisture has evaporated through the shell. If you put it into a bowl of water it will sink to the bottom. A less fresh egg will rise in the water because of air in the shell. A stale egg will come right up to the top of the water. This is because so much of its moisture has evaporated through the shell and has been replaced by air, making it lighter.

stale egg   fresh egg

2 If you break a fresh egg on to a plate, the yolk will be firm and prominent. You will be able to see two different parts in the white. The inner part of the white will be thick and gluey. If the white is watery and thin then the egg is not very fresh.

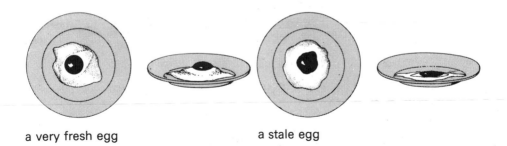

a very fresh egg   a stale egg

Buying and storing eggs

Eggs are graded for size from Grade 1 to Grade 7. Grade 1 is the largest. When you buy a box of eggs, look for the week number stamped on the lid. It will be between 1 and 52. The higher the number of the week, the fresher the eggs.

Eggs will keep fresh for two or three weeks in a cool place. There is no need to keep them in a fridge, but if you do, you should keep a few eggs out of the fridge ready for cooking. If they are not cold they are less likely to crack when boiled, they will mix more easily into a cake, and they can be whisked more quickly for a meringue or sponge. Store them with the pointed end downwards and keep them away from strong-smelling foods.

Recipes using eggs

When whisked – Swiss roll, sponge sandwich cake, sponge fruit flan or gateau.
To set a mixture – quiche Lorraine, cheese and onion flan, baked egg custard.
Glazing – most pastry dishes, e.g. sausage rolls, meat or fruit pies, scones.
Binding – fish cakes, duchess potatoes.
Coating – fish cakes, fish, baked chicken joints.
To emulsify – mayonnaise.
Other recipes – stuffed eggs, egg and cress sandwiches, lemon curd, Victoria sandwich and other cakes, pineapple upside-down pudding, steamed puddings.

Questions

1 **Eggs are used for many different purposes in cooking. Describe the five purposes for which you think they are most often used.**
2 **List the nutrients which eggs contain.**
3 **Describe, with the help of a diagram, why a very fresh egg sinks in a bowl of water.**
4 **When buying eggs in a supermarket, how would you know which are freshest?**
5 **Why is it better not to cook with eggs straight from the refrigerator?**

Milk

Milk is a valuable and useful food. It contains all of the nutrients that babies need; they live and thrive on a diet of nothing but milk for several months. Because it contains so many nutrients it is a good food for older children and adults too.

The food value of milk

Milk contains these nutrients:
    Protein
    Carbohydrate, in the form of a little sugar
    Fat, the creamy part of the milk
    Vitamins, especially retinol (Vitamin A)
        and riboflavin (Vitamin B_2)
    Minerals, especially calcium
        and phosphorus

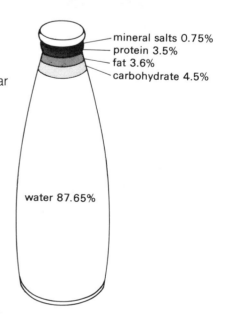

mineral salts 0.75%
protein 3.5%
fat 3.6%
carbohydrate 4.5%

water 87.65%

Different grades of milk

Grade Colour of bottle top	Description
Pasteurized *silver top*	The milk is pasteurized to kill any harmful bacteria. That is, it is heated to 71°C for 15 seconds, then quickly cooled to below 10°C. It will keep fresh for 2–3 days in a fridge. It is the kind of milk most often used for drinking, on cereals, and in cooking.
Homogenized *red top*	This milk has been treated to spread the fat or cream evenly through the milk so that there is no 'cream line'. It is pasteurized after this treatment and will keep for 2–3 days in a fridge.
Sterilized *metal crown cap or* *blue foil top*	This milk has been homogenized, bottled, then heated to a temperature above boiling point (100°C) for 20–30 minutes. This high temperature destroys any bacteria and sterilizes the milk so that it can be kept for a few weeks if it is unopened. Once opened, it will keep for a little longer than pasteurized milk. Because of the high temperature treatment, the flavour is different from pasteurized milk, and sterilized milk is usually less popular. It is sold in long necked bottles with a metal cap or else in plastic bottles with a blue cap.

Grade Colour of bottle top	Description
U. H. T. *pink top* (long-life milk)	The milk is heated to an ultra-high temperature, 132°C, for 1 second. It will keep for several months if unopened, so it is useful for keeping in the cupboard or for taking on holiday. It is packed in foil-lined cartons or plastic bottles. Once opened, it will keep for 2–3 days in a fridge.
Channel Islands *gold top*	This is milk from a Channel Island breed of cow, that is, a Jersey or a Guernsey cow. The milk itself has not come from the Channel Islands. It is a rich, very creamy milk which can be bought either pasteurized or untreated.
Untreated milk *green top*	This has had no heat treatment. The farm or dairy has to have a special licence to bottle this milk.
Skimmed milk	This has had the creamy 'top of the milk' skimmed off before it is pasteurized and put into bottles or cartons. It is suitable for anyone on a low-fat diet, a low animal fat diet, or a slimming diet.
Filled milk	This is skimmed milk, which has had the cream which was removed in skimming replaced by vegetable fat. It is sometimes used by people who are trying to replace the animal fat in their diet by vegetable fat (see page 10).

All milk in Britain today comes from cows which have been tested to make sure they do not have tuberculosis.

Storing fresh milk

You must be particularly careful when using milk to make sure that everything is scrupulously clean. Milk is an ideal food for bacteria to breed in and cause food poisoning. Keep milk 'Clean, Cool, and Covered'.

1   Never leave milk standing in the sun on your doorstep. Bring it in and put it in a cool place as soon as possible. The sun's heat will not only make the milk go off more quickly, but will destroy some of the Vitamin B and Vitamin C in the milk.
2   Do not mix milk from different days together. Put new milk into a clean jug, or leave it in the bottle. Pasteurized milk usually has the number of the weekday, 1 to 7, stamped on the top. Day 1 is Monday.
3   When you wash a milk jug or bottle, first rinse it in cold water. Hot water will 'set' the milk on to the jug. After rinsing in cold water, wash in hot soapy water, then rinse out and drain or dry with a clean cloth.
4   Do not store milk near strong-smelling foods such as onions or fish, as the milk will quickly pick up the smell.

Freezing milk

Pasteurized milk does not freeze well, as it tends to separate. You may have seen milk which has been standing outside in snow and has frozen. When it is thawed it separates and is not very appetizing.

Homogenized milk in cartons or plastic bottles can be frozen for up to one month, but it is just as easy to store a plastic bottle of U.H.T. milk in the cupboard. Never freeze any kind of glass bottle, as the liquid will expand when it freezes and crack the bottle.

Dried and canned milk

1 Dried milk can be sold in tins, packets, or plastic bottles in powder form. The watery part of the milk is removed and the dry powder will keep for a long time. Dried milk may be 'whole' dried milk, with its full fat content, or it may be skimmed to remove the fat before drying. Sometimes skimmed milk powder has vegetable fat added.
2 Evaporated milk. Some of the water in the milk is removed to make it more concentrated, then it is canned. It is useful as it has a flavour which many people like and can be used on puddings instead of cream or custard. It can be whipped to make it thicker and fluffy, as in jelly whip, page 193. It is a useful source of Vitamins A and D.
3 Condensed milk is milk which has been evaporated and has had a lot of sugar added to it. It is very thick and sweet and may be used for making puddings or sweets. You can buy it in a tube to take camping; it keeps for a long time as there is so much sugar in it.

Dishes made with milk

Mushroom soup.
Fish and cheese sauce, cheese and vegetable flan, toad in the hole, Yorkshire pudding, lasagne, macaroni cheese, chicken and mushroom pie, quiche Lorraine.
Gingerbread, jelly whip, fruit fool, crunchy chocolate flan, rice pudding, baked egg custard, custard, pancakes, Chelsea buns, Yorkshire teacakes.

Products made from milk

These include cream, butter, yogurt, and cheese.

Cream is available in different forms. The thickness of the cream depends on the amount of butterfat it contains.

Single cream must have a butterfat content of at least 18%. It cannot be whipped and is used for pouring.

Whipping cream must have at least 35% butterfat. It is pasteurized and can be whipped.

Double cream has at least 48% butterfat. It can be whipped.

Clotted cream (Devonshire cream) has at least 55% butterfat.

Tinned cream has at least 23% butterfat. It has been sterilized in the tin and will keep for several months. It cannot be whipped.

U.H.T. cream is heat-treated so that it has a long shelf life. It is sold in foil-lined cartons. Some U.H.T. creams can be whipped, others cannot; this is usually marked on the carton.

Frozen whipped cream is already whipped and is sold in waxed cartons or polythene bags.

Soured cream is not cream which has gone sour but is a specially prepared cream with a tangy flavour, which may be used in meat, fish, or other savoury dishes, or in salad dressings.

Butter is made from cream. It may be salted or unsalted. It has a very good flavour, either spread on bread or used for cooking, but as it is expensive it is sometimes replaced by margarine. Butter should be kept covered in the fridge or a cool place so that it does not go rancid. It should be stored away from strong-smelling foods as it quickly picks up any smell.

Yogurt may be made from either skimmed milk or whole milk, with a specially added culture of bacteria. Sometimes it has fruit or sugar added. Unsweetened yogurt can be added to meat or fish dishes, such as chicken curry (page 130), or it can be used instead of milk or cream on cereals or fruit dishes. It will keep fresh for 4–5 days in the fridge, and is usually sold with a date stamp.

Questions

1　**What nutrients does milk contain?**
2　**If milk is left on the doorstep in the sun, what effect does this have?**
3　**Describe exactly what these terms mean:**
　　(a) pasteurized, (b) homogenized, (c) sterilized, (d) U.H.T.
4　**You want to keep a store of milk at home for emergency use. What kind of liquid milk would be suitable? How long would it keep fresh in the cupboard?**
5　**What kind of milk is a suitable choice for someone trying to lose weight?**
6　**Name two kinds of milk suitable for someone on a low animal fat diet.**
7　**Describe how you would thoroughly wash a milk jug.**
8　**You have several unopened bottles of pasteurized milk in your fridge. How can you tell which is the freshest?**
9　**What is the difference between evaporated and condensed milk? Give two uses for each of them.**
10　**Plan the meals for a family for one day, including plenty of dishes made with milk.**
11　**What kind of cream would be suitable for each of these purposes:**
　a　**piping on to a cake or cold sweet to decorate it.**
　b　**keeping in store for a few weeks in the cupboard.**
　c　**pouring into coffee.**
　d　**putting into scones with strawberry jam for a 'Devonshire cream tea'.**
　e　**adding to a casserole.**

Cereals

Cereals are the seed grains of grasses, so called after Ceres, the Greek goddess of the harvest. They include wheat, oats, barley, rye, maize or corn, and rice.

The cereal crop grown in any particular country is usually a very important staple food in that country. Examples are rice in India and China, and wheat, used for flour for making bread, in western countries.

Cereals are useful foods because they are easy to grow and easy to store. They are inexpensive compared with animal foods and they are filling and nutritious.

Food value

Cereals are a valuable source of carbohydrate, vegetable protein, B-vitamins, and minerals. Whole grain cereals are a good source of dietary fibre.

Wheat

The most important cereal in this country is wheat. The wheat is milled to make flour, which is then used for bread, a staple British food.

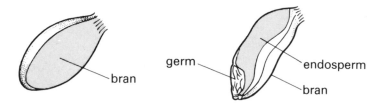

Grain of wheat.

The difference in the types of flour you can buy depends on the parts of the whole grain of wheat which are included in the flour.

Wholemeal flour is the whole grain of wheat ground up to produce the flour. It is said to have '100% extraction rate'. This means that 100% of the grain is included in the flour. Nothing is taken away or added.

Brown or wheatmeal flour will have between about 80% and 90% extraction rate. This is because some of the roughest outer layers of bran have been removed during milling to make a smoother flour.

White flour has an extraction rate of only about 70%. All the outer layers of bran are removed, leaving a smooth white flour.

You can buy white flour as either plain or self-raising flour. Self-raising flour is just plain flour with a raising agent (baking powder) added to it. Strong plain flour is always used for making bread. It contains a large amount of gluten, which becomes stretchy when mixed into a dough (see p. 194). This enables the bread to rise well and to hold a good firm shape once it is risen.

'Hovis' or 'Vit-be' flour is white flour with extra amounts of wheat germ added. This makes it a good source of the B-vitamins which are in the wheat germ.

Brown or white bread?

You can buy or make bread from wholemeal, brown or white flour. From the point of view of the nutrients they contain they are much the same. Although some of the nutrients in wholemeal flour are removed in the milling of white flour, all white flour in Britain is enriched with thiamin (vitamin B_1), niacin (B_3), iron, and calcium to make up for these losses.

The main advantage of wholemeal flour or bread is in the large amount of dietary fibre which it contains. This is becoming increasingly recognized as being a very important part of the diet. However, those people who prefer to eat white bread can include other high-fibre foods in their meals instead, for example whole breakfast cereals, bran or bran breakfast cereals, pulses, vegetables, and fruits (see page 15). Many people prefer the flavour and texture of wholemeal bread.

Other cereals

Oats

Traditionally these are widely grown and used in Scotland, for porridge, haggis, and oatcakes. Oats are most often prepared as 'rolled oats'. These are crushed between heated rollers to crush and partly cook them. They are the kind usually used in porridge, muesli-type breakfast cereals, and biscuits.

Barley

Most barley grown in Great Britain is used for malt, or for animal foods. You can also buy polished 'pearl barley', used for thickening soups and stews.

Maize or corn is used to make cornflakes, cornflour, and pop-corn. It is used also as a vegetable, as sweetcorn or corn on the cob.

Sago and tapioca are not cereals but they are starchy foods used for milk puddings, in the same way as rice and semolina. Sago is made from the pith of the trunk of the sago palm. Tapioca is made from the root of the cassava plant.

Semolina is produced from the starch in hard wheat when it is coarsely milled.

Arrowroot is prepared from a root. It is used for making a clear glaze for fruit flans, as it becomes transparent when boiled.

Rice and ground rice – see page 130.

Questions

1 **What nutrients do most cereal foods contain?**
2 **Draw and label the diagrams of a grain of wheat.**
3 **Describe what is meant by wholemeal, brown, and white bread.**
4 **What kind of flour is used for breadmaking?**
5 **What kind of flour contains extra wheat germ?**
6 **Would you give your family wholemeal, brown, or white bread to eat? Explain your reasons carefully.**

Vegetables and fruit

You can buy a great variety of fresh fruit and vegetables in the shops and markets today. There is usually a good selection of home-produced and imported fruit and vegetables to choose from. They are useful foods because:

1 There are so many to choose from that they can add a great variety of colour, flavour, and texture to meals.
2 They are a good source of many vitamins and minerals.
3 Many of them are inexpensive and widely available.
4 Many can be eaten either raw or cooked.
5 They fill us up but are low in calories, so they are not likely to make us put on excess weight.
6 They can be bought fresh, frozen, tinned, or dried.

Vegetables

Most vegetables can be roughly grouped as either:
root vegetables – e.g. potatoes, carrots, turnips, swedes.
green vegetables – e.g. cabbage, sprouts, lettuce, watercress.
pod or pulse vegetables – e.g. peas in their pods, broad beans, runner beans. When dried they are known as pulses, e.g. dried peas, lentils, red kidney beans (see page 135).

Choosing and storing vegetables and fruit

1 Look for fruit and vegetables which are in season, that means, at the time of year when they are growing plentifully. They will be cheap, easily available, and in good condition. This is the time to buy them to freeze for use later in the year.
2 Root vegetables should be firm and smoothly shaped so that they are easy to peel. They should not have a lot of dirt clinging to them.
3 Green vegetables should be firm, crisp, and a good colour. Avoid any which are soft, wilted, or discoloured.
4 Store vegetables in a cool, dark place. Do not buy large quantities of vegetables at one time as they soon lose their freshness.
5 The flavour of frozen, tinned, and dried vegetables and fruit is seldom as good as that of the freshly-picked kind, but they do have some advantages:
a the food value is usually as good as in fresh fruit and vegetables.
b they need little time spent in preparation.
c there is no wastage.
d their cost remains the same all the year round.
e they can be stored for use when you cannot obtain the fresh variety.

The food value of vegetables and fruit

This varies quite a lot, depending on the type of fruit or vegetable. In general, the main value of most fruit and vegetables in the diet is in the minerals and vitamins they contain, and also in the dietary fibre or roughage which they contribute.

Protein There is a small amount in all vegetables and fruit but there are good amounts in pod vegetables and pulses, that is, beans, lentils, and peas.

Carbohydrate Potatoes and pulse vegetables supply a useful amount of carbohydrate.

Vitamin A is found in the form of carotene in yellow, orange, and red fruit and vegetables, e.g. carrots, tomatoes, peaches; and in green vegetables. The carotene is converted by the liver into Vitamin A.

Vitamin B Some of the B-group vitamins are found in potatoes, pulses, and green vegetables.

Vitamin C Fruit and vegetables are our main source of Vitamin C. Blackcurrants, tomatoes, oranges, lemons, and grapefruit are all particularly rich sources. This vitamin is very easily destroyed and green vegetables must be carefully prepared and cooked if they are to retain as much Vitamin C as possible when you eat them.

These rules should be followed:

1   Use freshly picked vegetables; do not store them for a long time.
2   Shred finely before cooking, using a sharp knife.
3   Do not leave them to soak.
4   Cook in a small amount of boiling water, with the lid on. Do not overcook.
5   Serve straight away; do not try to keep them hot for a long time.
6   Use the cooking water in gravy if you can.

Questions

1   **Why are fruit and vegetables useful to anyone on a slimming diet?**
2   **Name three root vegetables, three green vegetables, three fresh pod vegetables, and three pulse vegetables.**
3   **Why should you look for fruit and vegetables in season?**
4   **Describe what you would look for when buying (a) root vegetables, and (b) green vegetables.**
5   **What are the points for and against choosing fresh vegetables rather than frozen or tinned?**
6   **Name the nutrients you would expect to find in (a) potatoes, (b) tomatoes, and (c) lemons.**
7   **Name three vegetables and three fruits which you would expect to supply useful amounts of carotene.**
8   **Describe how you would prepare and cook some Brussels sprouts, to ensure that they contain as much vitamin C as possible when you serve them.**

Recipes

For recipes using fruit, see the section on puddings, pp. 187–193.

Boiled potatoes *Serves 3*

500g/1lb potatoes, salt

Method
Scrub the potatoes in cold water if they are muddy. Peel them thinly in a bowl of clean water. Rinse and cut into even-sized pieces. Put into a pan, cover with cold water, and add a level teaspoon of salt. Bring to the boil and simmer very gently with the lid on until soft, about 20 minutes. Test with a skewer or a small sharp knife. Drain, using the pan lid, and return to the pan for a minute to dry off. Serve neatly in a vegetable dish.

Boiled potatoes can also be cooked with their skins on.

Creamed potatoes
Cook as above, but mash the potatoes in the pan when they are cooked. Add 15g/1½oz butter or margarine and a tablespoon of milk and beat well until smooth and creamy. Serve neatly in a vegetable dish, garnished with a little parsley.

Baked potatoes

Large potatoes, 1 for each person
Oil or melted fat
Butter and parsley

Method
1 Light the oven, Gas 6, 200°C. Place the shelf near the top of the oven.
2 Scrub the potatoes. Brush with oil and make a small slit in the top of each. Place on a baking tray.
3 Bake for about 1 hour until soft. Test carefully with a skewer.
4 Cut a cross in the top, add a knob of butter and a sprig of parsley.
5 Serve in a vegetable dish, on a coloured napkin if you have one.

New potatoes *Serves about 3*

500g/1lb new potatoes
Salt, butter, parsley

Method
1 Half fill a pan of water, add a level teaspoon of salt and put on to boil.
2 Wash the potatoes, scrape, and rinse. Put into the boiling water and simmer gently for about 20 minutes until cooked. Test with a skewer.
3 Drain, using the pan lid, and return to the pan with the butter. Shake the pan gently, to coat the potatoes in melted butter.
4 Serve in a vegetable dish, sprinkled with a little parsley.

Roast potatoes   *Serves about 3*

500g/1lb old potatoes
50g/2oz dripping or oil

Method

1 Light the oven, Gas 6, 200°C. Put the dripping in a roasting tin near the top of the oven.
2 Scrub and peel the potatoes, cut to even-sized pieces. Dry and place in the hot fat, using a little of this to baste the potatoes.
3 Bake for about 1−1½ hours until soft and golden brown. Baste occasionally during cooking. Serve in a vegetable dish.

Potatoes are often roasted in the fat around a joint or chicken. They will cook more quickly if boiled for ten minutes before roasting.

Duchess potatoes   *Serves about 3*

Small packet instant potato

Method
Make up the potato according to the directions of the packet. Put into a piping bag with a large star tube. Pipe on to a greased baking sheet and brown in a hot oven, Gas 6, 200°C, for about 20 minutes. Serve in a vegetable dish.

Buttered carrots   *Serves about 3*

250g/½lb carrots
25g/1oz butter
Salt, parsley

Method
Peel the carrots, rinse, then cut into neat 'sticks' or rings. Put into a pan, add enough water to cover the carrots and a level teaspoon of salt. Bring to the boil, then simmer very gently with the lid on for about 15 minutes until tender. Drain, then return to the pan with the butter. Shake gently until the carrots are glazed, then serve, garnished with a little parsley.

Turnip or swede   *Serves about 3*

1 small turnip or swede
25g/1oz butter
Salt, pepper, parsley

Method
Remove a thick layer of the outer skin. Cut the swede or turnip into slices about 1cm/½″ thick. Put in a pan, cover with cold water, add a level teaspoon of salt. Bring it to the boil and simmer with the lid on for about 20 minutes, until tender. Drain well, return to the pan, add butter and pepper, and mash well over the heat. Serve in a vegetable dish garnished with a little parsley.

Brussels sprouts   *Serves about 3*

250g/½lb sprouts
25g/1oz butter

Method
Put a pan of water, about one third full, on to boil. Add a level teaspoon of salt.
Remove any coarse outer leaves. Cut a cross through the stalk of each sprout.
Wash in cold water. Put into boiling water and simmer very gently with the lid on
for about 10–15 minutes. Drain very thoroughly. Return to the pan with the
butter and shake gently to coat the sprouts. Serve neatly in a vegetable dish.

Cabbage   *Serves about 3*

About 250g/½lb cabbage
25g/1oz butter

Method
Put a pan of water, about one third full, on to boil. Add a level teaspoon of salt.
Remove any coarse outer leaves and the stalk. Wash the cabbage, then shred
finely. Cook in the boiling water for about 10 minutes until tender. Drain very
thoroughly. Return to the pan with the butter. Serve in a vegetable dish.

Cauliflower   *Serves 3–4*

Wash the cauliflower, remove the leaves. Either leave it whole, cutting a cross
through the stalk, or cut it into sprigs. Half fill a pan with water, add a level
teaspoon of salt, and bring to the boil. Add the cauliflower and simmer very
gently for about 15 minutes until tender. Drain and serve in a vegetable dish.

Cauliflower cheese   *Serves about 3*

1 cauliflower   25g/1oz margarine
250ml/½pt milk   75g/3oz cheese, grated
25g/1oz flour   Salt, pepper, pinch of mustard

Method
Cook the cauliflower as above. Make the cheese sauce: put all the ingredients
except the cheese into a pan. Bring to the boil, whisking all the time. Stir in most
of the cheese until it is melted. Pour over the cauliflower. Sprinkle with the rest of
the cheese and brown lightly under a hot grill.

Peas   *Serves about 3*

500g/1lb fresh garden peas in pods
25g/1oz butter, salt

Method
Shell the peas. Put a pan about one third full of water on to boil, adding a level
teaspoon of salt. Put the peas into the boiling water and simmer very gently with
the lid on for about 15 to 20 minutes until tender. Test by tasting one of the peas.
Drain and return to the pan with the butter. Shake gently to glaze the peas then
serve in a vegetable dish. Frozen peas should be simmered for 2–3 minutes only.

Salads

Salads are made with raw or cold cooked vegetables and sometimes fruits. All the ingredients for the salad should be very fresh, crisp, and in good condition. Wash all the vegetables carefully but thoroughly in cold running water and shake gently to dry. Do not leave them soaking in water. A dressing served with a salad adds to the flavour and the food value. The two given below are both quick and easy to make. A salad may be made either as an accompaniment to the main dish in a meal, or as a complete dish in itself. There are recipes for both kinds below.

Some ways of preparing vegetables for a salad

Tomato 'waterlilies' Use a sharp knife with a narrow blade.

Cucumber Wash and dry, leave the skin on, mark with a fork then slice thinly.

thin slices

Cucumber cones Cut thin slices, then make one cut from the centre to the edge.
Cucumber twists Cut thin slices, then make a cut from the edge to just past the centre. Twist open.

cones

twists

Radishes Trim the ends, then cut through almost to the base. Leave in ice cold water to open.

Spring onions Remove the root and any discoloured leaves. Wash carefully and either leave whole or slice thinly.

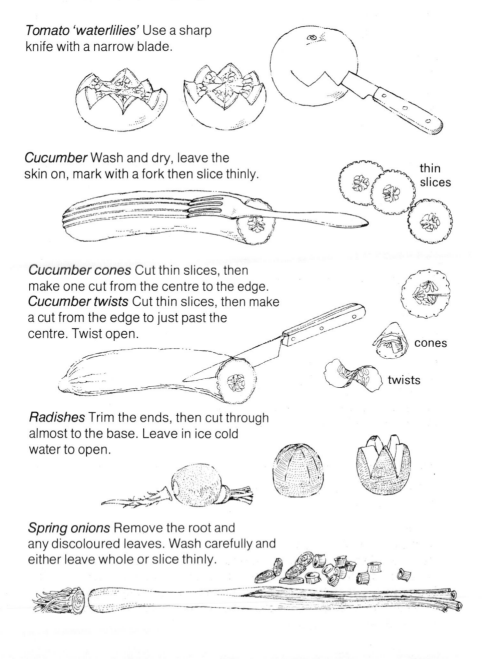

French dressing

1 tablespoon vinegar or lemon juice
2 tablespoons salad oil
Pinch of salt   Pinch of sugar
Pinch of dry mustard   Shake of pepper

Method
Put all the ingredients into a jam jar with a screw top or a plastic beaker with a leak-proof lid. Shake well together until thoroughly mixed. Shake again just before use.

Mayonnaise

Using a blender or liquidizer

1 egg (at room temperature, not cold)   ½ level teaspoon sugar
125ml/¼pt salad oil   ½ level teaspoon salt
1 tablespoon vinegar or lemon juice   Shake of pepper
½ level teaspoon mustard

Method
Put all the ingredients into the blender and mix on maximum speed for about 1 minute. If you want to make the mayonnaise a little thicker, add a little more oil through the lid. To make it thinner, add a little vinegar.

Side salads

Tomato salad   *Serves 4*

4 tomatoes
½ small onion or 2 spring onions
Parsley
French dressing (see recipe)

Method
1 Wash and dry the tomatoes. Slice and arrange neatly on a flat dish.
2 Chop the onion finely. Wash and chop the parsley.
3 Sprinkle the onion over the tomato. Spoon the French dressing over the tomatoes about 20 minutes before serving.
4 Sprinkle with chopped parsley.

Cucumber salad   *Serves about 3*

Half a cucumber
French dressing
Parsley

Method
1 Wash and slice the cucumber, arrange neatly on a shallow dish. Wash and chop the parsley. Make the French dressing.
2 Ten minutes before serving, shake the French dressing and spoon over the cucumber. Sprinkle with the parsley.

Lettuce and cucumber salad *Serves about 3*

Half a lettuce
Half a cucumber
Half a carton natural yoghurt
1 tablespoon salad cream
Salt and pepper

Method

1. Wash the lettuce and gently shake it dry. Wash and peel the cucumber, cut it into small dice.
2. Mix the yoghurt and salad cream, add a little salt and pepper, stir in the diced cucumber.
3. Put the lettuce on to the serving dish, spoon the cucumber mixture into the centre.

Potato salad *Serves about 3*

250g/½lb potatoes
Salad cream or mayonnaise
Parsley

Method

1. Peel the potatoes, cut into 1cm/½" dice. Put in a pan, cover with cold water. Add a level teaspoon of salt and one tablespoon of oil. Simmer very gently for about 5 minutes until tender.
2. Drain and cool. Carefully mix in enough salad cream to coat the potatoes.

Serve in a vegetable dish garnished with parsley.

Mexican salad *Serves about 3*

1 red or green pepper
100g/¼lb small button mushrooms
2 tomatoes
½ cucumber
French dressing

Method

1. Wash the mushrooms, remove the peel and stalks. Cut into neat slices about 0.5cm/¼" thick. (You can include the stalks in the salad or not, as your prefer.)
2. Peel the cucumber and cut into 1cm/½" dice. Wash the tomatoes and cut into wedges.
3. Wash the pepper, cut in two and remove the seeds and stalk. Cut into small pieces.
4. Make the French dressing and combine it with all the salad ingredients, mixing them gently until they are coated.
5. Serve in a salad bowl.

Kidney bean salad   *Serves about 4*

15oz tin kidney beans
½ a small onion or 2 spring onions
French dressing
Parsley

Method

1   Drain the kidney beans very thoroughly in a sieve.
2   Peel the onion and chop it finely. Wash and chop the parsley.
3   Make the French dressing and spoon carefully over the beans.
4   Put the beans into a vegetable dish or salad bowl and sprinkle with the chopped onion and parsley. Serve chilled.

Butter bean salad Make in exactly the same way but use butter beans instead of kidney beans.

Coleslaw   *Serves about 3*

Half a firm white cabbage
1 medium carrot
1 eating apple
Salad cream or mayonnaise
Parsley or cress to garnish

Method

1   Put aside some large cabbage leaves for serving.
2   Shred the cabbage and the peeled carrot on the large side of the grater. Peel and core the apple and grate it.
3   Mix the cabbage, carrot, and apple and add enough salad cream or mayonnaise to bind it together.
4   Serve neatly in a small vegetable dish, inside the cabbage leaves.
5   Garnish with a little parsley or cress.

Rice salad   *Serves about 3*

75g/3oz long grain rice
1 large tomato
25g/1oz frozen peas
25g/1oz sweetcorn
Parsley

Method

1   Cook the rice in boiling, salted water for 11 minutes. Drain and cool.
2   Cut the washed tomato in two, remove the pips. Dice the tomato.
3   Simmer the peas gently in boiling salted water for 3 to 5 minutes. Drain and cool.
4   Wash and chop the parsley.
5   Carefully mix all the ingredients and serve in a vegetable dish. You could add a little French dressing if you like.

You can vary the vegetables which you add to the rice, according to your taste.

Main-course salads

Cottage cheese and pineapple salad *Serves 2*

Half a lettuce
250g/8oz cottage cheese
A few slices or chunks of pineapple
2 tomatoes
Cress

Method
1 Wash the lettuce carefully under cold running water, gently shake dry. Wash the cress. Wash and slice the tomatoes.
2 Chop the pineapple and mix with the cottage cheese.
3 Arrange the lettuce to cover two plates. Put the cottage cheese in the centre of each plate. Put the slices of tomato around the edge of the cottage cheese and place a little cress in the centre of each salad.

Tuna fish salad *Serves 4*

500g/1lb potatoes
4 sticks celery
4 tomatoes
1 × 7oz can tuna fish (or mackerel)
French dressing
1 tablespoon chopped parsley

Method
1 Wash and peel the potatoes, cut to even sized pieces, cover with cold water and simmer for about 20 minutes until cooked. Drain and slice.
2 Slice the celery and tomatoes, drain and flake the fish. Chop the parsley.
3 Make the French dressing.
4 Put layers of ingredients into the salad bowl, sprinkling with the French dressing. Top with a layer of tomatoes and sprinkle with chopped parsley.

Sardine and tomato salad *Serves 2*

Half a lettuce
1 tin sardines (or small tin of pilchards)
Small carton cottage cheese (125g/4oz)
2 tomatoes

Method
1 Wash the lettuce under cold running water. Gently shake dry. Slice the tomatoes.
2 Use the lettuce to cover 2 medium sized plates. Put half the cottage cheese into the centre of each and place the sardines on top.
3 Garnish neatly with the tomato slices.

Making pastry

Shortcrust pastry

Recipe for 100g/4oz pastry

(this means pastry made with 100g/4oz flour)

100g/4oz plain flour, pinch of salt
25g/1oz lard
25g/1oz margarine
Cold water to mix, about 4 teaspoonfuls

Method

1 Sieve the flour and salt into a bowl. Add the margarine and lard to the flour and cut into small pieces.
2 Rub the fat into the flour using your fingertips, until the mixture looks like breadcrumbs. Do not rub it in too much or it will start to stick together and be very difficult to roll out later.
3 Add the water a little at a time and mix to a firm, smooth dough. Knead very lightly until it is smooth.
4 To knead the pastry: turn edges to centre and press firmly (1). Keep turning pastry round and turning edges to centre (2). Continue until underside and edges of pastry are smooth and free from cracks (3). Then turn underside to top.

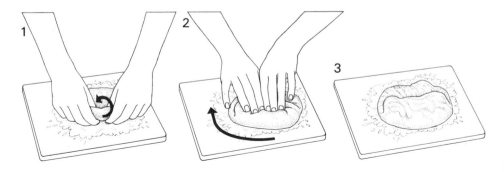

5 Roll out thinly and use as required. Bake in a hot oven (about Gas 6, 200°C).

Shortcrust pastry made with brown flour
Shortcrust pastry made with brown flour has a delicious, nutty flavour, and is particularly good for savoury flans and pies. For best results use either wheatmeal flour or a mixture of half wholemeal and half white flour. You may find that you need to add a little more water than usual.

Tips for making pastry

1 Keep everything cool, ingredients and utensils.
2 Handle very lightly.
3 Do not over-rub the fat into the flour.
4 Do not add too much water.
5 Roll out smoothly and evenly.
6 Bake in a hot oven.

Decorating pastry

To finish the edges of a pie or tart
Press the edges together with the fingers, and use a knife to 'knock up' the edges. Flute the edges with the left thumb and the knife.

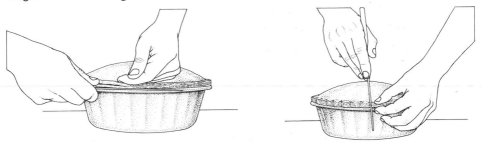

To brush the tops of pies before cooking, for an attractive finish
For a sweet pie, such as apple, use egg white and caster sugar, or milk and caster sugar. For a savoury pie, such as mince or corned beef and potato, use beaten egg and milk.

To make decorations for the top
Pastry leaves: roll out the trimmings and cut diamond shapes from 1"/2cm strips of pastry. Mark with a knife.

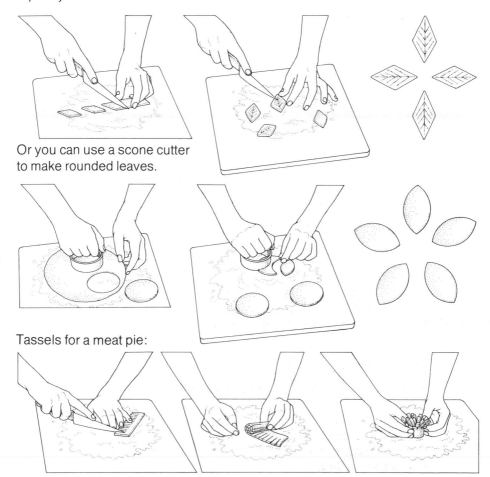

Or you can use a scone cutter to make rounded leaves.

Tassels for a meat pie:

To line a flan ring

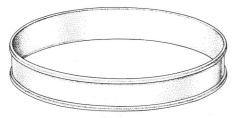

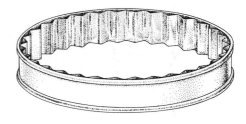

Plain flan ring for savoury fillings.

Fluted flan ring for sweet fillings.

1 Make the pastry and roll out to a circle about 2"/5cm larger than the flan ring.
2 Grease the flan ring and baking tray. Place the ring on the tray.
3 Place the rolling pin in the centre of the pastry. Fold one side over and lift the pastry into the ring. Press it firmly but gently against the base and sides. Be very careful not to stretch or make a hole in the pastry.

4 Use a rolling pin to remove the excess pastry from the top of the ring. Leave the flan in the fridge or a cool place while you prepare the filling.

To bake a flan case blind means to bake it before the filling is added. Place a large piece of greaseproof paper over the pastry in the flan ring. Add dried beans to weight the pastry down and stop it rising (or you can use foil, without the beans). Bake at Gas 6, 200°C, on the top shelf for about 15 minutes. Remove the paper and beans, or the foil, and the flan ring. Return to the oven for a further 5 minutes to dry the pastry out.

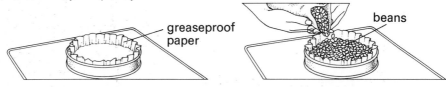

greaseproof paper

beans

Questions

1 **Write out and learn the basic ingredients for shortcrust pastry.**
2 **What are the rules to remember if you want to make good pastry?**
3 **Suggest a suitable finish for brushing the top of (a) a plum pie, (b) a bacon and egg pie.**
4 **Suggest suitable decorations you could make with pastry trimmings for (a) a chicken and mushroom pie, (b) a gooseberry pie.**
5 **Describe what is meant by baking a pastry case blind.**

Recipes using shortcrust pastry

Mince pie (savoury) *Serves about 4*

Shortcrust pastry
200g/8oz plain flour
Pinch of salt
50g/2oz margarine
50g/2oz lard

200g/8oz minced beef
1 level tablespoon plain flour
125ml/¼pt water
Salt and pepper, beef stock cube

Method

1   Light the oven, Gas 6, 200°C. Position the shelf at the top of the oven. Grease a pie plate about 20cm (8″) in diameter.
2   Put the mince into a small pan, stir over a low heat until brown. Stir in the flour, then add the water, salt and pepper. Bring to the boil, and simmer very gently with the lid on for 15 minutes, stirring occasionally, while you make the pastry.
3   Make the shortcrust pastry, divide into two, one piece slightly larger than the other. Use the larger piece to line the pie plate.
4   Place the meat on the pastry, damp the edges and cover with the other piece of pastry. Seal the edges and decorate the pie if you like (see page 161).
5   Brush with beaten egg and/or milk. Place the plate on a baking sheet and bake for 30–40 minutes until the pastry is cooked and golden brown.

Serve hot with freshly cooked vegetables or cold with a salad.

Meat and potato pie Add a little cooked mashed potato to the meat before you place it in the pastry. You could use a tin of minced beef or meat pie filling instead if you wanted to.

Quiche Lorraine *Serves about 4*

Shortcrust pastry
100g/4oz plain flour
Pinch of salt
25g/1oz lard
25g/1oz margarine

125ml/¼pt milk
2 eggs
Salt and pepper (black if you have it)
50g/2oz bacon
50g/2oz cheese
50g/2oz mushrooms (optional)
1 tomato (optional)
Parsley

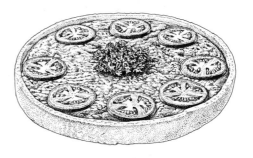

Method

1   Light the oven, Gas 5, 190°C. Place the shelf just above the centre. Grease a flan ring, about 18cm (7″) in diameter, and a baking sheet (or you could use a sandwich cake tin).

2   Make the shortcrust pastry and use it to line the flan ring.
3   Cut the rind off the bacon and cut into small pieces. Fry for a few minutes in a small pan. Wash and chop the mushrooms and add to the pan for a further couple of minutes. Grate the cheese.
4   Put the bacon, cheese and mushrooms into the flan. Beat the eggs and milk and add just a little salt and pepper. Pour into the flan.
5   Slice the tomato and carefully place on top of the flan.
6   Bake for 30–40 minutes until golden brown and firm to touch. Remove the flan ring for the last ten minutes. Garnish with a little parsley and serve hot or cold with a salad.

Cheese and onion flan Make and bake in exactly the same way, but instead of the bacon, add 1 onion, chopped and fried in 15g/½oz margarine until soft.

Both these flans are very good if the pastry is made with brown flour. Use either wheatmeal flour or a mixture of wholemeal and white flour (50g/2oz of each) for best results.

Chicken and mushroom pie   *Serves about 4*

Pastry
200g/8oz plain flour
Pinch of salt
50g/2oz margarine
50g/2oz lard

About 200g/8oz cooked chicken
100g/4oz mushrooms
15g/½oz margarine

Sauce
125ml/¼pt milk
15g/½oz margarine
15g/½oz plain flour
Salt and pepper

Beaten egg and milk to brush the top.

Method
1   Light the oven, Gas 6, 200°C. Place the shelf near the top of the oven. Grease an ovenproof plate about 20cm (8″) in diameter.
2   Wash the mushrooms. They need not be peeled if the skin is smooth. Chop them, then fry in the margarine for about 5 minutes.
3   Make the sauce: put all the sauce ingredients into a small pan. Bring to the boil whisking all the time. Simmer 2 minutes until thick. Stir in the chopped chicken and the mushrooms.
4   Make the pastry. Use half of it to line the plate. Add the chicken filling then cover with the other half of the pastry.
5   Decorate the pie. Brush with beaten egg and milk.
6   Bake for 25–35 minutes until golden brown.
    Serve with freshly cooked vegetables.

Leek and bacon pie   *Serves about 4*

Pastry
200g/8oz plain flour
Pinch of salt
50g/2oz lard
50g/2oz margarine

200g/8oz bacon rashers or bacon pieces
1 large or 2 small leeks
15g/½oz margarine

Method

1   Light the oven, Gas 6, 200°C. Place the oven shelf just above the centre. Grease an ovenproof plate, about 20cm (8″) in diameter.
2   Wash the leeks carefully under cold running water, then cut to 1cm/½″ slices. Fry for 10 minutes in the margarine.
3   Make the shortcrust pastry, cut into two pieces and use one piece to line the plate. Add the leeks.
4   Remove the rind from the bacon, cut into pieces and place it on the pastry with the leeks. Cover with the other piece of pastry. Seal the edges and decorate the top. Brush with a little milk.
5   Bake for 10 minutes then turn the oven down to Gas 5, 190°C, and bake for about 30 minutes more until the pastry is golden brown (about 40 minutes altogether).

Serve hot or cold, with fresh vegetables or a salad.

Sausage rolls

Pastry
200g/8oz plain flour
Pinch of salt
50g/2oz lard
50g/2oz margarine

200g/8oz sausagemeat
Salt and pepper
Beaten egg and/or milk to brush the top

Method

1   Light the oven, Gas 6, 200°C. Position the shelf at the top of the oven. Grease a baking tray.
2   Make the shortcrust pastry and roll it out. Cut it into a rectangle about 30cm × 25cm (12″ × 10″).
3   Cut in two, lengthwise.
4   Add some salt and pepper to the sausagemeat and roll it out the same length as the pastry. Place it on the pastry.
5   Brush the edges with water and seal them, place the join underneath. Cut into 5cm (2″) lengths, mark the tops with a knife and brush with the beaten egg and/or milk.
6   Place on the baking tray and cook for about 20 minutes until golden brown.

Serve them hot or cold.

Apple pie   *Serves about 4*

Pastry
200g/8oz plain flour
Pinch of salt
50g/2oz margarine
50g/2oz lard

500g/1lb cooking apples
75g/3oz sugar
Milk + 3 teaspoons sugar to brush the top

Method

1   Light the oven, Gas 6, 200°C. Position the shelf at the top of the oven. Grease a pie plate about 18cm (7″) in diameter.
2   Make the pastry, cut it into two pieces, one a little larger than the other. Use the larger piece to line the plate.
3   Cut the apples into four, remove the core and peel and slice them thinly. Spread over the pastry base and sprinkle with the sugar. Damp the edges of the pastry.
4   Roll out the rest of the pastry and use it to cover the fruit. Seal the edges of the pie and decorate it if you like (see page 161).
5   Brush with milk and sprinkle a little sugar on top.
6   Stand the plate on a baking sheet and bake for 15 minutes. Then turn the oven down to Gas 5, 190°C, and cook for about 20 to 30 minutes more until the fruit is cooked and the pastry is golden brown.

Serve warm or cold with custard.

Rhubarb, plum, or gooseberry pie Make and bake in exactly the same way but use 500g/1lb of whichever fruit you choose instead of the apples.

Suet pastry

Basic recipe
200g/8oz self raising flour
100g/4oz shredded suet
1 level teaspoon salt
Approximately 125ml/¼pt water

Method
Mix the flour, suet, and salt in a bowl. Add enough water to make a stiff dough, mixing it with a knife. Turn on to a floured board, knead lightly, and use as required.

Suet pastry is often cooked by steaming over boiling water. This keeps the pastry moist and prevents it becoming hard. It may be baked instead, for example, when making jam roly poly (page 188) or dumplings (page 125).

Rough puff pastry

Basic recipe
200g/8oz plain flour, preferably strong   75g/3oz block margarine
¼ level teaspoon salt   125ml/¼pt cold water
75g/3oz lard   1 teaspoon lemon juice

Method

1 Cut the lard and margarine into small pieces about 1cm/½″ square.
2 Sieve the flour and salt into a bowl, stir in the fat.
3 Mix the water and lemon juice, add enough of this water to the flour and fat to give a soft dough.
4 Turn on to a floured board and gently press the pastry together.
5 Roll out to an oblong, keeping the sides as straight as possible (1).
6 Fold the pastry in three, folding the lower third up and the top third down (2).
7 Seal the edges with a rolling pin, then turn the pastry a quarter turn (3).

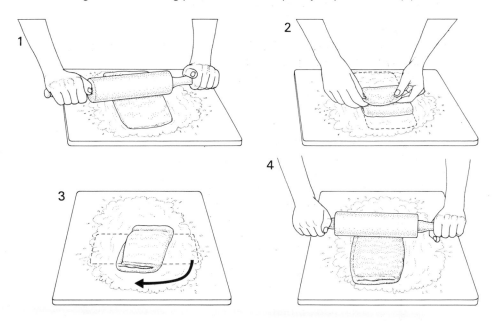

8 Roll out again, fold, seal, and turn in the same way (4).
9 Repeat the roll and fold again (3 times altogether).
10 Leave the pastry in a cold place for at least 15 minutes.
11 Roll and fold again twice more. Leave the pastry in a cold place for another 15 minutes if you have time.
12 Roll out the pastry and use as required.

Tips for successful rough puff pastry

1 Always use plain flour, strong bread flour if possible.
2 Use firm lard and margarine, not soft.
3 Use lemon juice in the water to soften the gluten in the flour and so make the pastry more elastic.
4 Keep everything as cold as possible and chill the pastry in the fridge between rollings. It will be much easier to handle.
5 Bake in a hot oven, about Gas 7, 220°C.

Using rough puff pastry

You can use rough puff pastry instead of shortcrust to make any of these recipes from the shortcrust pastry section:

Mince pie	Sausage rolls
Chicken and mushroom pie	Apple pie
Leek and bacon pie	

Recipes using rough puff pastry

Jam and cream slices   *Makes 8*

Rough puff pastry
200g/8oz plain flour, preferably strong
¼ level teaspoon salt
75g/3oz lard
75g/3oz block margarine
125ml/¼pt cold water
1 teaspoon lemon juice

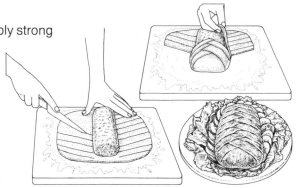

Small carton fresh double or whipping cream
About 3 rounded tablespoons jam
100g/4oz icing sugar

Method
1   Make the rough puff pastry as above. Light the oven Gas 8, 230°C. Place shelf near top. Grease a baking tray
2   Roll out the pastry to a rectangle 40cm × 10cm (16″ × 4″).
3   Cut into eight 10cm × 5cm (4″ × 2″) pieces. Place on the baking tray and leave in a cold place while you whip the cream.
4   Bake for 15–20 minutes until light and well risen, cool on a wire tray.
5   When cold, split in half. Spread one half with jam, then sandwich with cream.
6   Sieve the icing sugar into a bowl, add enough hot water, about 1 tablespoon, to make glacé icing which is thick enough to coat the back of a spoon.
7   Cover the tops with icing and leave to set. Do not move before the icing has set or it will crack.

Sausage plait   *Serves about 4*

Rough puff pastry
200g/8oz plain flour, preferably strong
½ level teaspoon salt
75g/3oz lard
75g/3oz block margarine
125ml/¼pt cold water
1 teaspoon lemon juice

250g/8oz sausage meat
Salt and pepper
Beaten egg and milk for top

Method
1   Make the rough puff pastry as above.
2   Light the oven, Gas 7, 220°C. Place shelf above the centre. Grease a baking tray.
3   Roll out the pastry to a rectangle, about 30cm × 20cm (12″ × 8″).
4   Season the sausage meat with salt and pepper. Roll it out and place in the centre of the pastry.
5   Cut the edge of the pastry diagonally into 2cm/1″ strips.
6   Fold the ends of the pastry over the meat, then fold over alternate sides. Place carefully on the baking tray.
7   Brush with beaten egg and milk, then bake for 15 minutes. Turn the oven down to Gas 5, 190°C and bake for a further 30 minutes.
8   Serve either hot or cold, with a salad.

Cake-making

Lining tins

When you are making cakes it is important to prepare the tins carefully, to ensure that the cakes can be removed from the tins without breaking. The best way to line the tin depends on its shape and on the mixture you are using.

To line a sandwich cake tin or a loaf tin
It is usually only necessary to line the bottom of the tin. The sides can be greased with margarine or lard. Stand the tin on a piece of greaseproof paper, draw around the base of the tin and cut the paper on the pencil line.

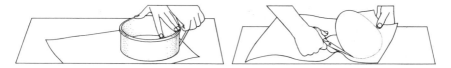

To line a Swiss roll tin, base and sides
Place the tin on a sheet of greaseproof paper and draw a pencil line around the base of the tin. Cut the paper about 1.5cm/1″ away from the pencil line. At the corners, cut into the pencil line. Place the paper neatly into the tin and the corners will fit smoothly against the sides and base.

To line a deep cake tin
Place the tin on a sheet of greaseproof paper, draw around the base and cut out this piece. For the sides, fold a sheet of greaseproof paper into two, lengthwise. Turn up about 2cm/1″ at the folded edge. Make diagonal cuts on this fold. Place the paper inside the tin with this fold on the base of the tin, then place the circle on to the base.

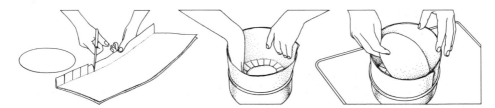

Methods of cakemaking

There are four basic methods of mixing the ingredients together when you make a cake. The method you use depends on the type and amounts of ingredients you are using. These methods are called:

1   The rubbing-in method
2   The creaming method
3   The melting method
4   The whisking method

The rubbing-in method

This is used for cakes, scones, shortcrust pastry, and some biscuits. It is used for 'plain' cakes, that is, cakes which do not have a large amount of fat compared to flour, for example, rock buns, which have 75g fat (margarine) and 200g flour. Recipes which are more than half the weight of fat to flour are made by another method as they would be too sticky to rub in. Block margarine is better than soft for rubbed-in mixtures as it is less sticky.

Basic method
The fat is cut up into small pieces, then lightly rubbed into the flour with the fingertips until it looks like breadcrumbs. The other dry ingredients are stirred in, then the liquids (egg and/or milk) are added.

These mixtures are baked in a fairly hot oven, Gas 5 or 6 (190°C–200°C). They will keep fresh for a few days but not longer because of the fairly small amount of fat they contain. The more fat used in a cake recipe, the longer it will keep fresh.

As well as the recipes below, the rubbing-in method is used for shortcrust pastry (see page 160), scones (page 185), apple crumble (page 187), and shortbread, lemon, and digestive biscuits (page 182–3).

Rock buns *Makes 10*

200g/8oz S.R. flour
Pinch of salt
75g/3oz margarine (from a block, not a tub)
75g/3oz sugar
75g/3oz dried fruit
1 egg
1–2 tablespoons water

Method
1 Light the oven, Gas 7, 220°C. Place the shelf just above the centre. Grease a baking sheet.
2 Sieve the flour and salt into the bowl, rub in the margarine, stir in the sugar and dried fruit.
3 Beat the egg lightly and add it to the mixture. If necessary, add the water. The mixture must be firm enough to stand in heaps.
4 Divide into 10 and place in rough heaps on the baking sheet. Bake for about 15 minutes until firm and golden brown. Cool on a wire tray.

Cherry buns Make and bake as above, but leave out the dried fruit, and add 50g/2oz of cherries which have been washed, dried, and chopped.

Chocolate chip buns Leave out the dried fruit and add 50g/2oz chopped chocolate.

Coconut buns Leave cut the dried fruit and add 50g/2oz coconut.

Date buns Leave out the dried fruit and add 50g/2oz chopped dates.

Raspberry buns Leave out the dried fruit. When the buns are on the baking sheet, make a slight dent in the centre of each and add half a teaspoonful of raspberry jam.

Fruit loaf

150g/6oz S.R. flour
1 level teaspoon mixed spice
Pinch of salt
75g/3oz margarine
75g/3oz sugar
100g/4oz dried fruit
25g/1oz peel, chopped nuts or cherries (optional)
1 egg +5 tablespoons of water

Method
1 Light the oven, Gas 4, 180°C, position shelf in centre.
2 Grease a small (1lb) loaf tin. Line the bottom with greaseproof paper.
3 Put the flour, spice and salt into a mixing bowl. Rub in the margarine, stir in the sugar and fruit.
4 Mix the egg and water, add to the mixture, mix well, put into the tin.
5 Bake for 1–1¼ hours, test with a skewer. Leave in the tin for 10 minutes before cooling on a wire tray.

Cherry cake Make the same way as the fruit loaf but leave out the spice and dried fruit and add 100g/4oz cherries instead. Wash and dry the cherries, cut them into four and add them when you add the sugar.

Wholemeal fruit cake Make in the same way as the fruit loaf, but instead of 150g/6oz S.R. flour, use 75g/3oz S.R. flour + 75g/3oz wholemeal flour and 1 level teaspoon of baking powder.

Granny loaf

200g/8oz S.R. flour
Pinch of salt
25g/1oz sugar (preferably soft brown sugar)
50g/2oz chopped walnuts or dates
75g/3oz raisins or sultanas
1 rounded tablespoon golden syrup
100ml/¼pt milk

<u>Sugar glaze</u>
1 tablespoon each of milk, water, sugar

Method
1 Light the oven, Gas 4, 180°C, position shelf in centre.
2 Grease a small loaf tin (1lb size), line the bottom with greaseproof paper.
3 Place all the dry ingredients in a bowl, add the nuts and fruit. Add the syrup and milk and beat well; the mixture will be very soft. Put into the tin and bake for 45–60 minutes.
4 Make the sugar glaze when the cake is nearly ready. Put milk, water, and sugar into a small pan, warm gently to dissolve the sugar, then boil for 2 minutes. Brush the loaf with the glaze while both are warm.

Serve sliced and buttered.

Fruit tea bread

225g/8oz S.R. flour
Pinch of salt
50g/2oz margarine

75g/3oz dried fruit
1 level tablespoon sugar
1 egg + 6 tablespoons milk

Method

1 Light the oven, Gas 6, 200°C. Position shelf just above the centre.
2 Grease a small loaf tin (1lb size), line the bottom with greaseproof paper.
3 Sieve the flour into a mixing bowl, add the salt, rub in the margarine, stir in the dried fruit and sugar.
4 Beat the egg and milk, keep back a teaspoonful to brush the top, pour the rest into the flour.
5 Knead lightly and shape to fit the tin. Place in the tin and brush with egg and milk. Bake for about 40 minutes until well risen, firm, and golden brown.
6 Leave in the tin for 10 minutes, then cool on a wire tray.

Serve sliced and buttered. This loaf does not keep well, so should be eaten the day it is made. If it is to be eaten the next day, it is delicious toasted and buttered.

Bran tea loaf

50g/2oz bran or All-Bran
100g/4oz dried fruit
100g/4oz soft brown sugar

200ml/7 fluid oz milk
100g/4oz S.R. flour
1 level teaspoon baking powder

Method

1 Put bran, dried fruit and sugar into a mixing bowl, pour the milk over them and leave to soak for about 20 minutes.
2 Light the oven, Gas 5, 190°C, put the shelf in the centre of the oven.
3 Grease a small (1lb) loaf tin, line the bottom with greaseproof paper.
4 Mix the flour and baking powder thoroughly, stir into the mixture.
5 Put into the tin and bake for about 1 hour. Test with a skewer.
6 Leave to cool in tin for 5 minutes, then turn out and cool on a wire rack.

Serve sliced and buttered.

Date and apple cake

150g/6oz S.R. flour
50g/2oz margarine
75g/3oz sugar

50g/2oz chopped dates
1 large cooking apple
1 egg + 2 tablespoons of water

Method

1 Light the oven, Gas 5, 190°C. Position the shelf in the centre.
2 Grease a small (1lb) loaf tin and line the bottom with greaseproof paper.
3 Put the flour in a mixing bowl, rub in the margarine, stir in the sugar.
4 Chop the dates, add to the mixture. Peel and core the apple and chop into small pieces, add to bowl.
5 Beat the egg and water, add to the flour and mix well together, put in the tin.
6 Bake for 1¼hrs, test with a skewer. Leave in the tin for 10 minutes, then cool on a wire tray.

Serve sliced, spread with a little butter if you wish.

All-in-one creaming method

This is used for cakes which have more fat and sugar compared to flour, usually about equal weights of each.

For example, a Victoria sandwich cake might have: 100g S.R. flour
100g margarine
100g caster sugar
2 eggs

These are called 'rich' cakes and they keep fresh for longer than plain cakes because of the extra fat. The flour is sieved into the bowl, then the other ingredients are all added and beaten together with a wooden spoon until the mixture is light-coloured and fluffy. The ingredients used are:

Self-raising flour is used, so there is no need to add extra baking powder.

Margarine Soft margarine in a tub is very easy to cream. Block margarine is also suitable and easy to use, provided it is not used straight from the refrigerator.

Caster sugar is better than granulated. It has smaller crystals which blend more easily into the mixture.

Eggs should be at room temperature, not chilled. For perfect results, weigh the eggs, then use an equal weight of each of the other ingredients. For example, if the 2 eggs weigh 120g, use 120g each of the flour, margarine, and sugar.

The all-in-one creaming method is quicker and simpler than the traditional creaming method and it is easier to achieve perfect results every time.

As well as the recipes below, this method is also used to make pineapple upside-down pudding (page 190), steamed sponge pudding (page 189), Hungarian chocolate biscuits (page 181), and crunchy bran biscuits (page 184).

The traditional creaming method
Using this method the fat and sugar are creamed together until light and fluffy. The eggs are whisked, then gradually beaten into the mixture, and then the flour is gently folded in.

Victoria sandwich cake

150g/6oz S.R. flour
150g/6oz caster sugar
150g/6oz margarine
3 eggs (size 3 or 4)
Jam to sandwich the cake

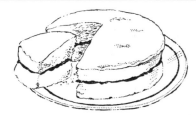

Method
1 Light the oven, Gas 3, 170°C. Place the shelf in the centre. Grease 2 sandwich cake tins, about 18cm/7″ in diameter, and line them with greaseproof paper.
2 Sieve the flour into a bowl. Add the sugar, margarine, and eggs and beat well with a wooden spoon (or mixer) until the mixture is light-coloured and fluffy.
3 Divide between the tins and smooth the top. Bake for 30–40 minutes, until firm and golden brown. Turn on to a wire tray to cool, then sandwich with jam.

Eggs can vary a lot in size. For perfect results you can, if you wish, weigh the 3 eggs. They will probably weigh over or under 150g/6oz. If, for example, they weighed 175g you would use 175g each of flour, sugar, and margarine.

Fairy cakes

125g/5oz S.R. flour
100g/4oz margarine
100g/4oz sugar, preferably caster
2 eggs

Method
1 Light the oven, Gas 5, 190°C. Place the shelf just above the centre. Place 18 paper cases into a bun tray.
2 Sieve the flour into a bowl, add all the other ingredients and beat well with a wooden spoon until light and fluffy.
3 Divide between the paper cases and bake for about 20–25 minutes until well risen, firm, and golden brown.

Queen cakes Make exactly as above, but add 50g/2oz currants or sultanas to the mixture.

Cherry cakes Make exactly as above, but add 50g/2oz cherries which have been washed, dried, and chopped.

Butterfly cakes Make some Fairy cakes as described above. Make some butter cream by sieving 100g/4oz icing sugar, adding 50g/2oz margarine or butter and 2 teaspoons milk, and beating together until smooth and light. Slice the tops off the cakes, cut each top in two to make 'wings'. Put a little butter cream on each case and replace the wings. Sieve a little icing sugar over the top of the cakes.

Chocolate cake

15g/½oz cocoa
100g/4oz S.R. flour
75g/3oz margarine
75g/3oz caster sugar
2 eggs
1 level tablespoon golden syrup

Butter cream
100g/4oz icing sugar
50g/2oz margarine or butter
1 level tablespoon cocoa (optional)
½ teaspoonful vanilla essence.

Method
1 Light the oven, Gas 3, 170°C. Place the shelf near the centre. Grease two 15cm or 18cm (6″ or 7″) sandwich cake tins and line them with greaseproof paper.
2 Sieve the flour and cocoa into a bowl, add the margarine, sugar, eggs, and syrup, and beat well until very light and fluffy.
3 Divide between the two tins and bake for 25–30 minutes until firm. Cool on a wire tray, then sandwich with the butter cream. Sieve a little icing sugar over the top.

To make the butter cream
Sieve the icing sugar into a bowl, with the cocoa if you are using it. Add the butter and vanilla essence and beat well.

Orange or lemon cake

150g/6oz S.R. flour
150g/6oz caster sugar
150g/6oz margarine
3 eggs (size 3 or 4)
1 orange or lemon

Glacé icing (optional)
100g/4oz icing sugar, sieved
1 tablespoon of juice from the orange or lemon
2 drops orange or yellow colouring
Mix the ingredients together until smooth.

Butter icing
100g/4oz icing sugar, sieved
50g/2oz margarine
2 or 3 teaspoons orange or lemon juice
Beat together until smooth and fluffy.

Method

1   Light the oven, Gas 3, 170°C. Place the shelf in the centre. Grease 2 sandwich cake tins, about 18cm/7″ in diameter, and line them with greaseproof paper.
2   Wash the orange or lemon. Finely grate the rind, then squeeze out the juice.
3   Sieve the flour into a bowl, add the sugar, margarine, eggs, and rind, and beat well with a wooden spoon until the mixture is light-coloured and fluffy.
4   Divide between the tins and smooth the top. Bake for 30–40 minutes until firm and golden brown. Cool on a wire rack.
5   When cool, sandwich with most of the butter icing. Spread glacé icing over the top and pipe the rest of the butter icing around the edge.

You could leave out either or both of the icings if you wanted to. You could use lemon curd to sandwich the cakes together.

Banana cake

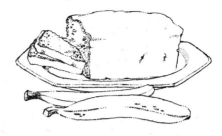

75g/3oz margarine
100g/4oz sugar
1 egg
1 large or two small ripe bananas
150g/6 oz wholemeal flour
1 rounded teaspoon baking powder
1 level teaspoon salt
1 tablespoon water

Method

1   Light oven, Gas 4, 180°C. Position shelf in centre.
2   Grease a small (1lb) loaf tin. Line the bottom with greaseproof paper.
3   Beat the margarine and sugar until light and fluffy. Beat in the egg. Mash the bananas and mix in.
4   Mix the flour, baking powder, and salt, and add to the mixture. Stir in the water.
5   Put into the tin and bake 1–1¼ hours. Test with a skewer. Leave in the tin for 10 minutes then cool on a wire tray.
6   Eat sliced, spread with a little butter if you wish.

The melting method

This method is less often used than the other methods. The flour and other dry ingredients are put into a bowl. The fat and syrup or treacle are melted in a pan and poured into the flour. Plain flour is usually used, with bicarbonate of soda as the raising agent. The bicarbonate of soda has quite a strong taste and darkens the colour of the cake, so it is a suitable raising agent in recipes like gingerbreads. The ginger flavour covers the taste and the darker colour improves the appearance of the gingerbread. These cakes usually improve with keeping, developing a good flavour and becoming more moist.

Ginger biscuits (page 183) are also made by this method.

Gingerbread

250g/8oz plain flour
1 rounded teaspoon ground ginger
1 level teaspoon mixed spice
1 level teaspoon bicarbonate of soda
50g/2oz sugar (any kind)

100g/4oz lard or margarine
150g/6oz syrup or treacle
1 egg
125ml/¼pt milk

Method

1 Light the oven, Gas 4, 180°C. Place the oven shelf just below the centre of the oven.
2 Line a tin about 18cm × 30cm (7″ × 10″) with greaseproof paper and grease it lightly. Beat the egg and milk together.
3 Sieve the flour, ginger, spice, and bicarbonate of soda into a bowl. Stir in the sugar.
4 Put the syrup into a pan, add the lard, and melt without boiling. Pour into the flour and beat well.
5 Add the egg and milk a little at a time, beating until smooth. The mixture will be very soft. Pour into the tin. Bake for about 40 minutes until firm.
6 Leave in the tin until almost cold, then remove the paper and cut into about 15 squares.

Ginger loaf

100g/4oz plain flour
50g/2oz wholemeal flour
50g/2oz sugar
Pinch of salt
1 level teaspoon bicarbonate of soda

2 rounded teaspoons ground ginger
100g/4oz black treacle
50g/2oz margarine
100ml/4 fluid oz milk

Method

1 Light the oven, Gas 4, 180°C. Position the shelf in the centre.
2 Grease a small (1lb) loaf tin, line the bottom with greaseproof paper.
3 Put flour, sugar, salt, and bicarbonate of soda into a bowl, mix well together.
4 Melt the treacle and margarine in a pan, pour into the flour and mix well.
5 Mix the egg and milk. Add to the mixture gradually and beat well. The mixture should be very soft.
6 Pour into the tin. Bake for about 1¼ hours, test with a skewer. Leave in the tin for 10 minutes, then cool on a wire tray.

Serve sliced, spread with a little butter if you wish.

The whisking method

This method is used for making sponge cakes. A sponge is a cake which contains no fat. As these cakes contain no fat they soon become stale, so they should be eaten within a day of being made. The ingredients used are flour, eggs, and caster sugar only.

Flour: self-raising flour is used to give extra lightness, though plain flour could be used. It must be well sieved.

Sugar: caster sugar is essential for this light mixture.

Eggs: these should be at room temperature. If cold, they will take longer to whisk.

Method
1   Put the eggs and sugar into a mixing bowl. Using an electric mixer, whisk until they are thick, white, and creamy. Test carefully to see if the mixture is ready. It should hold the mark of the beater trailed over the mixture for at least 10 seconds. This is called 'ribbon texture'.

2   Use a metal spoon to <u>gently</u> fold the sieved flour into the mixture, a little at a time. This must be done very lightly and carefully, but thoroughly.
3   Pour the mixture into the prepared tin and bake in a fairly hot oven, about Gas 6, 200°C.

Swiss roll

2 eggs
50g/2oz caster sugar
50g/2oz S.R. flour
2–3 tablespoons jam
Extra sugar for rolling up

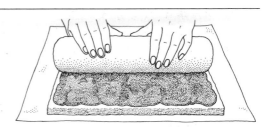

Method
1   Light the oven, Gas 6, 200°C. Place the shelf near the top of the oven.
2   Line a Swiss roll tin, 18cm × 30cm (7″ × 12″), with greaseproof paper. Grease the paper. Sieve the flour on to a plate.
3   Whisk the eggs and sugar until thick (see above). Gently fold in the flour using a metal spoon. Pour into the tin.
4   Bake for 8–10 minutes until golden brown and firm. Do not overcook, or it will break when you try to roll it up.
5   While the cake is baking, spread the extra sugar over a piece of greaseproof paper. Place a sharp knife and a palette knife beside the paper. Warm the jam.
6   When the Swiss roll is cooked, tip it on to the sugared paper. Peel off the paper. Trim the edges of the Swiss roll.
7   Spread quickly with the warm jam then roll it up, using the paper to help you. Cool on a wire rack.

If your Swiss roll tin is larger, about 30cm × 22cm (12″ × 9″), use 75g/3oz caster sugar, 3 eggs, and 75g/3oz S.R. flour.

Sponge fruit gateau

2 eggs
50g/2oz caster sugar
50g/2oz S.R. flour
Half a tin of fruit, such as mandarin oranges
 or pineapples, or a few fresh strawberries
About 50g/2oz toasted coconut, raspings,
 or grated chocolate for the sides
Small carton double or whipping cream

Method
1 Light the oven, Gas 6, 200°C. Place the shelf near the top of the oven.
2 Line a Swiss roll tin 18cm × 30cm (7″ × 12″) with greaseproof paper. Grease the paper. Sieve the flour on to a plate.
3 Whisk the eggs and sugar until thick (see above). Gently fold in the flour with a metal spoon. Pour into the tin.
4 Bake 10–15 minutes until firm. Then remove the paper and cool on a wire tray.
5 Drain the syrup from the fruit. Whip the cream and keep it cool.
6 When the cake is cold, cut it into 2 or 3 equal sized pieces and sandwich them together with a little cream. Spread a little cream on the sides (not the top).
7 Put the coconut/raspings/grated chocolate on to a piece of greaseproof paper. Dip the sides of the cake into this to coat them.
8 Spread a little cream on to the top of the cake, arrange the fruit on this, then decorate with piped cream.

If your Swiss roll tin is larger, about 30cm × 22cm (12″ × 9″), use 3 eggs, 75g/3oz caster sugar, and 75g/3oz self-raising flour to make the cake.

Sponge sandwich cake

3 eggs
75g/3oz caster sugar
75g/3oz S.R. flour
2 tablespoons jam
Small carton double or whipping cream (optional)

Method
1 Light the oven, Gas 5, 190°C. Place the shelf just above the centre.
2 Line two 15cm or 18cm (6″ or 7″) sandwich cake tins with greaseproof paper. Grease the paper and the sides of the tin.
3 Sieve the flour on to a plate.
4 Whisk the eggs and sugar until thick (see above). Gently fold in the flour using a metal spoon. Pour into the tins.
5 Bake for 20–30 minutes until firm and golden brown. Leave in the tins for a few minutes, then turn out to cool.
6 Sandwich with jam (and whipped cream if you have used it).

You can bake this cake in one 18cm or 20cm (7″ or 8″) deep cake tin if you prefer. It will take about 40–45 minutes to cook at Gas 4, 180°C. Split in two when cool and sandwich with the jam and/or cream.

Chocolate sponge cake Make and bake exactly as above, but use 50g/2oz flour and 25g/1oz sieved cocoa instead of 75g/3oz flour.

Sponge flan case

2 eggs
50g/2oz caster sugar
50g/2oz S.R. flour

Method

1   Light the oven, Gas 6, 200°C. Position the shelf above the centre.
2   Grease a 20cm/8″ sponge flan tin with melted lard. This must be done very thoroughly. Flour the tin lightly.
3   Sieve the flour on to a plate.
4   Whisk the eggs and sugar until thick (see above). Gently fold in the flour with a metal spoon. Pour into the tin.
5   Bake for about 20 minutes until firm and golden brown. Leave in the tin for a few minutes, then turn on to a wire tray to cool.

Sponge fruit flan

Flan case
2 eggs
50g/2oz caster sugar
50g/2oz S.R. flour

Small tin of fruit, e.g. peaches, pears,
   mandarin oranges, or fresh strawberries
1 rounded teaspoon of arrowroot
1 rounded teaspoon of sugar
2 drops of colouring
Small carton double or whipping cream (optional)

Method

1   Make a sponge flan case exactly as described above.
2   Drain the syrup from the fruit into a measuring jug. Add enough water to make 125mls/¼pt liquid.
3   Arrange the fruit neatly in the flan case.
4   Put the syrup, arrowroot, and sugar into a small pan. Bring to the boil, stirring all the time, and boil until transparent. Add the colouring if you wish, e.g. pink for pears.
5   Use a metal spoon to coat the fruit with this glaze.
6   When completely cold, decorate with the whipped cream if you are using it.

Apple sponge flan

Flan case
2 eggs   500g/1lb cooking apples
50g/2oz caster sugar   75g/3oz sugar
50g/2oz S.R. flour   Small carton double or whipping cream (optional)

Method

1   Make the sponge flan cake exactly as described above.
2   Cut the apples into quarters, remove the peel and core, slice.
3   Put into a pan with about 4 tablespoons water and simmer very gently with the lid on until soft. Add the sugar and beat until smooth. Put in the flan case.
4   When the flan is completely cold, decorate with the whipped cream.

Cold drinks

Lemonade

2 lemons
50g/2oz sugar
500ml/1pt water

Method
1 Wipe the lemons with a clean damp cloth. Peel the rind very thinly and put into a jug or basin with the sugar. Pour on the boiling water and leave until cold.
2 Strain into a glass jug, through muslin or a nylon sieve.
3 Add the lemon juice and some ice cubes and serve.

Orange squash Make in exactly the same way as the lemonade, but use two oranges and one lemon instead of two lemons.

Ginger and lemon punch

1 teabag or 1 rounded teaspoon tea
250ml/½pt boiling water
50g/2oz granulated sugar
250ml/½pt cold water
1 lemon, 1 orange
Small bottle of ginger ale
Ice cubes

Method
1 Make the tea with the boiling water. Leave to infuse for 3 minutes, then pour into a large jug or basin. Add the sugar and stir to dissolve. Add the cold water and leave until cold.
2 Cut the orange and lemon into halves. Remove two slices from each and save for decoration. Squeeze the juice from the orange and lemon halves and add to the tea.
3 Strain into a glass jug, add the ginger ale and ice cubes, and float the lemon and orange slices on the top.

Chocolate cream   *Makes 2–3 large glasses*

2 rounded tablespoons drinking chocolate
2 tablespoons boiling water
500ml/1pt cold milk
½ teaspoon vanilla essence
2 tablespoons double or whipping cream
Grated chocolate to decorate

Method
1 Dissolve the drinking chocolate in the boiling water.
2 Whisk in the milk and vanilla essence. Pour into glasses.
3 Whip the cream until thick.
4 Just before serving, spoon or pipe the cream on to the milk and sprinkle with a little grated chocolate.

Sandwiches

Sandwich fillings

Cheese and chutney – grated cheese with chutney or sweet pickle.
Egg and cress – chopped hard boiled egg, mixed with salad cream and cress.
Cooked meat and coleslaw – ham, chopped pork, corned beef, etc., with a little coleslaw (see page 158).
Cottage cheese and pineapple – chop the drained pineapple.
Cottage cheese and spring onion – chop the spring onion.
Cream cheese and cucumber – chop the cucumber, mix with the cheese.
Cream cheese and chopped walnuts.
Chopped pork and salad cream – chop the pork, mix with the salad cream.
Sardine and tomato – drain the sardines, mix with slices of tomato.
Salad – use a mixture of salad ingredients, with or without a little salad cream.

Making sandwiches

When you are making sandwiches, spread the butter or soft margarine right to the edges of the bread. There are many different kinds of bread available: wholemeal, brown, or white, and different shaped loaves and rolls. Make sure the sandwiches have plenty of filling. The filling should be moist so that the sandwiches don't taste dry. Serve them on a dishpaper, well garnished with cress, parsley, or lettuce to add some colour.

Afternoon tea or 'dainty' sandwiches
Use thinly sliced white or brown bread with
the crusts removed, cut into small squares,
fingers or triangles. Garnish with
cress or parsley.

Open sandwiches
Use bread buns, halved. Choose a moist
filling which will not fall off, and
colourful garnishes.

Vienna rolls or loaves
These look attractive if they are split along the side, well buttered, and filled with a moist filling. Use slices of tomato, cucumber, or hard-boiled egg, and lettuce or cress to add colour.

Toasted sandwiches
Most sandwiches can be toasted except those with lettuce or salad in the filling. Use any of the fillings above, or you could use grilled bacon and fried mushrooms, or any other filling.

Biscuits

Biscuits are easy to make at home and they usually have a better flavour than the bought variety. When you are making them, follow these rules for good results:

1 Grease the baking tray carefully, as biscuits are fragile and may break easily when you lift them off the tray.
2 Leave them to cool on the tray for a minute or two after removing them from the oven. Then cool on a wire tray.
3 Do not crowd them together on the baking tray, as some recipes will spread a little in the oven.
4 Make sure that you do not use too large a baking tray for your oven. If you do, the biscuits will not brown evenly and some may be overdone and dark before others are cooked.
5 Biscuits do not go crisp until they are cool, so do not leave them in the oven until they are crisp, or they will be overdone.

Lemon or orange biscuits

100g/4oz S.R. or plain flour
50g/2oz butter or margarine
50g/2oz caster, icing, or granulated sugar
    (plus a little extra to sprinkle on the tops)
1 egg
1 level teaspoon lemon or orange rind

Method
1 Light the oven, Gas 4, 180°C. Place the shelf in the centre of the oven. Grease a baking tray.
2 Separate the egg yolk from the white. Wash the lemon or orange, then grate the rind finely.
3 Put the flour into a mixing bowl. Rub in the butter, then stir in the sugar and lemon or orange rind. Add the egg yolk and mix to a smooth dough.
4 Knead lightly, then roll out thinly. Cut into about 15 biscuits with a medium-sized cutter.
5 Place on the baking sheet, brush with the beaten egg white, and sprinkle with a little sugar.
6 Bake for 12–15 minutes until pale gold. Leave to cool on the baking tray for a couple of minutes, then cool on a wire rack.

Currant biscuits Leave out the lemon or orange rind and add 25g/1oz currants when you add the sugar.

Cherry biscuits Leave out the lemon or orange rind and add 25g/1oz cherries (washed, dried, and chopped) when you add the sugar.

Spice biscuits Leave out the orange or lemon rind and add 1 level teaspoon mixed spice when you add the sugar.

Digestive biscuits

75g/3oz wholemeal flour
15g/½oz plain flour
Good pinch of salt
½ level teaspoon baking powder

15g/½oz oatmeal or porage oats
40g/1½oz butter or margarine
40g/1½oz sugar, preferably caster
3 tablespoons milk

Method
1 Light the oven, Gas 5, 190°C. Place the shelf in the centre. Grease a baking tray.
2 Sieve the plain flour, salt, and baking powder into a bowl, and mix well. Stir in the wholemeal flour and oatmeal.
3 Rub in the butter, stir in the sugar. Add the milk and mix to a stiff dough.
4 Roll out thinly and cut into about 12 biscuits with a medium-sized cutter.
5 Place on the baking tray and bake for 15–20 minutes until pale golden brown.

Shortbread biscuits

150g/6oz plain flour
100g/4oz butter or margarine

50g/2oz sugar (preferably caster)
Some extra sugar to sprinkle on the top

Method
1 Light the oven, Gas 3, 170°C. Place the shelf just above the centre of the oven. Grease a baking tray.
2 Put the flour into a bowl, rub in the margarine, stir in the sugar.
3 Squeeze together firmly with your fingers until the mixture forms a dough. Do not add any liquid.
4 Roll out to about 1cm thick (less than ½" thick). Cut into circles with a medium-sized cutter, or cut into fingers.
5 Carefully place on the baking tray. Bake for about 15–20 minutes until pale golden brown. The biscuits will not be crisp until they are cool.
6 Lift on to a wire tray to cool. Sprinkle with a little sugar.

Ginger biscuits

150g/6oz S.R. flour
75g/3oz sugar
½ level teaspoon bicarbonate of soda
1 level teaspoon ground ginger

1 level tablespoon syrup
50g/2oz lard
1 egg

Method
1 Light the oven, Gas 4, 180°C. Place the shelf near the oven centre. Grease a baking tray.
2 Sieve the flour into a bowl, stir in the sugar, bicarbonate of soda, and ginger and mix well.
3 Put the syrup and lard into a small pan. Warm until the lard is melted. Pour this into the flour and beat well. Beat the egg and gradually beat it into the mixture.
4 Divide into pieces about the size of a walnut (makes about 24). Roll in the palms of the hands until smooth. Place well apart on the baking tray and flatten slightly.
5 Bake for 12–15 minutes until firm and a rich brown colour.

If you tap the baking tray sharply against the table top as you bring it out of the oven, the biscuits will have the 'cracked' appearance of ginger biscuits.

Crunchy bran biscuits

50g/2oz sugar
50g/2oz margarine
1 egg
100g/4oz wholemeal flour
50g/2oz wheat bran
1 rounded teaspoon baking powder
Pinch of salt

Method
1 Light the oven, Gas 5, 190°C. Place the shelf in the oven centre. Grease a baking tray.
2 Cream the sugar and margarine until soft, beat in the egg.
3 Mix all the other ingredients thoroughly in a bowl, then add to the margarine and sugar. Knead into a dough.
4 Divide into about 20 pieces, the size of a walnut. Roll between the palms of the hands until smooth.
5 Place on the baking tray, well apart, and flatten slightly.
6 Bake for about 20 minutes until crisp and brown.

Hungarian chocolate biscuits

100g/4oz plain flour
25g/1oz cocoa
100g/4oz margarine
50g/2oz sugar
½ teaspoon vanilla essence

Chocolate butter cream
50g/2oz icing sugar
25g/1oz butter or margarine
1 level teaspoon cocoa + 1 teaspoon water

Method
1 Light the oven, Gas 4, 180°C. Place the shelf near the top of the oven. Grease a baking tray.
2 Sieve the flour and cocoa together on to a plate.
3 Cream the margarine, sugar, and vanilla essence. Stir in the flour and mix well.
4 Divide into about 16 pieces, each the size of a walnut. Place well apart on the baking tray. Flatten each one with a fork dipped in cold water.
5 Bake for 15 minutes. Cool on a wire tray.
6 When cool, sandwich with the butter cream. To make the butter cream: mix the cocoa with the water, which should be hot. Sieve the icing sugar into a small basin, add the butter and cocoa, and beat together until smooth and soft.

Melting moments Replace the 25g/1oz cocoa with another 25g/1oz flour. Roll each biscuit in 50g/2oz rolled oats (porage oats). Decorate each with a small piece of cherry (you do not sandwich these together with butter cream).

Viennese creams Replace the 25g/1oz cocoa with another 25g/1oz flour. Sandwich with plain butter cream, leaving out the cocoa.

Scones

Scones take only a short time to make and to bake. They should be eaten quite soon after being made as they contain little fat and so stale quickly. Scones should be light, well risen, and golden brown. Follow these rules for successful scone making:

1 The scone dough should be quite soft.
2 The scones should be at least 1cm/½″ thick before they are put into the oven.
3 They should be cooked at the top of a hot oven.

Plain scones

250g/8oz S.R. flour
Pinch of salt
40g/1½oz margarine
125ml/¼pt milk

Method
1 Light the oven, Gas 7, 220 C. Position the shelf at the top of the oven. Grease a baking tray.
2 Sieve the flour and salt into a bowl. Rub in the margarine.
3 Pour the milk in and mix to a fairly soft, but not sticky, dough.
4 Knead lightly, then roll out. The dough must be at least 1cm/½″ thick. Cut into rounds using a medium cutter and place on the baking tray.
5 Brush with a little milk, then bake for 12–15 minutes until golden brown. Cool on a wire tray.

Currant scones Make and bake in exactly the same way, but add 25g/1oz sugar and 75g/3oz currants to the mixture after you have rubbed in the margarine.

Cheese scones Make and bake in exactly the same way as the plain scones, but add 75g/3oz grated cheese and ½ level teaspoon mustard to the mixture after you have rubbed in the margarine.

Wholemeal scones

125g/4oz wholemeal flour
125g/4oz plain flour
2 level teaspoons baking powder

½ level teaspoon salt
40g/1½oz margarine
125ml/¼pt milk

Method
1 Light the oven, Gas 7, 220°C. Position the shelf at the top of the oven. Grease a baking tray.
2 Put the wholemeal flour into a mixing bowl. Sieve in the plain flour, baking powder, and salt and mix well. Rub in the margarine.
3 Save a little milk to brush the tops, pour the rest into the flour. Mix to a soft but not sticky dough.
4 Knead lightly then cut into 3. Shape each into a round and roll out to 1cm/½″ thick. Place on the baking sheet. Cut each one almost through into quarters.
5 Brush tops with milk, then bake for 15–20 minutes until firm and well risen. Cool on a wire tray.

Victoria scones

25g/8oz S.R. flour
Pinch of salt
50g/2oz lard or margarine
50g/2oz sugar
1 egg plus enough milk to make
   125ml/¼pt of egg and milk altogether
3 glacé cherries

Method

1. Light the oven, Gas 6, 200°C. Position the shelf near the top. Grease a baking sheet.
2. Sieve the flour and salt into a bowl. Rub in the lard or margarine and stir in the sugar.
3. Keep 2 teaspoonfuls of egg and milk to brush the tops. Pour the rest into the flour and mix to a soft dough. Knead it lightly until smooth.
4. Cut into 3 pieces and shape each to a round. Roll out to 1cm/½″ thick. Place on the baking sheet.
5. Cut across the top, almost into quarters. Brush with beaten egg and milk and put a piece of cherry on to each quarter.
6. Bake for about 15–20 minutes until golden brown.

Dropped scones

125g/4oz S.R. flour, pinch of salt
15g/½oz margarine
50g/2oz sugar
1 egg + 4 tablespoons milk
A little lard or oil for girdle or frying pan

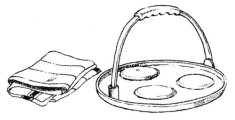

Method

1. Sieve the flour and salt into a bowl, rub in the margarine, and stir in the sugar.
2. Beat the egg and milk and add to the flour a little at a time, beating with a whisk until smooth.
3. Heat the girdle or frying pan with a little lard or oil.
4. Drop tablespoons of the mixture on to the girdle or pan and cook for about 3 minutes on each side. Cook about three at a time.
5. When the scones are cooked, pile them into a clean tea towel to keep them warm and moist. Serve as soon as possible.

Puddings

Hot puddings

As well as those given here, you will find other recipes for puddings in the pastry section.

Custard is served with most hot puddings, so the recipe is given here first of all.

Custard

250ml/½pt milk
2 level tablespoons custard powder
1 level tablespoon sugar

Method

1. Put a little of the milk into a jug or basin, add the custard powder and sugar, and mix until smooth and free from lumps.
2. Bring the rest of the milk to the boil and pour on to the mixture, stirring all the time.
3. The mixture may be thick enough now. If it is not, return it to the pan and simmer gently, stirring all the time until thickened.

Apple crumble   *Serves about 4*

500g/1lb cooking apples
125g/5oz sugar
100g/4oz flour
50g/2oz margarine

Method

1. Light the oven, Gas 5, 190°C. Place the shelf just above the centre of the oven.
2. Put the flour into a mixing bowl. Rub in the margarine, then stir in 75g/3oz of the sugar.
3. Cut the apples into quarters, then remove the peel and core. Cut into slices and place in a 1 litre/2 pint ovenproof dish.
4. Sprinkle the rest of the sugar on to the apples, then cover them with the crumble mixture.
5. Bake for about 40 minutes until the apples are soft and the crumble is pale golden brown.
6. Serve with custard.

For a change, you could make a crumble with a different kind of fruit:

Plum crumble – use 500g/1lb plums instead of apples.

Rhubarb crumble – use 500g/1lb rhubarb

Gooseberry crumble – use 500g/1lb gooseberries.

Blackberry and apple crumble – use 500g/1lb mixed blackberries and apples.

Jam roly-poly   *Serves about 4*

Suet pastry
150g/6oz self-raising flour
pinch of salt
75g/3oz shredded suet
Water to mix

3 tablespoons jam

Method
1   Make the pastry: mix the flour, salt, and suet in a bowl. Add enough water to mix to a firm dough.
2   Turn on to a floured board, knead lightly till smooth. Roll out to 20cm/8″ square.
3   Spread the jam to within 2cm/1″ of the edges. Damp the edges and roll up, pressing the ends firmly together.
4   To steam: Wrap the roll loosely in greased foil or greaseproof paper and steam for 2–2½ hours.
5   To bake: Place unwrapped on a greased baking tray and bake for 40–45 minutes, Gas 6, 200°C, just above the centre of the oven.
6   Serve with custard.

Apple charlotte   *Serves about 4*

100g/4oz caster sugar
100g/4oz white bread
500g/1lb cooking apples
1 lemon
75g/3oz butter, margarine, or suet

Method
1   Light the oven, Gas 5, 190°C. Place the shelf in the centre of the oven.
2   Grate the bread to make crumbs (or use a blender). Mix the crumbs and sugar together. Wash the lemon. Grate the rind finely, and add to the crumbs.
3   Cut the apples into quarters, remove the peel and core. Slice.
4   Put alternate layers of breadcrumbs mixture and apple into the dish, finishing with a layer of crumbs.
5   Melt the butter in a small pan and pour over the pudding.
6   Bake for about 45 minutes until the apples are soft and the pudding is golden brown.

Stewed fruit   *Serves 3–4*

500g/1lb apples, plums, gooseberries, rhubarb, or other fruit
75g/3oz sugar
125ml/¼pt water

Method

1   Wash and prepare the fruit.
2   Put the sugar and water in a saucepan. Stir gently over a low heat until the sugar has dissolved.
3   Add the fruit and simmer very gently on a very low heat until the fruit is cooked.
4   Serve either hot or cold with custard or a baked egg custard or a milk pudding.

Steamed sponge pudding (jam or syrup) *Serves about 4*

125g/4oz S.R. flour
125g/4oz margarine
125g/4oz sugar (preferably caster)
2 eggs
2 tablespoons jam or syrup

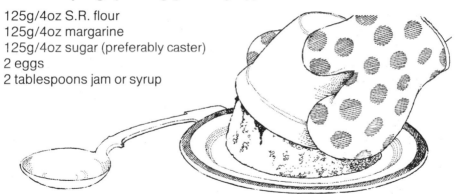

Method
1 Prepare a piece of double-thickness greaseproof paper or a piece of foil, and grease it in the centre. This is for the top of the pudding.
2 Grease a 750ml/1½pt pudding basin. It is important to use exactly the right size to make a well-shaped pudding.
3 Put a large pan, half full of water, on to boil. Fill a kettle with water and put it on a low heat.
4 Sieve the flour into a bowl. Add the margarine, sugar, and eggs, and beat well with a wooden spoon until the mixture is light coloured and fluffy.
5 Put the jam or syrup in the pudding basin, and the mixture on top. Cover with the greaseproof paper or foil.
6 Put in the steamer, put the lid on, and steam gently for 1¼ hours. Refill the pan with boiling water from the kettle, as necessary.

When cooked, turn out on to a plate and serve with custard.

Steamed chocolate pudding Use 100g/3oz flour and 25g/1oz cocoa instead of 125g/4oz flour.

Chocolate sauce to go with the pudding: Make custard as on page 187 but add one level tablespoon of cocoa to the custard powder.

Steamed currant pudding Add 50g/2oz currants to the pudding mixture, leave out the jam or syrup.

To make a smaller sponge pudding to fit a 500ml/1 pint basin:
100g/4oz S.R. flour
50g/2oz margarine
50g/2oz sugar (preferably caster)
1 egg
2 tablespoons water or milk
1 tablespoon jam or syrup (or 25g/1oz currants)
Make in the same way as above and steam for 1 hour.

To cook the puddings in a pressure cooker
1 Put 750ml/1½pts water and the trivet in the pressure cooker. Bring to the boil.
2 Place the covered pudding on the trivet, put on the lid but not the weight. Steam gently for 15 minutes.
3 Put the L/5lb weight on the cooker. Bring to pressure, then cook the larger pudding for 30 minutes, the smaller pudding for 20 minutes.

Pineapple upside-down pudding   *Serves about 4*

1 small can pineapple rings
2 glacé cherries
About 2 tablespoons golden syrup
100g/4oz self-raising flour
100g/4oz soft margarine
100g/4oz caster sugar
2 eggs

Method
1   Light the oven, Gas 4, 180°C. Place the shelf in the centre of the oven.
2   Grease the tin. Use either a deep 18cm/7″ cake tin or a 20cm/8″ sandwich cake tin or deep cake tin.
3   Cover the bottom of the tin with a thin layer of golden syrup. Drain the pineapple rings and place them on the syrup with half a cherry in the centre of each ring.
4   Sieve the flour into a bowl. Add the margarine, sugar, and eggs, and beat well until light and fluffy. Spread this mixture carefully over the pineapples.
5   Bake for about 45 minutes until firm. Turn out on to a plate.

Serve with either custard or pineapple sauce.

Pineapple sauce Put the syrup from the tin of pineapples into a measuring jug. Add enough water to make 250ml/½pt liquid. Put this into a small pan and add a rounded teaspoon of arrowroot or cornflour, a rounded teaspoon of sugar, and 2 teaspoons of lemon juice. Bring this to the boil, stirring all the time, until thick.

Pancakes   *Serves about 4*

100g/4oz plain flour
Pinch of salt
1 egg
250ml/½pt milk
Sugar, preferable caster
1 large lemon (or about 3 tablespoons lemon juice)
Lard or oil for frying

Method
1   Put the flour and salt into a bowl. Drop the egg in the centre, add a little milk and beat well with a whisk until smooth. Whisk in the rest of the milk a little at a time. Or blend all the ingredients for about 30 seconds until smooth.
2   Cut the lemon in two, squeeze out the juice.
3   Put a pan of water to heat, with a plate on top. This is to keep the pancakes warm until they are all made.
4   Heat a little lard or oil in a frying pan. There should be enough to cover the bottom of the pan. The pan should ideally be a small pan, about 15cm/6″ in diameter, but use whatever size is available.
5   When the fat is hot, pour in just enough batter to cover the bottom of the pan. Cook for 2 or 3 minutes until the bottom of the pancake is golden brown, then toss or turn it over and cook the other side.
6   Put it on to the plate to keep hot. Sprinkle it with a little lemon juice and sugar. Cook the rest of the pancakes.
7   When they are all cooked, roll each one up and serve on a warm serving dish.

Rice pudding   *Serves 3–4*

50g/2oz pudding rice
50g/2oz sugar
500ml/1pt milk
15g/½oz butter

Method
1   Light the oven, Gas 2, 150°C. Place the shelf in the centre or below. Grease a 750ml/1½pt ovenproof dish.
2   Put the rice into a sieve and wash it under cold running water. Put it into the dish and sprinkle it with sugar. Pour the milk over. Dot with the butter.
3   Bake for about 2 hours until the rice is soft and the top is golden brown.

Rice pudding cooked in a pressure cooker This is much quicker to cook and makes a very creamy pudding. Use the same ingredients as above.

Method
1   Melt the butter in the pressure cooker. Add the milk and bring to the boil. Add the washed rice and sugar and bring to the boil again.
2   Adjust the heat so that the milk continues to just boil in the bottom of the pan. Do not alter the heat again.
3   Put the lid and H/15lb pressure weight on the pan. Bring to pressure then cook for 12 minutes. Allow the pressure to reduce at room temperature.
4   Stir the pudding well and pour on to a serving dish. If you wish, you can brown the top under a grill or at the top of the oven.

Baked egg custard   *Serves 3–4*

2 eggs
375ml/¾pt milk
2 level tablespoons sugar
½ teaspoon vanilla essence (optional)
Nutmeg

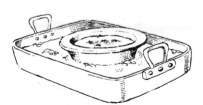

Method
1   Light the oven, Gas 3, 160°C. Place the shelf in the centre. Grease a 500ml/1pt ovenproof dish.
2   Beat the eggs, sugar, and vanilla essence together. Warm the milk until bubbles appear around the sides of the pan. Pour it on to the eggs and beat well.
3   Pour the mixture through a sieve into the pie dish. Place the dish in a roasting tin. Add enough warm water to come half-way up the side of the dish.
4   Sprinkle a little grated nutmeg on to the custard, then bake for about 45–55 minutes until the custard is set.

Serve hot or cold, with stewed fruit or fresh fruit salad.

Using the pressure cooker
Baked egg custard can be made very quickly in the pressure cooker; it will only take five minutes to cook. Make in the same way as above. Pour into a basin which will fit into the pressure cooker. Cover it with a double thickness of greaseproof paper. Put the trivet in the cooker, add 250ml/½pt water and place the basin on the trivet. Put on the lid and bring to H/15lb pressure. Cook for 5 minutes, then allow to cool at room temperature.

Cold puddings

Fruit fool   *Serves 4*

500g/1lb cooking apples or rhubarb or other fruit
75g/3oz sugar
About 5 tablespoons of water
250ml/½pt milk
1 rounded tablespoon of custard powder
1 level tablespoon sugar
Grated chocolate to decorate

Method

1 Cut the apple into quarters, remove the peel and core; or wash the rhubarb. Cut into slices and put these into a small pan with the water.
2 Simmer very gently with the lid on until the fruit is soft. Remove from the heat and stir in the 75g/3oz sugar.
3 Make the custard: put most of the milk into a pan, leaving about 4 tablespoonfuls in a jug or basin. Add the custard powder and sugar to the milk in the jug and mix until it is completely free from lumps. Bring the milk in the pan to the boil, then pour it into the jug, stirring all the time.
4 The custard may now be thick, but if it is not, pour it back into the pan and bring to the boil, stirring all the time until thick.
5 Put the custard and the fruit into the blender, blend until smooth then pour into glass dishes.
6 When it is cold, decorate with a little grated chocolate.

Fresh fruit salad   *Serves about 4*

1 apple (preferably red-skinned)
1 pear
1 banana
1 orange
50g/2oz grapes
1 lemon
250ml/½pt water
100g/4oz sugar

Method

1 Make the syrup by dissolving the sugar in the water in a small pan. When the sugar is completely dissolved bring the syrup to the boil. Boil for about 1 minute, then pour into a large bowl to cool.
2 Squeeze the juice from the lemon and add it to the syrup.
3 Wash the apple, cut it into quarters, remove the core. Cut into slices and put in the syrup. Cut the pear into quarters, remove the peel and core, add to the syrup.
4 Peel and slice the banana and orange, add to the syrup.
5 Wash the grapes, cut into two and remove the pips. Add to the syrup.
6 Serve the fruit salad when completely cold, with custard or baked egg custard.

Lemon cheesecake *Serves 4–5*

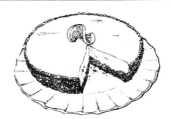

150g/6oz digestive biscuits
75g/3oz butter or margarine
225g/8oz cottage cheese
125ml/¼pt fresh double or whipping cream
50g/2oz caster sugar
1 lemon

Method

1 Put the biscuits into a polythene bag and crush with a rolling pin or else use a blender to make them into crumbs.
2 Melt the butter in a pan, stir in the biscuit crumbs. Use this to line the base and sides of a flan case or shallow dish, about 20cm/8″ in diameter. Put in a cold place.
3 Wash the lemon. Grate the skin finely and squeeze out the juice.
4 Whip the cream until thick. Sieve the cottage cheese into the cream. Fold in the sugar, lemon rind, and lemon juice.
5 Spread the mixture over the crumbs and chill before serving.

Jelly whip *Serves 4–5*

1 small can evaporated milk   Small carton of double or whipping cream (optional)
1 packet of jelly   Grated chocolate or flake to decorate

Method

1 Put the jelly into a small pan and add 125ml/¼pt of water. Warm gently, stirring until the jelly is dissolved. Do not allow it to boil.
2 Pour this into a large mixing bowl and add a further 125ml/¼pt cold water. Leave until completely cold.
3 Very slowly, pour the milk into the jelly, whisking all the time until the mixture is frothy. Pour into a serving dish. Leave in a cool place to set.
4 Decorate with whipped cream, and sprinkle with a little grated chocolate.

Crunchy chocolate flan *Serves 4–5*

150g/6oz digestive biscuits
75g/3oz butter or margarine
Packet of chocolate dessert mix
250ml/½pt milk
Grated chocolate to decorate

Method

1 Melt the butter in a pan. Use a little of it to grease a 20cm/8″ flan ring or a tin or dish with shallow sides.
2 Put the biscuits in a polythene bag and crush with a rolling pin, or use a blender to make them into crumbs.
3 Add the crumbs to the butter in the pan and stir until they are all moistened. Use them to line the sides and base of the flan ring, tin, or dish.
4 Make up the dessert mix with the milk as directed on the packet. Pour into the crumb case and chill. Remove the flan ring if you have used one.
5 Decorate with a little grated chocolate and serve cold.

Cooking with yeast

Making your own bread and rolls at home is very satisfying. It saves quite a lot of money and using the quick modern methods given here it does not take long. Provided you follow the instructions exactly, it is easy to achieve good results.

The flour to use

Choosing the right flour is important when you are making bread. It makes all the difference between getting good and poor results. You should use strong flour, which is marked 'strong' or 'bread' flour on the packet.

Strong flour is made from hard wheat, usually imported from North America or Canada. It contains more of a substance called gluten than does the soft wheat grown in this country. When the gluten is mixed with water and kneaded it becomes stretchy, elastic, and strong. It will rise easily and hold the bubbles of carbon dioxide gas which the yeast produces. In this way it forms a strong framework for the bread and gives a well-shaped loaf with a good texture. It is difficult to achieve good results with ordinary soft plain flour.

Wholemeal flour and brown or wheatmeal flour are also suitable for breadmaking, as they are ground from a hard wheat (see cereals, page 148).

Yeast

Yeast is a living, unicellular plant. If it is killed by excess heat it will not work and make the bread rise, so it must be carefully treated.

How the yeast works
In the right conditions the yeast cells will reproduce and increase in number. As they do this, alcohol and carbon dioxide gas are produced. The bubbles of gas are held in the stretchy framework of the dough and so the dough grows in size. Once it has increased in size sufficiently to give a light, well-risen loaf, it is put into a hot oven, the yeast is killed, and the dough does not rise any further.

Yeast needs moisture and food in order to grow. When you make bread, moisture is provided by the water or milk in the dough. The food is provided by sugars in the flour. Warmth encourages the yeast to grow more quickly, but it is not essential. Bread dough will rise in a refrigerator overnight and this cool rise produces a good, well-shaped loaf.

Too much warmth or heat will kill the yeast cells so you must be careful to avoid mixing the yeast with hot water or leaving it to rise in too hot a place.

The type of yeast to use
Wherever possible, use fresh yeast. All the recipes in this book are made with fresh yeast, mainly because it produces much quicker results and so saves a lot of time. Dried yeast will give good results but you will have to wait longer for the dough to rise.

Sometimes you cannot buy fresh yeast very easily. When you do find a shop where you can buy fresh yeast it is useful to buy a fairly large amount, perhaps 8oz/250g. Divide it into ½oz/15g portions, wrap each in greaseproof paper or foil and put it in a plastic box. You can store this in the freezer for several months, or in the freezing compartment of a refrigerator for up to a month. It keeps very well and this enables you to keep a store of fresh yeast in useful-sized portions. It does not need to be defrosted before use. Just put the frozen piece of yeast into the warm water and it will dissolve easily.

Dried yeast has the advantage of being more widely available in most shops and supermarkets. There are two types:

1 The kind which you stir straight into the flour while still dry. This is quick and easy to use.
2 Dried yeast which is mixed with water and left until it becomes frothy before you use it.

To use this dried yeast instead of fresh in any of these recipes, prepare the yeast and water mix before you do anything else, so that it will be ready to use by the time you have weighed out the other ingredients and prepared the tin and oven. Measure out the water as in the recipe so that it is just warm. Add 2 level teaspoons of dried yeast and a good pinch of sugar. Stir well, then leave until frothy. Continue exactly as in the recipe.

Fresh yeast.   Dried yeast.

Ascorbic acid tablets

You can buy these from the chemist as ascorbic acid or Vitamin C tablets. They are used in these recipes as they help strengthen the gluten while the dough is kneaded and rising.

Margarine and salt

A small amount of margarine or lard is added to the flour. It helps the bread to keep fresh a little longer, but it is not essential.

Salt is added to bring out the flavour of the bread. It also helps to prevent the dough from being too sticky.

The water temperature

It is important that you use water which is at the right temperature. It should be just lukewarm or at blood-heat. If you dip your finger into the water it should feel neither hotter not cooler than your finger. If the water is too hot, the yeast may be killed and the bread dough will not rise. If the water is too cold, it will rise much more slowly.

When you add the water to the flour the mixture should be fairly soft and sticky at first. If it is too dry and hard it will be difficult to knead and the bread may be heavy. As flours vary in the amount of water they absorb, you may have to add a little more than the recipe states. Wholemeal and brown flours particularly may need a little more water to ensure a soft pliable dough.

Kneading

This is an important part of breadmaking. It makes the gluten stretchy and strong so that the dough can both rise easily and hold its risen shape. Knead the dough as vigorously as you can, pulling and stretching it to develop the gluten. If you have a large electric mixer you can use a dough hook attachment.

Leaving the dough to rise

The dough can be left to rise in the tins in a warm place or on the kitchen bench or table, or in the refrigerator for a slower rise. In a warmer place the dough will rise more quickly, but too hot a temperature may kill the yeast. The dough should be covered loosely during rising to prevent a hard skin forming on the surface. Wrap the tin loosely in a polythene bag or cover it with a slightly damp tea-towel.

Traditional method
In recipes using larger quantities you can leave the dough to rise in the mixing bowl after you have kneaded it. Once it has doubled in size you knead it again lightly, shape it into loaves, leave it to rise again to the top of the tin, then bake it.

Baking

Bread should be baked in a hot oven, Gas 8, 230°C. The heat will cause the bread to rise a little more at first, then the yeast cells will be killed and the bread will be baked and 'set' in its risen shape. Test the bread to see if it is cooked by turning it out of the tin and tapping it underneath. If it is cooked it will sound crisp and hollow. Leave it to cool on a wire tray.

It is not necessary to brush bread before baking, but to give it a particularly attractive appearance you can brush bread rolls or round loaves with beaten egg and milk and sprinkle them with poppy seeds.

General instructions for making bread by the 'quick' method

1 Mix the flour, salt, and fat.
2 Mix the water, ascorbic acid, and yeast.
3 Mix the flour and water, knead well.
4 Shape into loaf or rolls.
5 Cover and leave to rise.
6 Bake in a hot oven.

Questions

1 **Why is it essential to use strong flour for breadmaking?**
2 **What is gluten?**
3 **What are the conditions needed for yeast to grow?**
4 **Explain how the yeast causes the dough to rise.**
5 **What is the advantage of using fresh yeast rather than dried?**
6 **How would you store fresh yeast in a freezer?**
7 **How much dried yeast would you use instead of ½oz/15g fresh yeast?**
8 **Describe how you would obtain water which was about blood-heat temperature. How would you test it before adding the yeast?**
9 **Why is it necessary to knead bread dough?**

Recipes

Bread *To make a small loaf, quick method*

250g/½lb strong white, brown, or wholemeal flour
1 level teaspoon salt
15g/½oz margarine
15g/½oz fresh yeast
125ml/¼pt water
1 × 25mg ascorbic acid tablet (optional)

Method
1   Light the oven, Gas 8, 230°C. Place the shelf just above the centre of the oven. Grease a small loaf tin.
2   Put the flour into a bowl, add the salt, rub in the margarine.
3   Put 4 tablespoons of boiling water into a measuring jug. Crush the tablet and dissolve it in the water. Add enough cold water to make 125ml/¼pt.
4   Add the yeast to the water and stir to dissolve it. Pour into the flour and mix together. The dough must be soft at this stage. If it seems dry, add another 2–3 tablespoons of water.
5   Knead firmly for 10 minutes, then shape into a loaf. To shape, turn the edges to the centre and press firmly. Repeat until smooth (1).
6   Place the dough in the tin, smooth side upward. Put the tin into a large polythene bag (2). Leave it in a warm place until the dough reaches right up to the top of the tin (3).
7   Bake for about 40 minutes. To see if it is cooked, remove the loaf from the tin and tap it underneath. It should sound crisp and hollow. Cool on a wire rack.

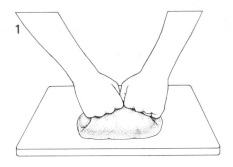

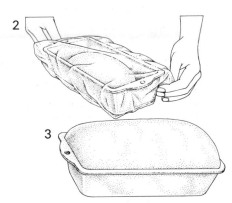

Quick bread buns

250g/½lb strong white, brown, or wholemeal flour
1 level teaspoon salt
15g/½oz margarine
15g/½oz fresh yeast
125ml/¼pt water
1 × 25mg ascorbic acid tablet (optional)

Method
1   Light the oven, Gas 8, 230°C. Place the shelf near the top of the oven. Grease a 20cm/8″ sandwich cake tin.

2   Put the flour in the bowl, stir in the salt, rub in the margarine.

3   Put 4 tablespoons of boiling water into a measuring jug. Crush the tablet, then dissolve it in the water. Add enough cold water to make 125ml/¼pt.

4   Add the yeast to the water and stir to dissolve it. Pour into the flour and mix together. The dough must be soft at this stage. If it seems dry, add another 2–3 tablespoons of water.

5   Knead firmly for 10 minutes, then cut into 8 pieces. Shape each into a bread bun and arrange in the tin.

6   Put the tin into a large polythene bag, then leave in a warm place to rise.

7   When the buns have risen to the top of the tin, bake for 15–20 minutes. To see if they are cooked, tap them underneath. If done they will sound crisp and hollow. Cool on a wire rack.

Pizza   *For a quick cheese pizza see page 140*

Dough
250g/½lb wholemeal flour,
   or brown or strong white
1 level teaspoon salt
15g/½oz margarine
15g/½oz fresh yeast
125ml/¼pt water

1 tin tomatoes (or 250g/½lb fresh tomatoes)
100g/4oz cheese
Salt, pepper, pinch of oregano or mixed herbs
50g/2oz mushrooms
1 onion
15g/½oz margarine
Tin of sardines, pilchards, or anchovies (optional)

Method

1   Light the oven, Gas 7, 220°C. Place the shelf near the top of the oven. Grease a baking sheet.

2   Put the flour and salt into a bowl, rub in the margarine.

3   Put 4 tablespoons of boiling water into a measuring jug. Add enough cold water to make 125ml/¼pt. Add the yeast and stir to dissolve.

4   Pour into the flour and mix to a soft dough. Add a little more water if necessary. Knead for 5 minutes. Roll out to a large circle, about 9″ in diameter, and leave in a warm place while you prepare the filling.

5   Drain the tomatoes, or slice if fresh ones. Grate the cheese. Peel and chop the onion, wash and slice the mushrooms. Fry the onions and mushrooms in the margarine until soft.

6   Put the tomatoes, cheese, onion, and mushrooms over the dough, add a pinch of oregano or mixed herbs and a little salt and pepper. Arrange the fish on top if you are using it.

7   Bake for about 30 minutes, until the base is cooked. Cool on a wire tray. Serve with a salad.

Chelsea buns

250g/8oz strong white flour
½ level teaspoon salt
15g/½oz margarine
125ml/¼pt milk
15g/½oz fresh yeast
1 × 25mg ascorbic acid tablet

Filling
25g/1oz butter or margarine
75g/3oz currants
25g/1oz sugar

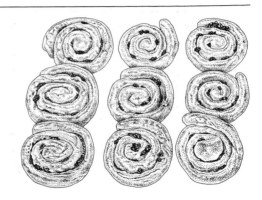

Method

1. Light the oven, Gas 7, 220°C. Place the shelf just above the centre of the oven. Grease a deep-sided roasting tin or Swiss roll tin.
2. Put the flour and salt into a bowl, rub in the margarine.
3. Crush the tablet, put it into a pan with the milk and stir until it is dissolved. Warm the milk till it is just lukewarm, not hot. Dissolve the yeast in the milk.
4. Pour the milk into the flour and mix well. The dough must be soft, so add another 1–2 tablespoons milk or water if necessary.
5. Knead the dough for 10 minutes until it is smooth and elastic. Roll out into a square, about 25cm × 25cm (10″ × 10″) (1).
6. Put the butter for the filling into a small pan, warm until melted. Brush it over the dough then sprinkle with the currants and sugar (2).
7. Brush the far side of the dough with water, then roll it up like a Swiss roll (3). Cut this into 9 slices and place these into the tin (4). Put into a large polythene bag and leave to rise right to the top of the tin (5).

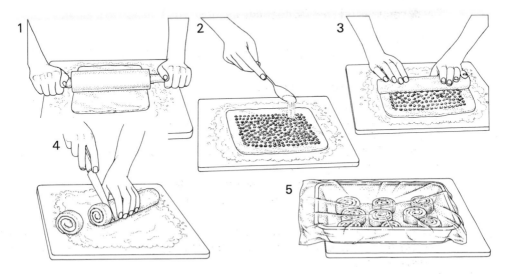

8. Bake for about 20 minutes, turning the oven down to Gas 5, 190°C, if the buns become too brown.

If you like, you can ice the buns when they are cooked. Make the icing by sieving 75g/3oz icing sugar and mixing with about 1 tablespoon water. Trickle lightly over the buns.

Jam and preserves

Making jam at home is an ideal way of preserving fruit in season for use throughout the year. Good home-made jam has a very good, fruity flavour, a clear bright colour, a firm set, and will keep well.

Jam is made from two main ingredients, fruit and sugar. The fruit has to contain plenty of pectin and acid if it is to set properly. Some fruits contain plenty of pectin and acid and so will set easily. These are often the hard sour fruits such as plums or damsons. Other fruits contain less pectin and acid, so to make sure that the jam sets well you have to add pectin or acid in some form.

Fruits which contain plenty of pectin and acid and so set easily	*Fruits with a moderate amount of pectin and acid*	*Fruits with low pectin and acid content which do not set well*
Gooseberries	Blackberries	Strawberries
Apples	Raspberries	Rhubarb
Plums, Damsons	Apricots	Cherries
Black-and redcurrants		

Pectin

Pectin is a gum-like substance found in the cell walls of ripe fruit in varying amounts. In under-ripe fruit it is in the form of pectose which can be turned to pectin when the fruit is stewed with an acid. In over-ripe fruit the pectin has turned to pectic acid and has lost its setting properties. This means that you should choose fruit which is either ripe or under-ripe for making jam. Avoid fruits which are over-ripe as results are likely to be poor.

If the fruit you are using is low in pectin you can add to it either:

1   Some fruit of a kind with plenty of pectin, e.g. apples to blackberries, gooseberries or blackcurrants to strawberries.
2   Pectin in powder or liquid form, e.g. 'Certo'. Buy this from a chemist or grocer.

Acid

Acid is needed in jam:
1   To convert any pectose to pectin and thus help it to set.
2   To improve the flavour and colour of the jam.
3   To prevent hard crystals of sugar forming in the jam when you store it.

If you are using fruits which are low in acid you can add it in the form of one of the following, before you start to cook the fruit:
1   Lemon juice (about 2 tablespoons to each 1kg/2lb of fruit).
2   Citric or tartaric acid, or cream of tartar (½–1 level teaspoon for each 1kg/2lbs fruit). You can buy this at a chemist's or grocer's.

Sugar

Use granulated sugar as it is cheapest and gives good results. You can buy special preserving sugar. This is meant to dissolve more easily and to produce a little less scum, but it is more expensive and not really necessary.

General method for making jam

1 Prepare the jam jars.
2 Prepare the fruit according to what kind it is and cook gently until completely soft.
3 Add the sugar and dissolve thoroughly.
4 Boil vigorously until setting point is reached.
5 Pour into the jars, cover, and label.

To prepare the jam jars
It is essential that these are clean, dry, and warm. Wash them thoroughly in warm, soapy water, rinse, and drain. Dry the outsides with a clean tea-towel. Warm the jars by standing them on a wooden board on the floor of a very low oven or by placing them above a warm cooker.

To test for setting point
Once the sugar has been dissolved in the cooked fruit, the jam is vigorously boiled until setting point is reached, usually in about 15–20 minutes. You have to test the jam to see if it has reached this point. There are several tests:

1 **The wrinkle test** This is the simplest method. Place a small saucer in the fridge. When you think that the jam may have reached setting point, remove it from the heat. Put a small teaspoon of jam on to the cold plate and let it cool a little. Push the jam with your fingertips over the plate. If it wrinkles on the surface the jam should set. If not, boil for a little longer and test again.

2 **The flake test** Use a clean, dry, wooden spoon to remove a little jam from the pan. Allow it to cool slightly. Gently pour the jam over the side of the spoon. If it comes off in wide flakes it is ready. If it pours off the spoon in a thin trickle it is not.

a good flake   jam not ready

3 **The thermometer test** The jam should reach a temperature of 104°C or 105°C before it has the sugar concentration of 65% which is necessary for it to set. Keep the thermometer in a pan of boiling water beside the jam pan. It enables you to check it for accuracy (the water boils at 100°C) and makes the thermometer easier to clean.

Removing scum
Scum is just made up of small bubbles of air which have been caught up in the sticky, boiling jam. It is harmless, but spoils the appearance of the jam. Once the jam has reached setting point, remove it from the heat. Stir in a small piece of butter or margarine. This will disperse most of the scum from the jam. If any remains, remove it with a metal spoon.

Filling the jars
This should be done while the jam is very hot, unless you are making strawberry jam or marmalade. With these, you allow the jam to cool for 15 minutes in the pan, so that all the fruit does not rise to the top of the jar.

Fill the jars very carefully as the hot jam can scald your hands badly. Use a jug to scoop the jam out of the pan. Scrape the bottom of the jug on the edge of the pan, then pour the jam into the jars. Fill them right to the top as jam shrinks when it cools.

Stand the jars on a board or baking tray and position each one right at the edge of the pan before you fill it. This keeps the outside of the jars clean and avoids splashes. Never hold a jar in your hands while pouring hot jam into it.

To cover the jars

As soon as you have filled them, place a waxed disc over the jam, wax side down. Damp the cellophane covers in a saucer of water, on one side only. Place the dry side down, and secure with an elastic band. You can use jars with screw-top lids instead of cellophane tops.

Remove any splashes from the outside of the jars with a damp cloth. Place a label on the jar with the name of the jam and date.

If you want to decorate the jars with small circles or squares of cotton fabric, place these over the cellophane cover or screw-top jar and secure with an elastic band. Store the jam in a cool, dry, dark place.

Common faults in making jam	Possible causes
Jam will not set.	The jam has not been boiled for long enough and so has not reached setting point. The fruit is over-ripe. Fruit is of a kind low in pectin or acid and you have not added anything to counteract this, e.g. lemon juice, cream of tartar.
Jam goes mouldy or ferments.	Not enough sugar. Storing in a damp, warm place.
Crystals in the jam.	Jam has been boiled too long. Too little acid.
Jam which is thick and stiff.	Boiled for too long past setting point.
Fruit which is tough and hard.	Fruit not properly cooked before sugar is added.

Questions

1 **What four ingredients are necessary for making well-set jam?**
2 **What is pectin?**
3 **Why is over-ripe fruit unsuitable for jam-making?**
4 **If you are making jam using fruit which is low in pectin and acid, how can you ensure the jam will set?**
5 **Describe the 'wrinkle test' for setting point.**
6 **How would you prepare the jars to be used for making jam?**

7 **What precautions would you take to avoid scalds when you are pouring hot jam into the jars?**
8 **What results would you expect if:**
a **you boiled the jam for too long?**
b **you boiled the jam for too short a time?**
c **you make strawberry jam without adding any ingredient except sugar?**
d **you stored jam in a cupboard which was slightly damp?**

Recipes

Strawberry jam *Makes about 1¼kg/2½lb*

1kg/2lb strawberries
1½ level teaspoons cream of tartar <u>or</u> 2 tablespoons lemon juice
900g/1¾lb sugar
15g/½oz margarine

Method
1 Hull and wash the strawberries. Cut them in half and put them in the pan with the cream of tartar or lemon juice.
2 Simmer very gently in their own juice for about 20 minutes until the fruit is soft. Add the sugar, stir until dissolved, then boil rapidly until setting point is reached.
3 Add the margarine and stir it around the pan. Allow the jam to cool for 15 minutes to prevent the fruit rising in the jars.
4 Carefully pour into the warm jars, cover, and label.

Plum jam *Makes about 2½kg/5lb*

1½kg/3lb plums
450ml/¾pt water
1½kg/3lb sugar
15g/½oz butter or margarine

Method
1 Wash the plums in a colander. Put them into a pan with the water. Simmer gently until the plums are cooked, about 15 minutes.
2 Add the sugar and stir until it is dissolved. Boil briskly until setting point is reached.
3 Take from the heat and remove all the stones with a perforated spoon. Stir in the butter to remove the scum.
4 Pour into clean, warm jars, cover, and label.

Raspberry jam   *Makes about 1¼kg/2½lb*

1kg/2lb raspberries
1kg/2lb sugar
15g/½oz butter or margarine

Method
1   Put the raspberries into the pan, simmer very gently to extract the juice.
2   Add the sugar and stir over a low heat until all the sugar is dissolved.
3   Boil quickly until the jam is at setting point. Stir in the butter to remove the scum.
4   Pot, cover, and label.

Rhubarb and ginger jam   *Makes about 2½kg/5lb*

1.5kg/3lb rhubarb
2 lemons
1.5kg/3lb sugar

3 level teaspoons ground ginger
15g/½oz margarine

Method
1   Wash and trim the rhubarb, cut it into short lengths. Put it in layers, with the sugar and the lemon juice, in a large bowl. Leave for 24 hours.
2   Prepare the jam jars.
3   Put the rhubarb and sugar into a pan, add the ground ginger. Stir gently over a low heat until all the sugar is dissolved.
4   Boil quickly until the jam is a fairly thick consistency. This jam does not set as firmly as other jams but is always firm enough to spread properly.
5   Stir in the margarine to remove any scum.
6   Carefully pour into the warm jars, cover and label.

Marmalade   *Makes about 2½kg/5lb*

750g/1½lbs Seville oranges
1 lemon
1¾litres/3pts water

1½kg/3lbs sugar
15g/½oz butter

Method
1   Scrub the oranges. Cut them in half and squeeze out the juice. Squeeze the juice from the lemon.
2   Tie all the pips in muslin.
3   Slice the orange peel very finely (or mince it).
4   Put the orange juice and peel, the pips, and the lemon juice into a large pan (a pressure cooker is very time-saving), and add the water.
5   Bring to the boil, cover and simmer gently for 1½–2 hours until the peel is soft (or pressure cook for 20 minutes at H/15lbs pressure, then reduce pressure at room temperature).
6   Remove the bag of pips and throw it away.
7   Add the sugar and stir over a low heat until all the sugar is dissolved.
8   Bring to the boil, boil until setting point is reached.
9   Stir in the butter, to get rid of any scum. Leave in the pan until a skin forms on the surface. Stir gently, then pot and cover.

Lemon curd   *Makes about 500g/1¼lb*

50g/2oz butter or margarine
3 eggs

200g/8oz sugar
1 large or 2 small lemons

Method

1 Melt the margarine or butter in a double pan. If you do not have a double pan, place a large bowl over a pan of water.
2 Wash and dry the lemon. Grate the rind finely, then squeeze out the juice. Add this to the pan. Then add the sugar.
3 Beat the eggs and add to the pan. Stir with a wooden spoon until the mixture is thick enough to coat the back of the spoon. Keep the water just <u>below</u> boiling point.
4 Pour into clean, warm, small jars. Keep in a cold place and eat within 2 weeks.

Mincemeat (sweet)   *Makes about 1½kg/3lb*

250g/½lb cooking apples
250g/½lb raisins
250g/½lb currants
250g/½lb sultanas
250g/½lb suet

1 lemon or orange
1 level teaspoon mixed spice
25g/1oz mixed peel (optional)
250g/8oz soft brown sugar
3 tablespoons brandy (optional)

Method

1 Cut the apples into quarters, remove the peel and core.
2 Grate the orange or lemon rind. Squeeze out the juice.
3 Mince the apples and the dried fruit. If you do not have a mincer, chop them finely.
4 Put them into a bowl with all the other ingredients and mix well.
5 Pack into clean, dry jars. Only fill to within 2cm/½" of the top. Cover and label as for jam. If possible, leave for a few weeks to mature before using.

Tomato chutney   *Makes about 1kg/2lb*

500g/1lb apples
500g/1lb tomatoes, green or red
250g/½lb sultanas or dates
100g/4oz sugar
500ml/1pt vinegar
1 level teaspoon salt

1 level teaspoon ground ginger
1 level teaspoon mustard
½ level teaspoon pepper
1 large onion
1 tablespoon brown sauce (optional)

Method

1 Cut the apple into quarters, remove the peel and core, chop roughly. Peel and chop the onion, chop the tomatoes.
2 Put all the ingredients into a large pan, bring to the boil and simmer very gently for about 1½ hours, until smooth and thick.
3 Pour into clean, warm jars. Cover with plastic lids (e.g. from instant coffee jars). Metal lids must not be used as they will affect the taste of the chutney. Label and date.

To cook in the pressure cooker Cook at H/15lb pressure for 15 minutes, but use only 250ml/½pt vinegar. Remove the lid and simmer until smooth and thick.

Cleaning the kitchen

To clean the kitchen thoroughly

You will need:
hot water
cleaning cloths
mop or floor-cloth
non-scratch cleaner
disinfectant
broom, dustpan and brush

1 Open the window to air the room.
2 Clean the refrigerator, defrosting if necessary.
3 Clean the cooker, including the oven.
4 Clean the larder or food cupboard.
5 Wash the paintwork, window sills, and cupboard doors with hot water and non-scratch cleaner. Rinse and wipe dry.
6 Wash the work surfaces with hot water and liquid detergent or non-scratch cleaner. Rinse and wipe dry.
7 Empty the waste bin. Wash with hot soapy water and disinfectant.
8 Sweep the floor. Wash with hot soapy water and disinfectant.
9 Thoroughly wash and dry the sink and draining-board. Use hot soapy water and a little non-scratch cleaner if necessary.

To clean a cooker

You will need:
steel wool soaped pads or a non-scratch cleaner
dishcloth, dry cloth
bowl of hot water, detergent

For the oven:
rubber gloves
oven cleaner
cloth

1 If electric, switch the cooker off at the wall.
   Turn off any gas pilot lights.
2 If you are going to clean the oven, apply the oven cleaner if required, wearing rubber gloves. Make sure you use this only on suitable surfaces, not on self-cleaning oven linings. Leave it to work while you clean the rest of the cooker.
3 Soak any removable parts in hot water at the sink.
4 Take a bowl of hot soapy water to the cooker. Start at the top and work downwards, using the steel wool pad or the non-scratch cleaner. Rinse the cloth frequently in the water, changing the water as it becomes necessary.
5 Clean all removable parts at the sink. Wipe them dry.
6 Rinse and dry the oven, wearing rubber gloves.
7 Rub over the cooker with a clean dry cloth to polish it. Replace the parts and turn any pilot lights back on.

To clean a refrigerator

You will need:
bowl of hot water, detergent
bicarbonate of soda
dishcloth
tea-towel

For the outside:
hot water, liquid detergent
dishcloth
furniture polish, cloth

To defrost
Switch off at the wall and leave to defrost. Empty the tray of water from time to time. Defrosting can be speeded up by putting a dish of hot water in the freezing compartment.

To clean
1 Remove all the contents.
2 Take out the shelves and trays. Wash at the sink with hot soapy water, then dry.
3 Dissolve a tablespoon of bicarbonate of soda in one pint of warm water and use this solution to wash the inside of the fridge. Do not use washing-up liquid or a cleaner as this will leave its smell in the fridge.
4 Rinse, dry with a tea-towel, replace the shelves and food and switch on.

To clean the outside
1 Wash with hot soapy water. Dry well.
2 Occasionally apply a little furniture polish with a soft cloth, to keep the outside in good condition.

To turn out a kitchen cupboard or drawer

You will need:
hot water, liquid detergent
scrubbing brush, cleaning cloths
lining paper, if you are using it

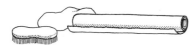

1 Remove the contents from the cupboard or drawer.
2 Scrub or wipe the shelves or drawer using the brush to get right into the corners to remove any dust. Rinse and wipe dry.
3 Check the contents of the cupboard or drawer, throwing away anything that is no longer useful. Wipe down all food containers and check that the labels are clear and firmly fixed on.
4 If you are lining the cupboard or drawer with kitchen paper, make sure it is completely dry first. Then cut the paper to fit and place it in position.
5 Replace all the contents neatly.

Practical work

1 **Thoroughly clean a cooker, inside and out.**
2 **Defrost and clean a refrigerator.**
3 **Turn out a kitchen drawer and line it with kitchen paper.**

Cleaning other rooms

To clean the living- and dining-room

You will need:
vacuum cleaner, duster, furniture polish
hot water, cleaning cloth, non-scratch cleaner
soft brush for chairs, or vacuum cleaner attachment

1 Open the window to air the room.
2 Empty ashtrays and waste-paper basket, remove old newspapers and dead flowers.
3 Tidy the room, straighten the cushions.
4 Vacuum the carpet.
5 Brush or vacuum dining-chairs and armchairs.
6 Dust and polish furniture, dust wall lights, skirting-boards, doors, window ledges.
7 Wipe marks from paintwork with a damp cloth, using a little non-scratch cleaner if necessary. Rinse and dry after use.

To clean the bathroom and lavatory

You will need:
lavatory brush, cleaning cloth and disinfectant
non-scratch cleaner, cloths
hot water, liquid detergent

1 Open the window, straighten towels, tidy room.
2 Brush the lavatory with the brush.
3 Wash the lavatory with disinfectant and warm water. Keep one cloth for this purpose and do not use it for any other cleaning job.
4 Clean the bath and wash-basin with non-scratch cleaner. Rinse well.
5 Wash the taps with hot, soapy water, being careful to clean underneath the taps. Rub with a dry cloth.
6 Wash the window sill, paintwork, and tiles with a cloth which has been wrung out in hot, soapy water. Wipe dry.
7 Wash the floor with disinfectant and warm water, or vacuum if a carpet is fitted.

Special cleaners for the lavatory
High standards of cleanliness are essential in the bathroom and toilet, to keep these areas fresh and free from harmful bacteria. Many special products are available for cleaning the lavatory. Some contain an acid to remove lime-scale, and bleach to kill bacteria and to keep the bowl white. They are available as powders or liquids. You can also buy preparations to put into the cistern, to soften and disinfect the water or to colour it blue.

To clean bedrooms

You will need:
vacuum cleaner, duster, furniture polish
hot water, detergent, cloths, non-scratch cleaner
cloths and cleaner for mirror

1 Open the window to air the room.
2 Tidy clothes, toys and books.
3 Make the beds – these should be turned down to air when you get up.
4 Vacuum or sweep the carpet.
5 Dust and polish the furniture. Dust skirting-board and door.
6 Wipe the paintwork and any furniture with a plastic finish with a cloth wrung out in hot, soapy water. Use a non-scratch cleaner to remove any marks.
7 Clean the mirror, if there is one.

Cleaning glass

Windows
There are plenty of products specially made for window cleaning. Rub on a little of the cleaner with a lint-free cloth (one that is not fluffy). Rub over with a soft clean cloth before the cleaner has dried.

Windows can also be washed with a chamois leather. Add a little methylated spirit to a bucket of warm water. Wash and wipe dry with the leather, wringing it out in the water. Change the water as it becomes dirty. Although these wash leathers are fairly expensive to buy, they last well, and you do not need to buy a special window-cleaning product as well.

Mirrors and glass-framed pictures
Use either a window-cleaning product or warm water and a wash leather. Be very careful not to mark the frame with the cleaner or water.

Cleaning plastics

Plastic surfaces might include kitchen work-tops or tables, lightweight stacking chairs, and polythene bowls, buckets, and cleaning brushes. Good plastic is light, strong, does not rust, and will last a long time if you keep very hot objects away from it. It is easy to keep clean. Plastic laminates on a kitchen work bench or table or on other furniture can be kept clean by washing with a cloth wrung out in hot, soapy water. Remove any marks with a little non-scratch cleansing cream, then rinse and wipe dry. Do not use a scouring powder as this will scratch the surface.

Polythene washing-up bowls, buckets, and cleaning brushes can be washed at the sink in hot, soapy water. A little non-scratch cleaner or scouring powder will remove any marks. Rinse well and wipe dry.

Practical work

1 **Describe how you would keep a bathroom thoroughly clean.**
2 **Clean a window or a mirror using either a window-cleaning product and a cloth or a chamois leather.**
3 **Clean a plastic washing-up bowl and brush.**

Cleaning wood and metals

Cleaning wood

Wood may have one of several finishes applied to it, to protect it from scratches, stains, and marks, and to improve its appearance. The way the wood should be cleaned and polished depends on which finish has been applied.

A plastic laminate such as Formica or Melamine may be applied to the wood. This is often used for kitchen work-tops or tables and for bedroom or living-room furniture. It often has a white or 'wood-effect' finish. Wash with warm, soapy water, using a little non-scratch cleaner if required to remove any marks. Rinse and wipe dry with a soft cloth.

Painted wood This may be used on window sills, doors, skirting-boards, and on furniture which has been painted to renovate it. Wash with warm, soapy water, rinse well, and dry with a soft cloth. A non-scratch cleaner will remove any marks.

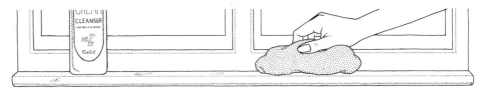

Teak Do not use ordinary furniture polish, but clean and feed the wood with teak oil about three times a year. Using a soft cloth, rub in a little oil, working it into the grain of the wood. Remove any excess with a soft, dry cloth.

Cellulose or polyurethane finish Used on tables, chairs, desks, and the legs of armchairs. Remove any marks with a damp cloth and dry. Polish from time to time with furniture polish or cream.

Pine or oak furniture Use a little wax polish, rubbing it into the grain of the wood with a soft cloth. Rub well with a soft, clean cloth to bring out the shine.

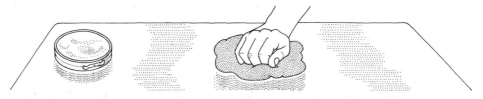

French polish This finish is found on older, more expensive furniture made of such woods as mahogany, walnut, or rosewood. It is easily scratched and marked by heat. Polish with a little furniture cream on a soft cloth, rubbing it well into the grain of the wood to produce a soft gloss. Marks may be removed by rubbing with a soft damp cloth. Dry well before polishing.

Salad bowls These should not be washed as the finish could be spoiled. Wipe with a damp cloth, then rub with a clean cloth to dry. Rub a little salad oil into the wood occasionally, using a soft cloth or kitchen paper, to keep the wood in good condition.

Wooden chopping boards Scrub with a brush and warm water, along the grain of the wood. Rinse in cold water to help keep the board a light colour, then dry.

Cleaning metals

Silver This is best cleaned with a special silver polish, which is available in different forms. Liquid silver polish is rubbed on with a soft cloth and polished off with another clean soft cloth. You can also buy thick wadding which is impregnated with silver polish. You remove a piece of wadding to clean the silver, then polish it off with a soft cloth.

Other cleaners are available which keep the silver free from tarnish for a much longer time than normal, so that you have to polish it less often.

Awkward shapes or silver jewellery can be dipped in a jar of special cleaner and held there for a few seconds until the tarnish disappears.

Copper and brass These are cleaned with a special metal polish which is available as a liquid or as wadding (like the kind used for silver). The polish is rubbed on, then rubbed off with a clean soft cloth.

Stainless steel This should stay in good condition if you just wash it in clean soapy water, rinse, and dry straight away. Do not leave stainless steel dishes or pans to drain as this may spoil their appearance. You can buy special stainless steel cleaners but this should not usually be necessary.

A stainless steel sink may sometimes need extra cleaning, in which case a non-scratch cream cleaner should be used. Do not use scouring powder or soap-filled wire-wool pads as they will scratch the surface of the metal and dull the shine.

Aluminium Many saucepans are made from silver-coloured aluminium. They can be safely cleaned with a soap-filled wire-wool pad, then rinsed and dried. Scouring powder can also be used for removing burnt-on food particles, or stubborn stains.

Enamel This metal is used for sinks and draining-boards, and for decorative saucepans and casseroles. It is more easily marked than aluminium, and neither scouring powder nor wire-wool should be used. Clean with a nylon pan-cleaner or brush. Sometimes the inside of the pan or sink is meant to be white and becomes discoloured. Cover the stained area with cold water, add a little bleach, and leave to soak. Rinse very thoroughly before using again.

Practical work

1 **Clean the following:**
   (a) a window sill or skirting-board, (b) an item of furniture made of pine or oak, (c) a salad bowl.
2 **Clean the following:**
   (a) some silver cutlery, (b) a stainless steel dish, (c) an enamel pan.

Washing and ironing

To hand-wash a delicate garment, or a garment made of pure wool

You will need:
A detergent specially made for washing by hand, e.g. Stergene, Lux, Dreft.
Water at the correct temperature for the fabric, that is:
<u>Warm</u> (40°C) for pure wool and acrylic fibres. It should feel just warm to the touch.
<u>Hand-hot</u> (50°C) for coloured nylon, polyester, polyester/cotton mixtures. The
water should be as hot as the hand can comfortably stand.
<u>Hot</u> (60°C) for white nylon and white polyester. This water temperature would be
too hot for the hands, so you can only wash these materials by hand if you use
rubber gloves. The higher temperature keeps the garments a good white colour.
Fabric conditioner, towel or spin-drier, iron, ironing-board.

Method
1 Dissolve the detergent thoroughly in the water.
2 Gently squeeze the garment in the water. Do not rub, twist, or wring. Squeeze
   out the soapy water.
3 Rinse well at least twice in clean warm water.
4 Add the correct amount of fabric conditioner to the final rinse, then gently
   squeeze the water out of the garment, but do not wring it.
5 Either fold the garment neatly and give it a short spin dry, or roll it in a towel to
   absorb any surplus moisture.
6 Dry carefully. A knitted garment should be laid flat on a clean towel to dry so that
   it will not become stretched. Dry away from direct heat such as fires or radiators.
   Do not put wool in a tumble-drier.

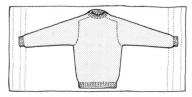

7 Ironing – a wool garment may be pressed lightly on the wrong side using a warm
   iron. For garments made of acrylic, nylon, or polyester, use a cool iron.
8 Leave to air after ironing until completely dry.

Ironing

One of the most difficult garments to iron and fold neatly is a shirt.

| 1 Cuffs: wrong side then right | 2 Yoke | 3 Collar: points to centre back | 4 Sleeves: under-arm seam first |

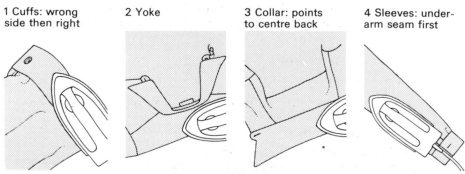

5 Right front,
back, left front

6 Lay flat,
button up, press

7 Place shirt
face downwards

8 Fold side
seams inwards

9 Place sleeves
along folded edges

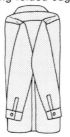

10 Turn up shirt
tail

11 Fold in half

12 A neatly
folded shirt

Products you can use when ironing

A 'pre-iron spray' is available which adds body to the fabric while you iron it. It improves the appearance of the garments and helps them to resist dirt. It is quite useful for clothes made of synthetic fibres, such as polyester/cotton shirts and blouses, which can quickly look limp.

Starch is available as an aerosol spray or in powder form. It gives a smooth glossy finish and adds body to fabrics. It is used mainly on cotton and linen fabrics, for table-cloths, tray-cloths, napkins, and pillowcases. Powdered starch is mixed with water according to the instructions on the packet. After washing and rinsing, articles to be starched are immersed in the starch mixture, then dried as usual. They should be ironed while still damp. Spray starch is ready to use in the aerosol can, and sprayed on just before ironing.

To iron table-cloths, table-mats, napkins, and tray-cloths

Wash, rinse, and dry as usual, but do not allow to become completely dry. Either starch lightly using a solution of powdered starch, or use a spray starch as you iron. With the iron set at the correct temperature for the fabric, iron until dry, pulling the edges straight as you do so. Fold neatly, but avoid folding table-mats and tray-cloths if at all possible, so that they will not show any creases.

Practical work

1 **Wash the following items by hand. Dry, iron, and fold them:**
a **a woollen jumper.**
b **a white nylon shirt.**
c **a polyester/cotton blouse or shirt.**
2 **Starch and iron a table-cloth or tray-cloth.**

Simple household mending

Mending tears and holes

Use Bondaweb or Bondina, which you can buy in department stores or drapers' shops. It is a sticky plastic spread on a paper backing.

For an L-shaped tear
Cut a patch from matching fabric, larger than the tear. Cut a piece of Bondaweb the same size as the patch. Put it on the <u>right</u> side of the patch, paper side up, and iron on with a warm iron. When cool, remove the paper backing and the right side of the patch will be sticky. Place this on the <u>wrong</u> side of the tear and press with a steam iron (or a dry iron and a damp cloth). Leave to set for ten minutes before moving.

For holes
Cut a piece of Bondaweb large enough to cover the hole, plus about 4cm/1½" around it. Cut a patch the same size. Iron the Bondaweb on to the wrong side of the garment. Remove the backing paper and cut away the sticky area over the hole. Place the right side of the patch to the wrong side of the garment which is now sticky. Press with a steam iron and leave to set for ten minutes. If there are any loose edges on the wrong side, trim them off.

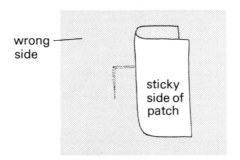
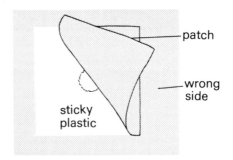

Holes or worn patches in children's clothes or in jeans
These can be covered with attractive iron-on or sew-on patches which you can buy.

For reinforcing material where it has worn thin
Machine darning is quick and easy to do on most modern sewing machines.

1   Adjust the machine for darning, according to the instruction booklet. This involves attaching a darning foot and lowering the feed mechanism.
2   Put the worn patch in the centre of an embroidery frame to hold it taut.
3   Draw the work steadily backwards and forwards through the machine to give neat, parallel rows of stitching to cover all the worn area.

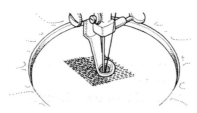

Sewing on buttons

These should always be sewn to double material. Buttons sewn on to thick material usually have a shank or stem. Buttons without a shank must be sewn on loosely to allow for the thickness of the material around the buttonhole.

1 Mark the position of the buttons. This should be in the centre of the buttonhole. Mark it with two pins.

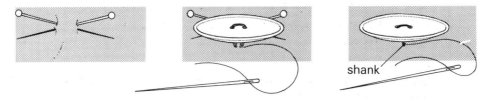

2 Take two or three stitches at this point, on the right side of the material, using strong thread.
3 Pass the needle up and down through the holes but do not pull the threads tightly.
4 Bring the needle up between the button and the material and wind the thread around the stem to form a shank.
5 Pass the needle through to the wrong side and work two stitches to finish off.

Darning a hole or worn area in socks or a woollen jumper

You need a darning needle, darning wool in a matching colour, a 'mushroom' tacking thread, and a sewing needle.

1 Mark the area of the darn with tacking thread. Include the hole and any worn area around it.
2 Working on the wrong side, darn up and down, picking up any loose stitches. Leave the wool loosely looped at the end of each row.
3 Darn across these threads, weaving under and over. Keep the stitches close to each other and do not pull them tightly.

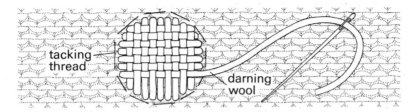

Practical work

1 **Mend an L-shaped tear in a piece of cotton material.**
2 **Sew a button on to a shirt.**
3 **Darn the worn elbow of a woollen jumper.**

Flower arranging

With a little practice it is easy to produce simple but very attractive flower arrangements. The basic equipment you need is not expensive and it can be used many times.

Bowls, vases, jugs, wineglasses, small baskets, or any other containers can be used to hold the arrangement. Plastic bowls such as empty margarine tubs make good containers. Wide, shallow containers are often more useful than the usual tall narrow vases.

'Oasis'

'Oasis' is a firm, sponge-like material which is extremely useful for flower arrangements. It enables flower stems to be held firmly in any position. It is cheap and can be bought from flower shops in many sizes. You cut it to the shape of your container with a knife. It should be soaked in water before use so that it is damp when you put the flower stems into it. Keep the Oasis continually damp while the arrangement is displayed.

To make this arrangement you will need:
about 15 daffodils
some green leaves, such as box leaves
Oasis in a plastic dish or bowl
a small basket (or a shallow bowl if you do not have one)

Soak the Oasis and put it in the plastic bowl. Place in the basket. Make the outline shape with long-stemmed daffodils and leaves.

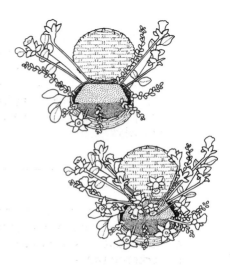

Fill in the centre with daffodils, cutting the stems to different lengths so that they are of varied heights. Add enough leaves to cover the plastic bowl or any Oasis which may show.

This arrangement can be made using only three blooms, for example, roses, chrysanthemums, irises, carnations, tulips, or freesias. You will also need green leaves or beech leaves, a shallow container, and Oasis.

Cut the three blooms to different heights and insert in the Oasis, which should be damp. The lowest flower should be just at the level of the Oasis.

Cut the stems of the leaves to varying heights and use them to frame the flowers. Put some short-stemmed leaves low down under the lowest flower.

A Christmas table decoration
Use a shallow base or dish, such as a piece of wood 'sliced' from the trunk of a tree, or a silver cake board. You will also need a coloured candle, holly, ivy, a few small glass baubles, Oasis in a shallow container, and an aerosol spray of glitter or snow if you wish.

Put the damp Oasis into the container, and put the candle into the centre of the Oasis. Add sprigs of holly of different heights, using short pieces at the base to hide the container.

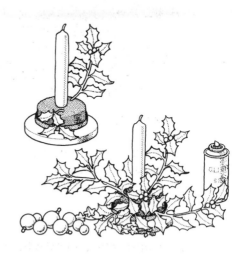

Trail some ivy over the edge of the container. Place the glass baubles on the holly leaves. If you are using glitter or snow, spray the holly leaves carefully. You could spray them before you put the arrangement together, if you wish.

Practical work

1 **Make one of the three arrangements described above.**
2 **Make an arrangement suitable for:**
a **an invalid's supper tray.**
b **a dinner party.**

Practical examination questions

1 Prepare a two-course lunch for three people. Clean an ornament made of brass or copper, a wooden salad bowl, and an aluminium pan.

2 Your family is going on a picnic. Prepare three dishes which would be suitable for them to take. Clean a liquidizer and a non-stick pan.

3 Make a small loaf and some bread rolls from one yeast mixture. Write down the cost of making them and the cost of the same sized items in the shops. Thoroughly clean the refrigerator. Clean a mirror.

4 You are not sure of the time the family will arrive home for their evening meal. Prepare a main course which will keep hot but include one vegetable to cook quickly on their arrival.

   Make a cold sweet.

   Iron a selection of garments to illustrate your knowledge of different fabrics (show at least <u>three</u>).

   Clean a cupboard in your unit. (EAEB)

5 You are spending the day doing odd jobs when you receive a telephone call from your aunt to say that she will visit you for lunch.
   (a) Prepare a suitable two-course meal.
   (b) Make a batch of scones.
   (c) Launder a small tablecloth.
   (d) Clean the top of your cooker. (EAEB)

6 Prepare, using eggs, a meal for two people.

   There is to be a committee meeting (four people) later that evening. Prepare a tray for coffee, also cook and serve a suitable item to hand around with it.

   Clean a selection of different metals.

   Use one metal container for a simple arrangement of twigs or green foliage. (EAEB)

7 (a) Show the use of <u>two</u> different types of flour. Adapt one item as part of a meal for two people.
   (b) Clean a piece of neglected brass or silver.
   (c) Launder <u>three</u> items of personal clothing, showing your knowledge of different fabrics. (EAEB)

8 You are going on holiday in a rented flat for one week. Prepare two dishes to help with the week's catering. One of these dishes must be made by the 'melting method'.

   Prepare a savoury dish that could be eaten on the evening of your arrival.

   Iron a long-sleeved shirt or blouse and show how to fold it for packing. (EMREB)

9   You are trying to lose weight. Prepare a two-course 'weight-watching' lunch for yourself and a friend. Include a drink. Iron the table linen to be used, make a floral arrangement, and set the table. (EMREB)

10 It is important to use the correct cleansing agent for cleaning surfaces and fabrics in order to achieve good results. Show practically how to use at least six of these agents effectively and make a clear chart to show the results. Make and serve coffee and biscuits within the first hour. (WMEB)

11 Plan and cook a tasty midday meal using 'left-over' food. Give a special clean to your kitchen working area, including the cooker. (WMEB)

12 Cook and serve a special evening meal. Make use of modern equipment, tableware, and easy-care fabrics in the preparation and serving of the meal. (WMEB)

13 Both your parents work and they have bought a home freezer to make meal planning easier and reduce the number of shopping expeditions.

    Make one dish from each of the following groups and pack one item ready for the freezer.
    (a) Casserole, stew or curry.
    (b) A suitable cake or cakes.
    (c) Scones or pancakes.
    (d) A dish of your own choice. (WMEB)

14 It is your day for a thorough house clean. Show <u>three</u> or <u>four</u> different tasks that you would expect to do. Also prepare a snack lunch which shows the imaginative use of convenience foods. (WMEB)

15 Cheese is an important source of protein. Show your imaginative use of it to make:
    (a) a dish suitable for supper,
    (b) a dish using cheese and a vegetable or vegetables, and
    (c) a dish using cheese and bread or pasta.
    Also clean a saucepan and a plastic washing-up bowl. (WMEB)

16 You are travelling to the Lake District by car with your parents and younger brother to spend the week-end with a relative.

    Prepare a satisfying packed lunch including a hot drink.

    On arrival use your aunt's new electric mixer with liquidizer attachment to make something interesting. (WMEB)

17 Your mother is away on a visit. Cook and serve a substantial breakfast for your father and yourself. Prepare a packed lunch for him to take to work. Iron a shirt which you have washed previously. (MREB)

18 Your brother is working on a building site. Prepare four dishes to illustrate food which would be suitable for his packed lunches. Launder a shirt and sweater for him. (SREB)

19 Your town is twinned with a continental town and a family are coming to stay with you. Prepare a typically British meal and make a regional British cake or some biscuits. Serve on a tray with coffee for their arrival, having cleaned the tray and laundered the tray cloth. (SREB)

20 Cook four dishes to show the use of different fats and oils. Label each dish to show the fats or oils used.

Launder a selection of kitchen cloths. (SREB)

21 Using your skill in planning, choose, prepare, and cook four dishes showing the economical use of fuel. Launder the table-cloth upon which the dishes will be displayed. (SREB)

22 To show the use of eggs in cookery, prepare, cook, and display four different dishes. Launder a knitted sweater or pullover. (SREB)

23 Your small niece is coming to stay and will be having her second birthday whilst with you. Prepare, cook, and serve a selection of sweet and savoury dishes for the birthday tea. Include a birthday cake. Set the table for the party. (SEREB)

24 Your mother has asked you to look after your two young sisters aged 3 and 6 years while she is away for the day. Plan, cook, and serve a suitable two-course mid-day meal and an appropriate drink for the three of you.

While your mother is away clean two of her favourite ornaments, and make a simple flower arrangement as a surprise for her return.

Prepare a fruit salad for the children's tea. (WJEC)

25 Make 8oz (200 grams) of short crust pastry and 8oz (200 grams) of a mixture made by the creaming method of cake making. Show how each of the above can be used to make two different dishes.

Launder a small table cloth and serve your cooking on this cloth.

Thoroughly clean your working surface and a kitchen drawer or cupboard. (WJEC)

26 A student from abroad is staying with your family for a month in the summer. Cook a two-course evening meal for two people including either some traditional food from this country or traditional food from his country.

Mend the worn elbow of a sweater.

Make a few bread rolls to use in packed lunches. (O)

27 Make two inexpensive protein dishes. Use textured vegetable protein in one of the dishes. Cook one vegetable to accompany each dish.

Mend a sheet with a tear in the middle. (O)

Books for further reading

About the House Helen McGrath (Oxford University Press)
Particularly useful for practical work such as stain removal, washing by machine, comparing household cleaning products, wiring a plug, first aid, and writing letters.

Don't Forget Fibre in your Diet Denis Burkitt (Martin Dunitz)

Manual of Nutrition H.M.S.O.

Success in Nutrition Magnus Pyke (John Murray)

Elementary Science of Food E. M. Hildreth (Mills and Boon)

The Value of Food Fisher and Bender (Oxford University Press)

The Dairy Book of Home Cookery Sonia Allison (Milk Marketing Board)

The Dairy Book of Home Management (Macdonald Educational)

Food Science Birch, Cameron, and Spencer (Pergamon Press)

'O' level Cookery Abbey and Macdonald (Methuen Educational)

Index